Inside the Volcano

Series in Political Economy and Economic Development in Latin America

Series Editor
Andrew Zimbalist
Smith College

†*Inside the Volcano: The History and Political Economy of Central America,* Frederick Stirton Weaver

†*Sexual Politics in Cuba: Machismo, Homosexuality, and AIDS,* Marvin Leiner

"Everything Within the Revolution": Cuban Strategies for Social Development Since 1960, Thomas C. Dalton

Industrialization in Sandinista Nicaragua: Policy and Practice in a Mixed Economy, Geske Dijkstra

†*The Making of Social Movements in Latin America: Identity, Strategy, and Democracy,* edited by Arturo Escobar and Sonia E. Alvarez

Peasants in Distress: Poverty and Unemployment in the Dominican Republic, Rosemary Vargas-Lundius

The Latin American Development Debate: Neostructuralism, Neomonetarism, and Adjustment Processes, edited by Patricio Meller

Distorted Development: Mexico in the World Economy, David Barkin

State and Capital in Mexico: Development Policy Since 1940, James M. Cypher

Struggle Against Dependence: Nontraditional Export Growth in Central America and the Caribbean, edited by Eva Paus

The Peruvian Mining Industry: Growth, Stagnation, and Crisis, Elizabeth Dore

Cuban Political Economy: Controversies in Cubanology, edited by Andrew Zimbalist

†Available in hardcover and paperback

Inside the Volcano

The History and Political Economy of Central America

Frederick Stirton Weaver
Hampshire College

Westview Press
Boulder • San Francisco • Oxford

Series in Political Economy and Economic Development in Latin America

Published in 1994 in the United States of America by Westview Press, Inc., 5500 Central Avenue, Boulder, Colorado 80301-2877, and in the United Kingdom by Westview Press, 36 Lonsdale Road, Summertown, Oxford OX2 7EW

Library of Congress Cataloging-in-Publication Data
Weaver, Frederick Stirton, 1939–
Inside the volcano : the history and political economy of Central America / Frederick Stirton Weaver.
p. cm.—(Series in political economy and economic development in Latin America)
Includes index.
ISBN 0-8133-0978-6.—ISBN 0-8133-0979-4 (pbk.)
1. Central America—Economic conditions. 2. Industries—Central America—History. 3. Central America—Politics and government.
I. Title. II. Series.
HC141.W42 1994
330.9728—dc20

93-47319
CIP

Printed and bound in the United States of America

The paper used in this publication meets the requirements of the American National Standard for Permanence of Paper for Printed Library Materials Z39.48-1984.

10 9 8 7 6 5 4 3 2 1

Contents

Tables and Illustrations

Maps

Tables

Figures

Acknowledgments

I have been working on this book for several years and have been fortunate throughout to have received a lot of help from a range of people and institutions. Among those whom I wish to thank are Carollee Bengelsdorf, Paul Dosal, Michael Ford, Jeanne Hahn, Marc Linberg, Rodolfo Torres, Tom Walker, Patricia A. Wand, D.W.S. Weaver, and Serena Arpené Weaver. They contributed to this book in a variety of ways, although this public announcement of their involvement may dismay some of them. I also wish to thank my Westview editor, Barbara Ellington.

Several cohorts of first-year Hampshire College students read early drafts of the manuscript, and with inimitable Hampshire irreverence and commitment they helped make it a clearer and more interesting book. I thank them as well as the Hampshire students who directly enhanced my understanding of the region by writing senior theses on Central American topics.

I have presented the ideas in this book to various people in different forums over the past few years, but I wish to single out the members of the history and economics faculties of the Universidad Estatal de Cuenca who participated in the seminar during my first Fulbright fellowship in Ecuador. Their lively, challenging, and supportive responses forced me to rethink several key points.

I am also grateful for the financial support for travel that I have received from the Hewlett-Mellon Presidential Discretionary Fund at Hampshire College and for the excellent and cordial help from the librarians at Hampshire College, the University of Massachusetts–Amherst, the Hispanic Division of the Library of Congress, and the Inter-American Development Bank.

My greatest debts are to María Elena Fieweger, Frank Holmquist, Roberto Márquez, Sharon Hartman Strom, and Andrew Zimbalist. All of them carefully read and trenchantly criticized drafts of chapters, and they argued with me and listened to me. There is no question that the book is far better as a consequence.

Frederick Stirton Weaver

Source: Richard Fagen, *Forging Peace: The Challenge of Central America* (Basil Blackwell, Inc., 1987), p. xii. Copyright © PACCA 1987.

Introduction

Central America has experienced more than five hundred years of social and economic change and transformation, more rapid and disruptive at some times than others, and the 1970s to the present have to be seen as part of a continuing, dynamic process of conflict, accommodation, and resistance. "Crisis," the word that dominates book titles and media coverage about Central America, is not a new reality for the five nations I cover in this book (Guatemala, Honduras, El Salvador, Nicaragua, and Costa Rica). The convulsions of the past two decades in Central America did not suddenly erupt from random or idiosyncratic sources, nor were they simply determined by foreign powers' manipulations.

I have written this book with the conviction that knowledge of the historically changing character of social and political life in the region is necessary for understanding and explaining events and prospects in Central America. The purpose of this book is to provide a historical background to recent Central American social unrest, repression, and revolution to help readers engage in current arguments, claims, and debates in a critical and historically informed manner.

As Table I.1 shows, the Central American nations are small, and although the size of these nations is important in a number of ways, its importance can easily be exaggerated. Being small does not condemn a nation to poverty and economic stagnation, as is demonstrated by Switzerland, Belgium, the Netherlands, Luxembourg, and Taiwan and even more so by the tiny and economically dynamic city-states of Singapore and Hong Kong. Moreover, small is not the same thing as insignificant, nor should the size of the Central American nations suggest that these societies are homogeneous or uncomplicated.

In studying Central American history, if one mistakes small national size for the lack of social complexity, it is easy to conclude that the only important impulses of economic and political change in Central America have been from outside the region. But this conclusion is indeed a mistake; it is historically inaccurate, analytically misleading, and patronizing to attribute too much influence to external forces. This is true whether an author argues that everything "good" or everything "bad" in Central America is primarily the result of outside influence.

TABLE I.1 Area and Population of Central American Nations

	Area (1,000 sq. km.)	Population (millions,1990)	Population per square kilometer
Guatemala	108.9	9.2	84
Honduras	112.1	5.1	46
El Salvador	21.0	5.3	250
Nicaragua	130.0	3.9	30
Costa Rica	51.1	3.0	59
Total	423.1	26.5	64

Source: United Nations, Department of Economic and Social Information and Policy Analysis, *Statistical Yearbook, 38th Issue, 1990/91* (New York: United Nations, 1993), pp. 61-62.

Examples of such interpretations are legion in writings about Central America. When a U.S. writer even critically ascribes a peculiar potency to U.S. influence, it is a form of nationalist celebration: The United States is presented as all-powerful in a world of weak and passive nations. In addition, this interpretation is convenient for Central American elites because it allows them to point an accusing finger at the gargantuan north (that is, the United States or Mexico), represent themselves as victims, and deflect criticisms about the way in which local social relationships impede economic growth and sustain immense inequalities and injustices. But even though I am impressed by some Central Americans' ability to manipulate U.S. fears and acquisitiveness for their own ends and by how frequently U.S. Central American policy has been ineffectual, it is still true that many acting in the name of the United States have been complicit in what have frequently had very unpleasant consequences.

The very real importance of foreign influences has to be understood in the contexts of the Central American nations' internal dynamics. The five nations are very individual social formations in which social power has been and continues to be organized and exercised in distinct ways that reflect, in part, the influences of foreign intervention. So although foreign influences, including the Aztec and the Spanish, have been pervasive, their effects on the nations have been significantly different. Throughout the book, I have stressed the mutual and historically changing relation between domestic social structures and external influences.

Closely related to my attempt to highlight the central importance of the social and political contradictions within the five nations are my strong reservations about the usefulness of speaking of a nation as a historical actor. That is, I am very uneasy about such formulations as "Guatemala desired to . . . ," "Guatemala managed to achieve . . . ," or

"Guatemala experienced. . . ." Guatemala, like all societies, is composed of many groups and individuals with opposing interests and aspirations, and conflict among these opposing interests and aspirations is one of the primary sources of historical change.

For instance, when a national government implements a particular policy, it represents the victory of one set of social actors (class, regional interests, religious institution, or whatever) over others. This understanding is severely undercut by describing the policy as a nation's determination to do something. For purposes of variety, I occasionally do lapse in my effort to avoid personifying nations, but I hope that my conviction about the primacy of internal dynamics is sustained and reinforced by my effort to identify with some precision who is doing what within a nation.

All of the points I have been arguing here derive from a general methodological principle. As I maintain throughout the book, one cannot adequately understand economic growth, social structure, or political change without studying the relationships among the three. All three both reflect and influence the others. Although this idea is very demanding and requires comparative history, I believe that it offers the best approach for a satisfactory understanding of Central America.

Unlike the size of national societies, the small size of this book does mean a reduction of complexity. Because of my desire to write a book short enough to be useful for several purposes, I have selected the particular aspects of historical development that I consider to be especially important in comprehending the social and political events of the past twenty years and in assessing the prospects for the near future. One result is that I focus on only five nations in the region: Guatemala, Honduras, El Salvador, Nicaragua, and Costa Rica. Panama became an independent nation only in the first decade of the twentieth century, and its unique relationship with the United States and the canal limits the value of comparative study with the other five nations. Belize became independent from Great Britain in 1981, and again it is less useful to compare the nature of change in Belize to that of the five larger nations with their common legacies of Spanish colonization.

The book's selectivity also pertains to substantive issues. For example, I discuss early nineteenth-century efforts to create a unified political entity among the five newly independent Central American nations, and I describe the post–World War II Central American Common Market in some detail. I do not, however, deal with attempts to integrate the Central American nations into a unified whole during the later nineteenth and early twentieth centuries. Although these integration efforts have a long and interesting history, they have not, in my opinion, significantly shaped the experience of the people in these nations.

The first chapter begins with the Spanish conquest of Central America and the ways in which the colonial society that the Spaniards established reflected the people whom they found there, in both their numbers and social organization. The second chapter discusses the sweeping colonial reforms in the eighteenth century and the character of the movement that succeeded in securing independence from Spain but failed in creating durable political systems.

Both of these chapters emphasize the ways in which economic activities were primarily the consequence of political initiatives and control. The third chapter, in contrast, deals with the rise of coffee and banana production for export during the late nineteenth and early twentieth centuries. The large-scale economic expansions profoundly changed the bases of social relations and the organization and exercise of political power.

With the severe economic contraction of the Great Depression in the 1930s and the special circumstances of World War II—the subject of Chapter 4—political impulses were again the chief sources of change and development. In Chapters 5 and 6, however, economic expansion returns as the principal source of social and political change during the 1950s through the mid-1970s. New agricultural exports, selective agricultural modernization, and urban manufacturing growth encouraged by the Central American Common Market led to extensive economic growth during the 1960s and 1970s. The fifth chapter draws together the themes presented in earlier chapters to fashion an organizing framework to identify and explain the relationships among economic growth, increased misery, and the limits of political containment.

The last chapter is a brief political narrative that brings events up through the early 1990s. In it, I pay particular attention to the nature of electorally oriented political reforms and to the intent and effect of U.S. foreign policy in the region.

In each chapter, I have set Central America firmly in the broader context of Latin America to indicate which processes and events are parts of more general currents and which are more specific to the isthmus.

This history is highly interpretive, both implicitly by the selection of historical materials and explicitly by the connections I make among them. The historical "facts" that I present are not new; I simply make new and, I believe, more fruitful connections among them than has heretofore been the case. Because of the nature of this enterprise, my endnotes not only serve the purpose of corroboration and indications of good faith, but they are also intended to guide the reader who wishes to explore issues in more depth. The Suggested Readings at the end of the book, organized by topic and period, includes most of those sources included in the notes as well as some additional ones.

Many of my arguments are presented in a deliberately provocative manner to stimulate thought and debate. There is a lot to argue about here, and the book demands an active, critical reading. I would be delighted to respond to readers' critical challenges (and to praise, too).

1

Conquest and Colony, 1500 to 1700

The initial Spanish contacts with Central America gave little hint of the drama and travail that would soon follow. In 1495, an unsuccessful Spanish expedition explored the Caribbean coast of present-day Colombia and made a brief foray along the coast of Panama. And in 1502, during his fourth voyage, Columbus explored along the Central American coast from Honduras to Panama without finding much that interested him. The Great Navigator did name some places, including Costa Rica, which turned out to be not at all rich. Indeed, the Spaniards were decidedly unimpressed by their first experiences with Central America. Nevertheless, soon after the Spaniards established Santo Domingo on the island of Hispaniola—now Haiti and the Dominican Republic—as their headquarters for exploring the New World (or Indies), the immediately disastrous decline in the numbers of indigenous peoples throughout the Caribbean islands increased Spanish interest in Central America as a source of slaves.

The first Spanish invasion of the Central American isthmus—Panama in 1509—was, if not a complete failure, certainly less than an outstanding success. Disease, hostile Indians, and the loss of ships and provisions almost wiped out the expedition. The surviving members did manage to establish the town of Darién, but shortly afterward a dispute with another band of Spaniards ended in the execution of the first expedition's leader. This style of dealing with each other and with the local peoples predominated in the Spanish conquest of Central America and of the Indies in general.

Geography and Peoples

Once the Spaniards began systematically exploring Central America, they found highly varied and difficult terrain. The mountain range that runs through North and South America constitutes the spine for the narrow isthmus of Central America, where the mountains are highly volcanic. The higher elevations are found in western Guatemala, and the lowest are in Honduras, around the Nicaraguan lakes, and in Panama. With this geography, it is no mystery why these three low-lying areas have consistently been the sites favored for constructing an interoceanic canal.[1]

The mountains run from the northwest to the southeast, as does the isthmus as a whole. Only Belize and Nicaragua are situated so that the Caribbean (or Atlantic) forms the eastern borders. The Caribbean defines the northern coasts of Guatemala, Honduras, and Panama and the northeastern edge of Costa Rica; El Salvador has no Caribbean coast. The Pacific Ocean generally lies to the south.

Although the whole of Central America is within the tropics, the position of the mountains and the range of elevations (which result in transportation and communication difficulties) create a surprising variety of terrain and climate within such a small area. The line created by the mountain chain forms a primary geographical division, and in general the northern and eastern sides of the mountain chain are much less fertile than the southern and western sides. There is considerably less volcanic ash, and the heavy rains typical of the Caribbean side of the mountains leach out much of whatever nutrients the soils possess.

This is especially true of the northern and eastern areas below 2,500 feet of elevation. Prior to the Spanish invasion, most of the entire coast from the Cape of Gracias a Dios (the northeastern end of the border of Honduras and Nicaragua) through Panama was sparsely populated swamps and rain forests. The area around the Gulf of Honduras, especially the small part of the Caribbean coast that now belongs to Guatemala and extending to the east about halfway along the Honduran coast, differs from the rest of the Caribbean coast because it received more volcanic ash, and the land is better drained, reducing the leaching effects of the rains.

Even though this area, like the rest of the Caribbean coast, is vulnerable to fierce hurricanes from the Caribbean, it was densely populated by people who managed to achieve the most complex cultural levels found in Central America and perhaps in the New World. By the first millennium A.D., the Maya had developed a complex written language, even today only partially deciphered, and a level of mathematical and astronomical sophistication that may have surpassed that of their European contemporaries. Along with these cultural accomplishments, the Maya had created a strongly hierarchical (and unremittingly patriarchal) social order, an elaborate system of religious beliefs and ceremonies, a powerful priesthood, and creative artistic and architectural works. Moreover, the Maya traded actively in products and slaves within their region and with areas as far away as the southeastern coast of Mexico. The trading activities may be what first drew the Mexican Aztecs into Mayan territory. By the end of the fifteenth century, the Aztec empire had established a definite presence in the region.[2]

The Maya's highly sophisticated culture, religion, and strata of non-producing social elites were erected upon an extremely undeveloped economic base. Mayan scientific knowledge and investigations were not applied to production, which remained at rudimentary levels of technique and organization. For instance, wheels were used in children's toys, but they were not used for transportation or plowing. Lacking large draft animals, the Maya depended on human labor to pull, push, lift, and carry, and they did not develop a metallurgy useful in production. Slash-and-burn agriculture remained the principal source of food. Most of the work was done by people in formally subordinate positions and subject to direct coercion. Workers were sharecroppers, tenants, peasants beholden to the central state, and slaves. Some of the slaves were local inhabitants being punished for transgressions, but most were captured in raids on neighboring peoples.

In considering who did the work, it is interesting to note that when twentieth-century North Americans talk about pre-Columbian Mayan culture, they are usually referring to the high culture of the Mayan elite. In contrast, references to twentieth-century Mayan culture are to the more durable, everyday living patterns of the tillers of the soil—a very different cultural form. Mayan high culture had been in decline for five or six hundred years by the time of the Spanish invasion in the sixteenth century, but it did still exist in written documents, religious ceremonies, and architecture. The Spaniards deliberately set out to destroy that culture and its representatives—the political and ecclesiastical elites—as heretical and politically dangerous.

As the vitality of Mayan civilization declined over the centuries before the Spaniards arrived, the Mayan people became dispersed throughout the highlands of Guatemala without completely deserting the Gulf of Honduras. Although cultural commonalities among them were obvious, the political unity disintegrated and the different tribes identified themselves by a variety of names other than Maya, a designation used here as a general category. Frequent wars among tribes, often for the purpose of acquiring slaves, made it easier for the Spaniards to conquer them.

Large numbers of these people who had historical and cultural roots in the Mayan empire settled on the other side of the Central American isthmus—to the south and west of the mountains. Here the soils have been enriched by thousands of years of volcanic ash deposits, and because the area receives considerably less rain than the Caribbean side they are more fertile. The higher populated elevations (between 5,000 and 8,000 feet above sea level) are made up of mountain valleys in western Guatemala and in Chiapas, now the southern state of Mexico bordering Guatemala. These cold-zone valleys are fertile but susceptible to frosts. The temperate zone, between 2,500 and 5,000 feet in elevation, runs through the interiors of western Guatemala, El Salvador, Honduras, northwest Nicaragua, and Costa Rica.

The lowest elevations, including the Pacific coast, are hot. Because these areas have more fertile soils and less rain and humidity than the Caribbean coast, however, the Spaniards preferred them to the Caribbean coast.

The temperate zone has pleasant weather and fertile soils, and at the time of the Spanish conquest it had plentiful labor. This zone was favored by the Spaniards, but it had some definite drawbacks as a place to live. Active volcanoes, earthquakes, and avalanches seriously damaged virtually every colonial city the Spaniards founded in the temperate zone, and many cities were moved several times or simply abandoned. The capital of Guatemala, which was also the capital of the Central American colony (other than Panama), was founded in three different places after disasters during the colonial period. The region continues to be rocked periodically, occasionally with heavy loss of life.

A second disadvantage of this temperate zone, shared with the Pacific coast, was the direction it faced. It was unfortunate for the Spaniards that the most desirable regions of Central America opened to the west and south because their economic, political, and cultural orientation was to Europe—east and north. And the topography of the isthmus, including few good natural harbors on that side, made access to Europe difficult.

The Spaniards found very different patterns of indigenous settlement in other areas of Central America. In contrast to the areas that are now Guatemala, El Salvador, northwestern Honduras, and the Pacific coast of Nicaragua, the rest of Honduras along with Nicaragua, Costa Rica, and Panama were inhabited by descendants of tribes that had migrated north from South America. Many of the peoples west and south of the mountains lived in farming communities that only occasionally moved, but the communities were small and dispersed with nothing like the density or cultural and organizational complexity of the Maya. And also unlike the Maya (and other more advanced, hierarchically organized societies in the New World), women did most of the agricultural field work. The social structure of the peoples of the Caribbean coast was even more loosely organized, and they relocated their villages more often.

In the spectrum of social and cultural patterns among the Indian population, Central America was a microcosm of the New World. Because these indigenous patterns indelibly marked Spanish colonial society,

Central America continued to contain much of the variety of New World social formations in miniature, as it were, throughout the colonial era and beyond. Although in land area and demography the scale is small, the extent of regional heterogeneity was (and continues to be) surprisingly great. This local distinctiveness is interesting for travelers, but at the same time it impedes political unity and sharply reduces the value of generalizations about Central America.

Conquest and Social Destruction

The Spanish Crown tried to control all exploration of the vast area of the New World, but there were few Spanish officials in the Indies at that time, and great distances, poor communications, and overwhelming uncertainties about what was involved made tight control impossible. Nonetheless, although the Spanish exploration and conquest of the New World was by and large conducted by entrepreneurs who organized and financed expeditions, the Spanish Crown was able to enforce, to a surprising degree, the need for official approval. The Crown tried to shape the composition of the expeditions (for instance, excluding non-Catholics and often preferring people from certain regions in Spain), but both leaders and followers were an extremely mixed lot of adventurers.

In virtually all aspects, royal officials had difficulty in controlling the Spanish conquest of the Indies, and the conquest of Central America, like that of the rest of the hemisphere, was anything but orderly. The first major campaign began from Panama, and its most notable member was Vasco Núñez de Balboa, who fled creditors in Hispaniola by joining the expedition to Panama that founded Darién.[3] Balboa quickly usurped authority from the victor of the squabble between competing leaders and sent the deposed leader back to Spain under arrest. With a small band, he then pushed south to the Pacific (the "South Sea"), which he reached in 1513. Balboa returned with substantial booty from coastal Indian villages to find that the Spanish Crown had replaced him as leader with Pedrarias Dávila. But the word of Balboa's discoveries and plunder made such an impression in Spain that the royal authorities reversed themselves and sent word that Balboa was to be honored. Before the message reached Panama, however, Pedrarias had arrested, summarily tried, and beheaded Balboa and four associates.

This was Pedrarias's style of operation, practiced throughout the years in which he administered Spanish colonies in Panama, Costa Rica, and Nicaragua until his death in 1531. It was under his leadership that Panama City was founded on the Pacific coast in 1519 and disease-ridden Darién abandoned. Shortly thereafter, he sent expeditions north and east; the first of these met and established amicable relations with Nicaoa, the principal chief of the area that later became Nicaragua. Subsequent expeditions, however, went to conquer.

Equally able, shrewd, and ruthless, the third major figure in the Spanish conquest of Central America—Pedro de Alvarado—entered Guatemala from Mexico. Hernán Cortés, who conquered the Aztecs in 1519 and 1520, sent this trusted lieutenant to explore Central America, following up Indians' stories about rich tribes farther south. It appears that Indians frequently told Spaniards about fabulous riches just a hundred or so miles further in order to keep the Spaniards moving on. Nevertheless, when Alvarado arrived in Guatemala from the Valley of Mexico in 1524 with 120 cavalry, 300 Spanish foot soldiers, and 20,000 Indian allies, he found the densely populated and relatively advanced descendants of the Maya. After the usual treachery, fighting, and skillful use of intertribal rivalries, Alvarado established himself as the most powerful figure in what is now Guatemala and El Salvador. Although his dominance was constantly challenged by both Spanish contenders and rebellious Indians, he brutally and successfully beat them down until he was killed in battle in 1541.

Because there was fragmentation and rivalry among the Central American Indian communities, the Spaniards were able to avoid fighting a unified empire, but they did have to conquer each tribe separately. Moreover, Indian tribes initially allied with the Spanish invaders soon realized that the Spaniards were more dangerous than their traditional enemies. Therefore, the conquest of Central America, and especially of Guatemala, was a more protracted and bloody process than in other parts of the Indies. The highlands of Costa Rica were not effectively controlled by the Spaniards until the 1570s, and some areas, such as northern Guatemala, were not subdued until the late seventeenth century.

There was less effective Indian resistance to the Spaniards in Honduras than in Guatemala, but 30,000 to 50,000 Indians died in the conquest. And in Honduras, fights among the Spaniards were especially bitter. In the early years of the conquest, Honduras was simultaneously claimed by Cortés, Pedrarias, and the governor of Hispaniola. Even Cortés's marching into Honduras from Mexico in 1525 failed to settle the conflicting claims.[4]

The reasons for the Spaniards' ability to subjugate so many people so far from Spain continue to be debated, although the major elements are clear. There is no question that animosities among various Indian groups throughout the New World helped considerably, and as has been noted, a divide-and-conquer strategy was successful in almost all parts of the Indies. The Spaniards also had the advantage of terror. Bearded white men clad in steel armor, mounted on horses, and armed with firearms were an extremely fearsome sight to people not familiar with any of the components. And worse yet, the whole picture was not entirely alien; at least parts of it often seemed to confirm some apocalyptic elements of Indian religion and mythology. Finally, the Spaniards were experienced, tough, and ruthless soldiers, products of a Spanish military tradition forged by centuries of struggling to reconquer the Iberian Peninsula from the Muslims.

But perhaps the most important factor in the conquest was disease. The indigenous peoples of the New World, like the aborigines of Australia and New Zealand, had been completely isolated from the pestilences that had been passed among the residents of Europe, Africa, and Asia for centuries. As recently as the fourteenth century, Europe experienced the Black Plague, which killed nearly half the population. When the Spaniards arrived in the New World, they brought a range of diseases against which the local populations had no immunities. Smallpox, measles, bubonic plague, typhus, influenza, malaria, and, later, yellow fever killed millions of Indians.[5]

Diseases greatly facilitated the conquest throughout the Indies. In Mexico, for instance, Cortés and his troops were initially invited into Tenochtitlán (now the site of Mexico City), the Aztec capital. While guests there, they kidnapped the Aztec leader and held him for ransom, which resulted in his death, although the specifics are unclear. It is not surprising, then, that the Aztecs drove the Spaniards out of the city; several months later they returned with reinforcements, including large numbers of Indian allies who for generations had chafed against Aztec oppression and cruelty. But by the time the Spaniards returned, the city was in the throes of a terrible smallpox epidemic caused by initial contact with the Europeans. The Aztecs' ability to repel the Spanish siege was seriously weakened.

The ravages of smallpox also helped Francisco Pizarro in his conquest of Peru. When Pizarro, a member of the original Darién expedition, invaded Peru with his henchmen in the 1530s, he found the Inca empire just beginning to recover from the convulsions of a civil war fought to determine which of two brothers would succeed their father as emperor. The emperor had died of smallpox (or perhaps measles), which had preceded the Spaniards' arrival by five years, and the resulting struggles between the sons vastly simplified the Spaniards' military task.

Disease paved the way for the conquest of Central America as well. By the time Alvarado began fighting the Maya in Guatemala, these organized, urban societies had already been severely weakened by smallpox epidemics.

Although some Spaniards, especially in the tropical coastal settlements, also became sick, they were much less affected than were the

Indian populations, who were ravaged by wave after wave of epidemics throughout the colonial period. During the sixteenth century, the Central American Indian population was reduced by almost 5.5 million people. This population loss—around 90 percent—was similar to that in other areas of Latin America. In fact, the sixteenth- and seventeenth-century depopulation of the New World was perhaps the worst demographic disaster in history. At the beginning of the sixteenth century, there were about 80 million people in the Americas, compared to 60 million in Europe. This 80 million constituted about 20 percent of the world's population; within a century, the population of the Americas had declined to about 3 percent of the people living on earth.

Population losses were not evenly spread. In Central America, the greatest losses occurred along the coasts and in Panama, where the local inhabitants virtually disappeared. In an attempt to maintain a work force, Spaniards repeatedly tried to replenish the Indian populations along the coast by forcing Indians from the interior to relocate there, but high death rates frustrated these attempts. Although still staggering, the rates of loss were lower among the highland Indians of Guatemala and Chiapas, the major centers of population and political authority throughout the colonial era.

The sharp reduction in the Central American Indian population was not all directly attributable to disease. The extended wars of conquest killed hundreds of thousands of Indians in battle and also led to starvation. After the Conquest, a terrible toll was taken by the amount and types of work forced on the Indians; the displacement of indigenous crops of corn (maize) and beans by wheat, sugar, grapes, and olives, introduced for the consumption of the Spaniards; and the destruction of Indian crops by the rapidly multiplying cattle introduced by the colonists. Moreover, the destruction of Indian cultures, communities, and social orders led to high rates of suicide, infanticide, fertility restriction, and alcoholism. These and other factors directly reduced the numbers of Indians and increased their vulnerability to disease.

Another reason for the declining numbers of Indians was their enslavement for sale to other regions during the first twenty years of Spanish domination. In this period, the material benefits of conquest were primarily from looting of both goods and peoples, especially the gold and silver that had been accumulated by the Indian communities over the years. One-fifth of the value of all precious metals appropriated by the Spaniards was supposed to be paid over to the Crown through a tax called the royal *quinto* (one-fifth of the value), which applied to virtually all economic activities. Most of this type of loot came from the highly organized societies of Mayan peoples.

The Indians themselves were another kind of booty. Because disease, overwork, and other hardships virtually destroyed the indigenous populations of the Caribbean islands and Panama in the first years of Spanish colonization, there were lucrative markets for slaves to work in the islands and to carry goods across the isthmus of Panama—the route of the rapidly growing commerce between Peru and Spain.

Although Spanish law prohibited Indian slavery except for those captured in war or those who had already been slaves in Indian societies, these rules were observed in the breach during the first decades after the Spanish conquest. Indians were indiscriminately rounded up, branded on the face or thigh, and sold abroad. Again, one-fifth of the proceeds, the quinto, was to go to the Spanish Crown. The major sources of Indian slaves for sale abroad were not the most densely populated areas of Central America, where already existing systems of labor organization could be used by the Spaniards. Rather, it was the less populous regions where social structures of the semisedentary and nomadic peoples did not lend themselves so readily to Spanish purposes. For instance, from Nicaragua alone, Spaniards exported over 400,000 Indian slaves to Panama, where few indigenous peoples still survived, and to Peru, where the Inca population had not yet been sufficiently subdued.[6] This commerce was the basis of an active boat-building industry on the Pacific coast of Nicaragua, which was well endowed with wood, pitch, and fibers for rope and canvas. And it also contributed to the virtual disappearance in Nicaragua of the indigenous population, stimulating the conquest of the Costa Rican highlands, which was a relatively densely populated area in the 1560s. Waves of epidemics in the late 1570s, however, decimated that population as well.

Production in the Early Years of the Colony

Neither looting nor slaving for export can be regarded as productive activities, although they were profitable, at least for a few Spaniards for a while. Pillaging, by its very nature, is an ephemeral source of income; longer-term profitable relationships require levels of sustained production and work force in a social framework that can be reproduced over time.

In early sixteenth-century Central America, commodities with strong markets outside the immediate area were the most obvious source of individual wealth for Spaniards. But the lack of adequate numbers of docile workers at this time was the most critical limit on the production and transportation of these commodities. The most desirable situation, of course, was when a valuable natural resource (e.g., minerals, good soil, and climate) was located close to large numbers of Indians who lived in stable and hierarchically organized societies. In this circumstance, the

Spaniards could simply appropriate for their own use the existing system under which a minority had already controlled the allocation and products of the work of the majority. The silver mining areas of the Valley of Mexico and of highland Peru were ideal in this respect. They both had a valuable economic resource in close proximity to large numbers of people with previously developed labor mobilization mechanisms capable of being adapted to Spanish purposes.

In Central America, something approximating this ideal was found in the areas of cacao cultivation, a major economic activity during the early years of colonial Central America. For years before the arrival of the Spaniards, Indians had raised cacao along the extreme southern Pacific coast of what is now Mexico and along the adjacent Pacific coasts of Guatemala and El Salvador to supply markets in Guatemala and especially in the Valley of Mexico. In pre-Columbian society, consumption of the chocolate drink made from cacao was restricted to the elites. After the Conquest, when the elites had for the most part been destroyed, social norms broke down, and cacao became popular with all Indians. They drank it with spices, including powdered chili pepper, a delicacy that did not initially find favor with the Spanish palate. Only later, perhaps after sugar cultivation was introduced to the Indies, did the Spaniards begin to use chocolate, which later became popular in Europe. Nevertheless, in the early years of Central American colonial history, the market for cacao was other Indians, and after looting, the Spaniards recognized the value of cacao beans, which were frequently used as money both before and after the Conquest.

The cultivation of cacao, a going concern long before the Spanish invasion, required considerable knowledge and skills and took place in areas where indigenous mechanisms of labor mobilization were well developed and could be taken over by the Spaniards. As a consequence, the Spaniards did not have to become directly involved in cacao production. They had come to the Indies not to become farmers but to become lords. Therefore, they were much more interested in controlling labor than land during the first decades of the colony. This interest was in line with the desires of the Spanish monarch, who from bitter experience in Spain was reluctant to grant land to the conquerors, who might become a landed class powerful enough to challenge royal authority.

Instead of land, then, the Crown granted people to the conquerors, or more precisely, their products and services. These grants, known as *encomiendas* and their holders as *encomenderos,* put a Spaniard in charge of an Indian village or group of villages but was awarded no property rights in land. The encomendero was obligated to convert the Indians to Christianity, support a priest, and look after the Indians' general welfare. In exchange for these services, the encomendero could levy a tribute in kind from the villages and in the early days conscript a certain amount of labor service from them. Encomenderos were prohibited from living in Indian villages, exactions from the villages were restricted by law, and the right to pass encomiendas to succeeding generations was limited.

It was not long after the Conquest that encomenderos were prohibited from demanding direct labor services, but local officials levied labor quotas (*repartimientos*) from villages for the construction of public roads and buildings, for instance, and for allocation to private individuals to use for their own projects. Even though the direct control of labor services was uncertain, the encomienda was the basic device for mobilizing Indian agricultural labor in general and cacao labor in particular through the control of products of Indian labor. It was primarily through the encomienda system that Indian labor supplied foodstuffs to the cities and cacao to the Spaniards in the first century or so in colonial Central America.

This tribute system for requisitioning the products of Indian labor worked through a village headman and left the production decisions in the hands of Indians. The significance of this can easily be overstated, because the Spaniards imposed a headman system when one had not already existed in a village, and they frequently appointed the headman. Nevertheless, Spaniards did not actually organize and direct production, and this relatively indirect relationship contained the potential of preserving aspects of traditional Indian life and thereby maintaining a sharp distinction between the world of the Indian and that of the Spaniard. While this occurred in some places, the flexibility (for the encomendero) of the encomienda tribute system often undercut the possibility of social and cultural preservation.

Unlike Mexican encomenderos, for whom the size, composition, and payment schedule of the tribute soon became standardized, those in Central America had considerably more latitude in determining the volume and form of tributes. The imposition of very heavy tributes could press the material standard of living of an Indian community to the point that the community and many of its individuals were destroyed. This was common in the early days of the Central American colony, but the composition of the tribute also could destroy Indian communities.

Cacao production illustrates the destructive effects of both the level and product mix of encomienda tribute. The quantitative burden of the tributes levied by encomenderos in cacao-growing areas contributed to the disappearance of something on the order of 97 percent of the Indian population. The resulting labor shortage made it feasible for encomenderos in the highlands to share some of the profits from this lucrative crop by changing the products they demanded from the Indians in their own encomiendas. The highland encomenderos demanded tribute in cacao, thus forcing Indians from their encomiendas to migrate to the Pacific coast and augment the declining cacao labor force. The radical change in climate and the work with unfamiliar crops made these immigrants especially susceptible to disease and debilitation, and cacao production, which was labor intensive because of the delicacy of the bushes, continued to be threatened by serious labor shortages. Moreover, long absences of large numbers of able-bodied males from the highland communities made it difficult for those remaining in the highlands to produce enough for subsistence. Moreover, this situation must have had a serious effect on community gender relations, including those related to power. Both consequences greatly affected the communities' cultural patterns.

Encomenderos manipulated the composition of the tribute to the disadvantage of Indian communities in other ways as well. For example, some demanded tribute in silver, gold, wheat, wool, woven cloths, and other kinds of goods desired by Spaniards. As in the case of cacao, tributes in these products often forced Indians to leave their communities to work in areas in which that particular commodity was available or, in the best of circumstances, to remain in their communities but to change traditional patterns of cultivation and work in order to produce unfamiliar European goods.

As noted, the encomienda as well as labor conscription by the public authorities worked best in areas where stable and hierarchically organized indigenous societies had developed systems by which a minority controlled the allocation and products of the work of the majority. The Valley of Mexico, the highlands of Peru, and the Mayan regions of Central America were the sites of the most extensive and successful use of the encomienda and repartimiento, adapted from pre-Conquest institutions.

Outside the Mayan regions, the organization of indigenous societies had been less complex and more egalitarian. As a consequence, it was much more difficult to coerce Indians to work for Spaniards, even apart from the continuing decline in numbers. After slavery was abolished, the encomienda system survived, but sometimes, as in the case of Honduran and Nicaraguan cattle ranches, local conditions militated against easy implementation. In such unpropitious circumstances, the encomienda system was replaced by something closer to debt peonage or even a wage system. These devices were based more on coercing or attracting individuals to a particular activity rather than on imposing tribute on a collective. In any case, the system was less rigid and did not result in the sharpness of the distinction between Spanish and Indian worlds. There was more of a cultural continuum rather than the either/or of the purer encomienda system, where tribute was imposed on Indians as Indians.

In colonial Central America, contrary to the logic of neoclassical economic theory, severe labor shortages seldom worked to the advantage of workers. These shortages were more likely to lead to tighter controls over labor than to higher wages. In the early decades of the sixteenth century, outright slavery was a common Spanish response to labor scarcity where the organization of Indian communities did not lend themselves to the encomienda system. In addition to the large number of Indians sold outside the region as slaves, Indian slaves were also used within Central America, especially where labor needs were intense and there were obstacles to mobilizing indigenous labor through indigenous mechanisms.

Among the most common occupations assigned Indian slaves was that of porter, and it was also one of the most brutal. Chroniclers report that when an Indian porter fell because of exhaustion or accident, instead of unlocking the neck ring that connected the fallen individual by chain to the other porters, Spanish overseers frequently severed his or her head in order not to hold up the line. (There are also numerous documented accounts of Spanish brutality unrelated to efficiency, no matter how defined.) Starvation and injuries were also frequent causes of the death of Indian porters. On one journey, which began in Honduras with 4,000 porters, fewer than 50 returned.

Large numbers of Indian slaves were also put to work in procuring precious metals. The Spaniards quickly discovered that many streams in Honduras, Guatemala, and later the northern mountains of Nicaragua contained substantial amounts of alluvial gold and silver. Gangs of up to 100 slaves washed the gold, mined surface deposits of silver, and then moved on to other sites. In mining as well as other tasks to which Indian labor was allocated, African slaves, who appeared more able than Indians to withstand the rigors of systematically organized work and to adopt Spanish ways, were frequently employed as overseers, artisans, and skilled workers. Although African slaves were expensive, it seems to have been increasingly worth the extra cost, especially as the numbers of Indians declined. For example, there were 1,500 African slaves working in one Honduran mining region by the 1540s.

The Beginnings of Colonial Society

For the Spanish Crown and its agents in Central America, the question was how to make their control of the region yield long-term material benefits. Based on earlier experience in the Caribbean islands and on reports reaching Spain from Central America, it was becoming clear to authorities in Spain that shortsighted Spanish settlers were using such predatory practices that they could not be trusted to further the interests of the empire (and often not even their own). The encomienda system was killing Indians at an unacceptable rate, and Indian slaves were dying at an even higher rate. As a consequence, Indian slavery was abolished and the encomienda system became subject to greater regulation and taxation by the middle of the sixteenth century.

The arrival, at about this time, of the Catholic religious orders, primarily Dominicans and Franciscans, also increased political and moral pressure on the Spanish settlers to change their treatment of the Indians. The pope had decreed that the entire Spanish American Church structure, including the regular Catholic orders, be placed under the direct and immediate control of the Spanish Crown. The Church, therefore, was a formal arm of the state, and royal officials even collected the tithe. But the Dominican and Franciscan friars, unlike the priests who had accompanied the early conquerors, were not subordinate to the individual conquerors, and they moved forcefully to ameliorate the conditions of the Indians and to convert them to Christianity. In this first generation of Churchmen in Central America, the most notable protector of the Indians was Bartolomé de las Casas, the fiery first bishop of Chiapas. He was the driving force behind the New Laws of 1542, which prohibited many practices that exploited and brutalized the Indians.

The enthusiasm displayed by the members of the religious orders for sheltering and Christianizing the Indians included some actions that certainly were not in the Indians' earthly interests. Especially notable in this regard was their massive and largely successful project to "congregate" Indians into centralized settlements. Between 1543 and 1550, the Spanish friars, by persuasion and coercion, relocated over half of Guatemala's Indian population into new towns. The principal reason for this forced resettlement was to facilitate evangelical efforts, to monitor relations with the Spaniards, and probably for the Church to mobilize the labor necessary for an ambitious program of church construction. But the forced congregation also had some unintended consequences: It increased the spread of communicable diseases, disrupted subsistence agriculture, and freed up land for Spaniards. The immediate importance of the last can easily be exaggerated. With the death of so many Indians, empty land was already plentiful, whereas the labor necessary to make the land valuable for Spaniards uninterested in working it themselves was increasingly scarce. The control of labor rather than of land was key to the good life.

Independent of reformist zeal, however, Indian slavery, both as commerce and as a way to utilize labor within Central America, was already in sharp decline by the 1540s. In addition to the increasing shortage of Indians, there was a reduction in market demand for Indian slaves: Indian porters in Panama and Central America were replaced by mules and horses as roads became better, and the number of African slaves in the Caribbean islands and in Central America rose, reducing the need for Indian slaves. Even the most humanitarian voices in colonial Latin America had no qualms about enslaving Africans. Unlike Indians, Africans were not considered to be vassals of the Spanish Crown and therefore could be enslaved. Moreover, many of the Africans were tainted with Islam, and again unlike the Indians, they could be seen as infidels rather than innocents. The importance of these rationales is questionable, however, because African slavery functioned profitably for important segments of Spanish colonial society haunted by severe labor shortages.

To make effective the restrictions on Indian slavery, the encomienda, and repartimiento, the Crown substantially strengthened its administrative authority in Central America. But given the frontier conditions in Central America and the distances separating Spain from the Indies, and the fact that bribes were an important and expected part of the reward for underpaid officials, it was extremely difficult to implement policies that protected Indians from rapacious treatment. For instance, in an outlying, impoverished area like Costa Rica, Indian slavery (and even the export of Indian slaves to the English Caribbean) persisted into the early eighteenth century, thinly disguised as encomienda and repartimiento. Even in cases involving flagrant violations of laws, a group of encomenderos could appeal a local ruling to authorities in Spain and be able to count on at least a year passing before they would hear about the appeal's disposition. Still, by the middle of the sixteenth century, greater numbers of Spanish officials and Churchmen improved law enforcement and juridical procedures in Central America. As the Crown asserted control over Central America, royal officials and Churchmen increasingly assumed the poorly executed custodial functions of the encomienda, regulated the amounts and composition of tributes, and monitored repartimiento labor.

The geographical lines of Central American colonial administration did not change significantly in the 300 years that Central America was a Spanish colony. The five republics of modern Central America were a part of the Captaincy General of Guatemala, with its capital in the province of Guatemala, and in an ill-defined way, subordinate to the viceroyalty of New Spain (Mexico). Panama, attached to New Granada (northern South America), was outside the administrative sphere of Central America and Mexico.

The transition from the anarchy of personal rule by individual conquerors to governance by a colonial state, staffed by Spanish civil and ecclesiastical bureaucrats, was feasible by midcentury, in part because most of the powerful figures of the Conquest were by then either dead or getting on in years. Nevertheless, the enforcement of more restrictive

Spanish laws did provoke strong protests from Spanish settlers. In one such incident, Nicaraguan encomenderos murdered a reformist bishop and attempted to revolt against Spanish authority. Although this is an extreme example, the incident reflects the Spanish settlers' passions, and much of what we know of colonial Latin America, including Central America, comes from the voluminous letters of complaint and supplication written to the Spanish Crown by disgruntled Spaniards in the New World.

With the establishment of effective Spanish political authority in Central America, the Spanish Crown and its agents developed an elaborate colonial policy. A clear understanding of the Spanish state's interests and intentions in colonial Latin America is necessary to make sense of this policy.

Spain in the Era of Mercantile Colonialism

First of all, it is important to remember that "Spain" was quite new as a consolidated national entity in the sixteenth century. In the first great burst of Islamic expansion, which began during Mohammed's lifetime in the seventh century, the Muslims and their religion swept through North Africa and had conquered the Iberian Peninsula by the eighth century. Over the centuries, the Christians pushed back the Moors, as they were called in Spain. The first successful drive south by Christian forces was along the west coast of the Iberian Peninsula, which became the nation of Portugal.[7]

Subsequent Christian efforts resulted in the creation of two additional kingdoms. The largest and most powerful, Castile, occupied the center of Iberia, and the other, Aragon, ran along the east coast (and included Naples, Sicily, Sardinia, and Navarre). The centuries-long struggle against the Moorish invaders, a process known in Spanish history as the *Reconquista,* was not completed until 1492, when the Christians took Granada, the Moors' last stronghold on the Iberian Peninsula. The marriage in 1469 of Isabella, future Queen of Castile, to Ferdinand, future King of Aragon, was an important dynastic merger. When the monarchs inherited their respective kingdoms, the unification of the nation known today as Spain began.

The Reconquista gave the Spaniards a strong militaristic legacy, and many early conquerors of the Indies were veterans of those campaigns. There is no question that they were a rough bunch, and for individual Spaniards the conventional triad of gold, glory, and the gospel adequately represents their motivations. But whatever their personal motivations, they operated in a framework of forces broader than individual aspirations and broader than Spain's recent history.

Western Europe's vigorous exploration and empire building in the fifteenth and sixteenth centuries, which incorporated large parts of Africa, Asia, and Latin America into a world economy dominated by Europe, was a general western European phenomenon not limited to Spain. These western European imperial projects were not the first large-scale empires the world had known, but the character of these earlier empires—primarily based on looting and tribute—differed significantly from early modern empires and reflected the changing social organization and technical conditions of production in the imperial center.

The role of merchants and monarchs—the sponsors of western European expansion—reveals the domestic roots of early modern imperialism. The merchants' desire for mercantile profits requires no explanation. However, it is important to understand why that desire became translated into national policy in sixteenth- and seventeenth-century Europe. The answer lies in the need felt by European monarchs of the period for revenues from overseas activities.

Throughout western Europe, monarchs were struggling against the political remnants of feudalism with its decentralized system of local barons and lords. The monarchs were trying to establish centralized national political systems with monarchical control over internal affairs, and they were persistently pressed financially. One major expenditure for ambitious monarchs was to buy the services of mercenary armies that had no allegiances to local barons.

Revenue from overseas commerce was highly desirable because it was derived from an activity that did not strengthen local barons or require their consent. Monarchs gained such revenue by directly investing in foreign expeditions and by selling franchises for mercantile monopolies that also facilitated efficient tax collection. The merchant-monarch alliances varied in their mix of relative power between the two groups, and Holland with its mercantile oligarchy and Spain with its powerful monarchy probably defined the endpoints of the continuum in the sixteenth and early seventeenth centuries.

Although the Spanish Crown certainly desired new sources of revenue to short-circuit rival power blocs within Spain, its need for fiscal resources went beyond the exigencies of domestic politics. Isabella died in 1504, Ferdinand in 1516, and their grandson, offspring of a daughter and a Hapsburg prince, became Charles I of Spain. Charles was the first of the Spanish Hapsburg dynasty, which was to rule Spain for 200 years. After devious and expensive machinations, he soon also became Charles V, emperor of the Holy Roman Empire, and it is as Charles V that he is known in history. Along with the Holy Roman Empire, Spain assumed primary responsibility for defending Europe from the second great wave of Islamic expansion, the Ottoman expansion with its center in Turkey. In the early sixteenth century, the Ottomans controlled the lands around the eastern Mediterranean, were rapidly taking over the Balkans, and were soon knocking on the gates of Vienna.

As though again defending Christianity from the infidels were not enough of a strain, Spain also became the leader in the major schism among Christians: Catholicism versus the Protestant Reformation. Because the Spanish king had to bribe or otherwise neutralize the nobility and other centrifugal tendencies within Spain, fight the Ottomans, and mount the Counter-Reformation, the Spanish government was very eager, often desperate, for new fiscal resources.

At the time, an ideal source of such revenues would be to take over an established, lucrative trade and extract high profits through a commercial monopoly protected by cannon. The obvious target in the fifteenth century was the trade with the Orient in articles whose high value for volume was profitable in spite of high transportation costs. This trade included Chinese silks, porcelain, rhubarb (used as a medicine), Indian cottons, and precious stones, but the real prize of East-West commerce was the trade in spices: pepper from India, ginger from China, cinnamon from Ceylon, and especially the nutmeg, mace, and cloves from the Spice Islands of present-day Indonesia.

Some of the demand for Eastern spices was definitely a luxury demand, reflecting the creation in Renaissance Europe of a distinctive cuisine for privileged palates. The new cuisine was qualitatively rather than merely quantitatively different from what the majority of people ate, and stylized table manners were part of this general development of increasing the cultural distance between classes at this time.[8] But because most peasants had to preserve meat since they could not feed livestock over the winter, even peasants bought Eastern spices to complement the use of other, less satisfactory, preservatives (e.g., salt and West African pepper).

In the fifteenth century, although having to accommodate to changes brought about by Ottoman expansion, the Venetians exercised a near monopoly in the last geographical link of the spice and Asian trade: from the purchase of the spices from Arab traders in the Levant and Egypt to their sale in western Mediterranean ports. This monopoly was the initial target of the Iberians, whose intentions were not to destroy it but to take it over intact.

In spite of the great strides taken in the design and construction of Iberian sailing ships and naval cannon, these vessels were still no match for Venetian or Ottoman galleys in the Mediterranean. But on the high seas, the many small cannon of the Iberian vessels, their more efficient use of wind, and their greater seaworthiness and maneuverability gave them the decisive edge over the great galleys, which continued to depend on ramming and boarding tactics supplemented by one or two large siege cannons located in the bows.

The inability to confront directly either the Venetians or Muslims within the Mediterranean indicates the critical importance for Portugal of Bartholemeu Dias's sailing around the southern end of Africa in the 1480s and Vasco de Gama's successful expedition around Africa to India in the last years of the fifteenth century. Having found a sea route to India free from the Venetians and Ottomans, the Portuguese could break the Mediterranean traders' hold on Asian trade and establish their own monopoly.

Sticking to the seas and establishing posts on the coast that could be protected and supplied from the seas, the Portuguese successively took over each link on the spice trade—Venetian and Ottoman, Arab, Hindu, and Chinese—until they were dealing directly with the princes of the Spice Islands. By the third decade of the sixteenth century, the bulk of trade between Asia and western Europe was going around Africa in Portuguese ships. In the late sixteenth century, however, Spain invaded Portugal, and the Dutch, who had recently succeeded in throwing off a century of Spanish rule, took the Asian trade (and the colony of Brazil) away from the Portuguese.

The purpose of this historical and geographical excursion has been to establish the distinctive principles that underlay sixteenth- and seventeenth-century European expansion. Looting and tribute—central features of earlier expansions—were still important, but the Portuguese and Dutch were principally pursuing a more modern goal: mercantile profits. There was no strong drive to find investment outlets, raw materials for local production, sources of food supplies, areas to settle excess populations, or markets for domestically produced goods. These were features of international expansion by later, more advanced capitalist economies. The principal purpose of the sixteenth-century western European penetration into new areas was mercantile: controlling the flow of desired commodities for sale to all of Europe to ensure high profits. The establishment of Brazilian and Caribbean sugar plantations in the sixteenth and seventeenth centuries reflected a similar mercantile impulse.

The Spaniards in the fifteenth century were also after the Asian trade, but because of the Reconquista and struggles around national consolidation, the entire effort of exploration and mercantile expansion began later than Portugal's and was not as systematic. In addition, the national base of commercial institutions and power was not as secure. Because the African coast was already controlled by the Portuguese, the Spaniards sponsored Columbus's expedition. Reflecting her position as the most powerful of the two monarchs, Isabella was the actual sponsor who with her advisers decided to take the chance that our planet was small enough to make going west a commercially feasible route to the Spice Islands. This, rather than uncertainties about whether the world was round or flat, was the principal issue.

On the way to the Indies, however, the expedition bumped into the New World. There was considerable initial confusion over the next few years over what had been found and where it was, thus the inaccurate naming of "Indies" and "Indians." The first circumnavigation of the globe, by Ferdinand Magellan's expedition in the early 1520s, graphically demonstrated that Columbus's Spanish critics were right: The world was indeed so large that going west from Europe was not a practicable route to the Spice Islands. As Amerigo Vespucci (after whom the Americas were named) had contended, what Columbus had run into was a very large land mass unknown to Europeans except in unconfirmed tales and legends.

The Spanish Crown was interested in protecting its claim in the New World on the chance that something valuable might come of it, but new exploration, though monitored by the king's agents, was initially haphazard and left to individual initiative. It was not until Cortés, the quintessential military entrepreneur, defeated the Aztecs and looted Tenochtitlán (Mexico City) that royal attention was seriously engaged. The Spanish Crown became thoroughly committed to the New World enterprise with the pillage of the Inca empire and the opening of the rich silver mines in Mexico and Peru. Silver was a very useful commodity, and its high value for bulk made it worthwhile to mine in the Indies for use in Europe.

But in light of the discussion of the spice trade, it is crucial to stress how limited, by modern standards, were the Spanish Crown's aims in the New World. Royal interest, for all intents and purposes, was confined to precious metals, and the institutions of colonial society were deliberately designed to ensure the flow of labor and provisions to the mines and the flow of metals from the mines to Spain. The most important mines (and therefore the most important colonial administrative centers) were in Mexico and Peru.

Even though it was the hopes of mercantile profits (and consequent fiscal resources) that led to the Spaniards' stumbling onto the New World, this motive was quickly overshadowed by the availability of monetary metal. The Crown enthusiastically grasped the opportunity of achieving greater and more immediate sources of revenue through mining specie (gold and silver), and this meant the subordination of the commercial possibilities of Spanish colonization in the New World in favor of promoting unilateral transfers of gold and especially silver from the mines in the New World.

Monetary metal has an ambiguous status as both commodity and money. The fundamental relationship between Hapsburg Spain and Spanish America was not the typical mercantile arrangement that combined political control and market opportunities to realize fiscal receipts through commercial profits. Instead, the colonial relationship quickly became a tribute relationship, predicated exclusively on political control to wring fiscal resources from the area by tribute. As such, the relationship of the Spanish imperial center to its New World was already archaic in the sixteenth and seventeenth centuries, and the success of the Spaniards was also their failure. By operating a successful tribute empire, the Spaniards limited subsequent national economic and political development by stunting the growth of commercial and industrial sectors within Spain. The tribute core of the imperial project was much closer to that of the Ottoman, Inca, Aztec, and even Roman and Egyptian empires than to the seventeenth-century mercantile empires of Holland and England.

Plantations worked by Indians and African slaves on the Caribbean islands and the coasts of Mexico, Central America, Venezuela, Colombia, Ecuador, and Peru did grow and export sugar, cacao, tobacco, dyes, spices, and other tropical produce. But Spanish policy until the middle of the eighteenth century so restrained their development that Spanish plantations lagged far behind those of the French and English Caribbean islands and of Portuguese or Dutch Brazil. Spanish planters constantly complained about inadequate supplies of African slaves, and their exports and imports were taxed heavily, funneled through interlocking monopolies of trading guilds (*consulados*) that blatantly manipulated prices to the disadvantage of initial sellers and final purchasers, and transported to Europe by an unreliable Spanish fleet system.

For the Spanish authorities, the primary importance of these plantations, whose crops competed with those from the Canary Islands and Andalusia, was to encourage the settlement and protection of strategic areas with minimum expenditure. The lack of Crown interest in the outlying ranching areas in Argentina, Chile, southern Venezuela, and northern Mexico also demonstrated the Crown's indifference toward any productive or commercial activity apart from that which directly and indirectly supported the extraction and transport of precious metal.

Spanish colonial aims certainly did not represent the progressive edge of contemporary European expansion. Although Spanish society and economy were capable of benefiting from an authentic mercantile imperialism, the opportunities discovered in the New World were such that Spanish colonial policy essentially regressed. The Crown saw in the silver mines the clearest and most obvious source of fiscal revenues, and they were developed at the expense of other possibilities. The interests of the Spanish merchant consulados, which were the most powerful commercial interests in Spain, lay in expanding trade with the New World, even though in that trade Spain was principally an entrepôt for goods produced in other nations. But the interests of the merchant guilds were consistently and effectively subordinated to those of the Spanish Crown. The flow of specie was paramount, and the Crown tolerated the development of commercial potential only when it supported (or at least did not compete with) the acquisition of specie.

It is necessary, however, to appreciate how important the New World colonies were to the Spanish Crown. One interesting illustration of Spanish seriousness of purpose in the Indies is the Crown's efforts to prevent migration to the New World by people from Spain deemed undesirable (for example, Jews, Moors, heretics, and in the early years even those from Aragon). This contrasts sharply with English migration policy in the North American colonies, which in the seventeenth century appeared to be used as a dumping ground for social undesirables, including prisoners and political and religious dissidents.

Marginalization and Economic Decay in Central America

With this understanding of Spanish imperial aims, one can more readily understand the reasons that Central America was becoming peripheral to the Crown's interest in the New World by the second half of the sixteenth century. Despite initial discoveries of gold and silver deposits, Central American mining declined after the midsixteenth-century peak, around the time the rich silver mines in Mexico and Peru were discovered. Many Spaniards, frustrated by a conquest that took more effort and yielded fewer easy benefits than in other regions, left Central America for what seemed to be greener pastures elsewhere.

The economic promise of Central America for profitable colonial exploitation was limited to tropical agricultural produce, and it might have been realized if the Spanish Crown had pursued a systematic policy of mercantile imperialism. But Hapsburg colonial policy remained indifferent to developing this agricultural potential beyond what was necessary to maintain a Spanish presence to secure the area from foreign penetration.

Cacao production and export, so important in the sixteenth century, declined precipitously in the seventeenth century. In addition to being strangled by the prohibitions, restrictions, and high taxes imposed by Spanish commercial policy, cacao production in Central America was severely limited by competition from Venezuela and Ecuador and most of all by labor shortages. Although Spaniards in the cacao-producing areas of the Pacific coast supplemented the Indian work force with substantial numbers of African slaves in the seventeenth century, the sixteenth century was the peak years for Central American cacao output.

Nevertheless, cacao continued to be produced in various parts of Central America throughout the colonial period. For instance, there was a minor cacao boom on the Caribbean coast of Costa Rica in the seventeenth century. Despite Spanish commercial policy as well as frequent attacks by pirates, Miskito Indians, and escaped African slaves, the plantations achieved some prosperity through illegal trade with the Dutch and English. And even in Guatemala, cacao continued to be the economic base for a small but powerful group of merchants and growers.

So while the Crown asserted control over local strongmen and the Indians through its officers and the clergy, Central America was becoming a colonial backwater, whose principal importance in Spain's overall colonial design was its strategic proximity to Mexican and Peruvian mines and trade routes. But even in matters of transit, Panama continued to be the major route for the riches of Peru and the site of annual fairs at Porto Bello despite Central American efforts to develop competing routes through Nicaragua and Honduras.

The economic influence of Panama was especially strong in the southern areas of Central America. Although Costa Rica was administratively part of the Guatemalan Capitancy General, the Panamanian fairs and fleets were the principal markets for Costa Rica's marketed produce as well as for a very large proportion of Nicaragua's mules. The seventeenth-century decline of the Spanish fleet system therefore contributed to Central America's general economic malaise and confirmed Costa Rica's status as a poor outpost of a colonial backwater.

A major exception to Hapsburg Spain's desultory attitude toward commercial development of tropical agriculture in Central America was the Crown's strong support for cochineal in early seventeenth-century Guatemala and Nicaragua. This fast, scarlet dye was produced in pre-Conquest Mexico. It is made from the bodies of a female insect that lives on the nopal cactus. In spite of official encouragement, however, locusts, rains, and shortages of the skilled Indian labor needed to nurture and harvest the insect curtailed the growth of cochineal production.

Other efforts to find new high-value exports on which to build personal fortunes in seventeenth-century Central America either failed or had only limited success. For instance, balsam and sarsaparilla, used for salves and cosmetics, were temporarily promising, but local supplies were limited and were soon harvested at rates exceeding the ability of the wild plants to regenerate. Hides and leather from Honduras and Nicaragua had better long-term prospects, but Spain itself produced quality leathers, and the high transportation costs and the consulados' monopoly on trade put Central American ranchers at a competitive disadvantage and kept returns at modest levels.

Indigo was seen as the salvation for the sagging economy and personal prospects. In the last two decades of the sixteenth century, Spaniards began to organize plantations of the hardy plant that produced the fast blue dye and to build crude dye works for processing it. Indigo was grown on the Pacific coast from what is now El Salvador through Nicaragua, areas formerly devoted to cacao. Unlike cacao, however, indigo required large numbers of unskilled workers only three months a year.

By 1600, indigo was Central America's most valuable export, and the future looked bright. Although indigo production and export remained important throughout the seventeenth century, the bright future never materialized. Many factors conspired to keep indigo from becoming a dynamic sector that might have energized the slowing economy of sixteenth-century Central America: labor shortages, official prohibitions on the use of Indian labor in the corrosive process of dye making, restrictive trade regulations, high taxes, the decline of the Spanish textile industry (and thus the demand for indigo), high transport costs, pirates in the Caribbean, and the increasingly erratic and unreliable Spanish fleet system (which had virtually collapsed by 1630).

At the same time, Spanish Central America was experiencing increasing external pressure that both contributed to and reflected these problems. During the seventeenth century, the British seized Jamaica and established a permanent settlement in Belize. On the one hand, with Belize in English hands, Spaniards were better able to avoid the restrictive and expensive Spanish commercial system through smuggling. On the other hand, the English and their Indian allies could easily interdict legal colonial commerce through the Gulf of Honduras. These same forces, along with free-lance pirates, made commerce from other points along the Caribbean coast of Central America increasingly risky. The sacking of the town of Granada, in western Nicaragua, by Caribbean pirates in the middle of the seventeenth century underscored the pirates' growing boldness and Spanish weakness. Central American losses from the reduction in trade with Europe through the Caribbean coast were partially offset by increased trade with Peru and Manila from the Pacific coast, but only partially.

The aggregate consequence of all these factors was that Central America slid slowly downward into the seventeenth century. The seventeenth century was a time of economic depression for all of Spanish America, indeed for Europe, but Central America was in the lead. Perhaps because of this leadership in economic decay, the size of the Central American Indian population reached its nadir in the early seventeenth century, several decades before the end of the contraction of Indian populations in other parts of the continental empire.

The slowdown of economic activity in the region put severe strains on the living standards of Spanish urban dwellers. Their incomes shrank while the costs of maintaining their life-styles rose. The rising costs of aristocratic standards of consumption resulted primarily from the decline in the Indian working population, who provided most of the goods and services consumed by urban Spaniards, and to the prohibitive costs of high-status imported goods.

The decline in urban living standards prompted many of those Spaniards who remained in Central America to move from the cities into the countryside during the seventeenth century. They occupied some of the lands left empty by the population decline, or the Spaniards removed Indians settled on desirable parcels by force or chicanery. Spanish settlers in poorer, outlying areas of southern Central America were always much closer to the land than their more urban counterparts in the northern provinces, but this seventeenth-century rural movement was the beginning of the Guatemalan and Salvadoran *hacienda,* which, unlike the encomienda, was privately owned land. The hacienda was like the encomienda, however, in that the work was done primarily by Indians.

While haciendas were replacing encomiendas as the most important form of controlling agricultural production for individuals, both the Crown and the Church still controlled extensive holdings in the form of encomiendas, and Indian tribute from the encomiendas accounted for more than three-quarters of the Spanish Crown's fiscal receipts from Central America during the seventeenth century. The Church held haciendas as well as encomiendas, and their magnitude made it a formidable economic power by the end of the seventeenth century. The Church's agricultural holdings were principally in Guatemala and included substantial interests in sugarcane fields and mills, and the Church was the major source of credit throughout the isthmus.

The means by which Indians were recruited into the growing private hacienda sector varied. Some Indians became members of a permanent work force on a hacienda through the transformation of encomienda tributes, but more frequent was the change from corporate responsibilities—the tribute levied on a village of Indians as Indians—to individual contracts. In addition to a range of coercive devices, such as debt peonage, there was a fair amount of voluntary movement to haciendas by Indians. Although there is no question that life on Central American haciendas for Indians was far from pleasant, the haciendas did offer an Indian family a parcel of land and protection from the endless depredations to which corrupt agents of the Crown, predatory clergy, and local Indian officials subjected Indians living in tributary villages. That "free choice" simply illustrated how bad the alternatives were.

Some haciendas were rather grand affairs, but the vast majority of them were quite modest, even poor, semisubsistence units with a handful of workers. The haciendas expressed, to a real extent, the end of the Spanish dream. The conquerors had come to the Indies not to operate farms or ranches but rather to be supported luxuriously in a city by a docile and productive work force. The ultimate hope for many was to amass enough wealth to return to Spain, live like barons, and be prominent in royal court activities. For those two or three generations removed from the conquerors, the dream was dead, and succeeding generations of Spaniards struggled simply to get by.

These later generations were not even regarded as true Spaniards by their peninsular contemporaries. People born in the Indies to Spanish parents were known as *criollos,* quite distinct from those New World residents born in Spain, known as *peninsulares.* The Crown was always a bit uncertain about the loyalty of the criollos, and the upper reaches of governmental and ecclesiastical bureaucracies in the Indies were staffed, to all intents and purposes, exclusively by peninsulares who were appointed with the expectation that they would return to Spain after leaving office.

The other new population group, much more numerous than the criollos, was the *castas,* who combined the blood of Indians, Spaniards, and Africans. People of mixed Indian and Spanish parentage were known as *mestizos,* those of African and Spanish parentage were known as *mulatos,* and children of Indian and African parentage were called *zambos.* Needless to say, Spaniards fathered offspring in the first two categories in the early years, and escaped African slaves and unconquered Indians were the principal sources of zambo communities. The largest concentrations of zambos, sometimes allied with Miskito Indians, pirates, and the English navy, controlled large stretches of the Caribbean coast, where they were known as Caribs—not to be confused with the indigenous people of the Caribbean Islands.

These were the basic categories, and for a while, Spaniards in the Indies had specific names for each combination and proportion of racial mix. This is in sharp contrast to Anglo-American either/or practices (e.g., people with any African ancestry being categorized as "Negro"). But racial combinations soon became too complex and the vocabulary too cumbersome even for race-sensitive, "pure-blooded" Europeans in seventeenth-century Central America. Therefore, they adopted a more general term, *ladino.* Ladino is a cultural rather than strictly racial term, a label for people who are hispanicized to the extent of speaking Spanish, wearing European apparel, and so on. Ladinos could be of completely

Indian ancestry or they might be mestizos or zambos, as long as they demonstrated definite assimilation with the rulers' ways of life and the ability to operate in the Spanish world of colonial Central America. In current usage, ladino includes those of pure European origins, but during the colonial period, criollo and peninsulare were distinguished from ladino.

Throughout the colonial period, ladinos were the most rapidly growing sector of the population, and they usually lived in the interstices of Spanish and Indian societies, working as brokers between the two groups. In this role, one found many ladinos in the lower echelons of rural officialdom and the police and in occupations such as small traders and foremen on haciendas, construction projects, and indigo works. In addition, ladinos were also prominent in transportation (mule drivers) and as cowboys, artisans, owners and operators of small commercial farms and in a wide range of entrepreneurial activities. Ladinos as a group were notorious among Indians for preying on the native communities, and some groups of ladinos—especially cowboys, many of whom were of African descent—were feared by Spaniards as well.

The major ladino areas were those where Spanish economic activity was most intense as well as where the indigenous populations had all but disappeared.[9] The former included areas of El Salvador used for intensive indigo production. As previously noted, indigo required only a seasonal and unskilled labor force, and as such Spaniards organized and supervised production with ladino help. Yet the zones of El Salvador that experienced intensive cacao but not indigo production did not become as ladinoized. Because of high skill requirements, Spaniards left cacao cultivation in Indian hands and taxed off the product by way of tribute. The difference in the effects of the two crops on the material welfare of workers, however, was much less significant.

In regions with relatively few surviving indigenous peoples, such as the cattle-ranching and wheat-farming areas of southeastern Guatemala, Honduras, and the plains of El Salvador and Nicaragua, highly ladinoized populations also were prominent. The highlands of Costa Rica, with few indigenous peoples and a small number of Spaniards engaged in semisubsistence agriculture on small plots, were principally European.

The Indian communities and their ways of life were battered by the demographic catastrophe, the friars' enthusiastic evangelical efforts, the forced agglomeration of Indians into new communities, and the continuing pressure on the Indians to supply labor in myriad ways. They fought back: Resistance occasionally took the form of local revolts in which exceptionally brutal or greedy Spaniards or ladinos were killed. Indians also petitioned through the Spanish colonial legal system, but most often indigenous resistance was passive, and this tactical preference helped to bolster the Spaniards' stereotype of Indians as passive, stupid, fatalistic, and humorless. The stereotype was a convenient one for the Spaniards, and often for the Indians, so it has stuck, despite the overwhelming body of evidence to the contrary about how Indians deported themselves within their villages and how they actively, at times fiercely and effectively, resisted new incursions into their lives.

The seventeenth-century depression reduced the value of Indian labor. This took some of the pressure off the Indians, especially those in the Guatemalan highlands, where the vast majority of those clearly identified as Indians lived. The number of clergy also declined, and some of the congregated Indian villages formed by the religious orders in the midsixteenth century broke up, with the Indians either returning to their original villages or starting new ones. As a consequence, these people were able to revive some traditional practices, including internal governance systems. The survival of so much pre-Conquest Indian culture, in the form of language, diet, worship, dress, and custom, is a testimony to the strength and tenacity of the indigenous peoples.

But it is important not to confuse the survival of some Indian cultural forms with indigenous cultural authenticity. The cultural and political practices of Indian communities as well as the organization and composition of indigenous production had been significantly and irreversibly affected by the Spaniards. Given the shock of conquest and colonization, manifestations of Indian culture reasserted in the seventeenth century were an amalgam of pre-Conquest and Hispanic cultures, with the mix varying substantially in different communities and locales. Murdo MacLeod uses the apt term "the seventeenth-century reconstituted Indian" to describe the result, and what we today call Indian culture has its roots more solidly in this colonial syncretism than in pre-Conquest times.[10]

Although the central questions of colonial culture revolve around that of indigenous peoples, it is worth looking quickly at the other side. The elements of Spanish culture that became established in Spanish America (including Central America) were much more homogeneous than one would have expected from the great variety of cultural forms and practices evident in sixteenth- and seventeenth-century Spain.

What were the principles and mechanisms of selection by which some aspects of Spanish life traveled to the New World and others were left behind? George M. Foster demonstrates that the backgrounds of the Spanish settlers (region, class, and other elements) do not account for the cultural selectivity, nor do a range of other initially plausible explanations. He argues cogently that the Spanish culture in the New World was a "culture of conquest."[11] That is, certain elements of Spanish culture were much more appropriate for the subordination and control of large numbers of non-European peoples, and these became the hallmarks of Spanish culture in the New World.

Returning to the seventeenth-century depression, it is clear that the slowdown in production, commerce, and migration sharply reduced both outside influences on Central America as well as interprovincial communications within Central America. The provinces, which never had been integrated into an organic whole, thereby became politically and culturally even more diverse. The region, which had always been fragmented, became increasingly so as more producers became oriented strictly to local markets or indeed to no market at all.

Major political and economic changes in the eighteenth century, however, transformed the Central American social order, and the resulting conflicts carried the isthmus into political independence.

Notes

1. The first officially sanctioned survey, made in 1534, concluded that the route that became the Panama Canal 380 years later was the best.

2. M. J. MacLeod, *Spanish Central America: A Socioeconomic History, 1520–1720* (Berkeley and Los Angeles: University of California Press, 1973), is the most thorough exposition of the history of the period, including a good background on the geography and pre-Conquest indigenous peoples. Ciro Cardoso and Héctor Pérez Brignoli, *Centroamérica y la economía occidental (1520–1930)* (San José, CR: Editorial Universidad, 1977), is also a valuable general source. Hector Perez-Brignoli, *A Brief History of Central America* (Berkeley: University of California Press, 1989), pp. 1–32, is an exceptionally graceful description of the peoples and places prior to the arrival of the Spaniards. For more detailed information on the demographic and cultural patterns of the peoples of Central America before the sixteenth century, with extensive bibliographic essays, see Miguel León-Portilla, "Mesoamerica Before 1519," and Mary W. Helms, "The Indians of the Caribbean and Circum-Caribbean at the End of the Fifteenth Century," in Leslie Bethell (ed.), *The Cambridge History of Latin America, Volume 1: Colonial Latin America* (Cambridge: Cambridge University Press, 1984), pp. 3–36 and 37–58.

3. In addition to MacLeod, *Spanish Central America,* see W. L. Sherman, *Forced Labor in Sixteenth Century Central America* (Lincoln: University of Nebraska Press, 1979), and the three essays by MacLeod, Sherman, and R. J. Carmack in M. J. MacLeod and R. Wasserstrom (eds.), *Spaniards and Indians in Southeastern Mesoamérica: Essays on the History of Ethnic Relations* (Lincoln: University of Nebraska Press, 1983), for the effects of the Conquest on the Indians. John H. Parry, *The Spanish Seaborne Empire* (New York: Knopf, 1971), and Leslie Bethell (ed.), *The Cambridge History of Latin America, Volume 2: Colonial Latin America* (Cambridge: Cambridge University Press, 1984), especially the essays by M. J. MacLeod and James Lockhart (pp. 219–264 and 265–320), are good surveys of the political economy and social institutions of the Spanish American colonies.

4. Linda Newson, *The Cost of Conquest: Indian Decline in Honduras Under Spanish Rule* (Boulder, CO: Westview Press, 1986), is a meticulous study.

5. Alfred W. Crosby, *The Columbian Exchange: Biological and Cultural Consequences of 1492* (Westport, CT: Greenwood Press, 1972), is an excellent study of the biological consequences of the Spanish conquest, including that of disease. For a fascinating argument about the role of disease in world history, see William H. McNeil, *Plagues and Peoples* (Garden City, NJ: Anchor Press, 1976). Nicolás Sánchez-Albornoz, *The Population of Latin America: A History* (Berkeley: University of California Press, 1974), is the standard demographic history, and it and the bibliography are updated in the same author's "The Population of Colonial Spanish America," in Bethell, *The Cambridge History of Latin America, Volume 2*, pp. 3–36.

6. Sherman, *Forced Labor in Sixteenth Century Central America;* MacLeod, *Spanish Central America.*

7. For the historical background of Spain of the period, see Jaime Vicens Vives, *An Economic History of Spain* (Princeton: Princeton University Press, 1969), pp. 155–467. For the more general setting of Spain's colonial ventures, see Eric Wolf, *Europe and the People Without History* (Berkeley: University of California Press, 1982), and John H. Parry, *The Age of Reconnaissance: Discovery, Exploration, and Settlement* (Berkeley: University of California Press, 1981).

8. Fernand Braudel, *Capitalism and Material Life* (New York: Harper & Row, 1967), pp. 121–191.

9. Murdo J. MacLeod, *Spanish Central America: A Socioeconomic History, 1520–1720* (Berkeley and Los Angeles: University of California Press, 1973).

10. Ibid.

11. George Foster, *Culture and Conquest: America's Spanish Heritage* (New York: Quadrangle Books, 1960).

2

Colonial Reform, Political Independence, and the Liberal Experiment, 1700 to 1850

The eighteenth century was a time of economic vitality and political reform in Central America, contrasting sharply with the stagnation of the seventeenth century. But the early years of the eighteenth century were not promising. There was an unremitting series of natural disasters. Between 1680 and 1730, epidemics, locusts, and earthquakes wreaked havoc throughout the region and especially in its demographic and political heart, Guatemala and El Salvador. These blows, one after another, over and over again, reduced even the elite to dire straits in spite of their attempts to maintain their standards of living at the expense of workers in general and Indians in particular. This increased pressure on the Indian communities resulted in the Indian uprising in Chiapas in 1712, the most extensive and dangerous revolt up to that time in colonial Central America.

Beginning in the fourth and fifth decades of the eighteenth century, however, the Central American economy began a period of growth that lasted fifty years. This dynamism had three major sources: a qualitative change in the energy and direction of leadership from the Spanish throne; the discovery of silver in Honduras; and the boom in indigo, the blue dye.

Bourbons, Reason, and Reform

The Spanish Hapsburg dynasty, which had produced a series of unremarkable kings throughout the seventeenth century, came to an end in 1700 when Charles II died without an heir. Strongly influenced by Louis XIV of France (the Sun King), Charles II named one of the French king's grandsons, Philip, to succeed him. England, Holland, Austria, and Prussia considered this appointment unacceptable, and they fought Spain and France in the War of Spanish Succession to forestall the unification of the French and Spanish royal families.

Divisions among the northern European allies weakened their effectiveness in prosecuting the war, and eventually hostilities ended with the agreement that Philip could ascend the Spanish throne as long as the Bourbon crowns of Spain and France were never united. Spain lost some of its holdings in continental Europe and ceded Gibraltar and Minorca to England along with some trading rights with Spanish America, including a monopoly over the slave trade. England also gained Newfoundland, Acadia, and Hudson Bay from the French.

Thus, in the early eighteenth century, Spain had a new king from a new dynasty—the Bourbons. Determined to reverse the Spanish decline and influenced heavily by French Enlightenment rationalism, the Spanish Bourbons moved energetically to reform the Indies.[1] Over the eighteenth century, the Bourbons reorganized and centralized the loose, ramshackle colonial administrative system of Spanish America that was the Hapsburg legacy. Changes initiated by the Bourbons included a redefinition of administrative districts in Central America along lines that for the most part corresponded to what became the borders of five independent nations (with the exception of Chiapas, joined to Mexico after independence). In addition, they loosened restrictions on colonial commerce with Spain, with other nations, and within the colony.

The Bourbons also moved decisively against Church power, which by the end of the seventeenth century had become a political and economic rival to the colonial state. The Church was politically vulnerable because the pope, fearing the anticlerical strains within France, had opposed the Bourbons during the War of Spanish Succession. New policies reduced Church influence over Indian communities, weakened the Inquisition, restricted Church landholdings, prohibited clerics from collecting tribute or controlling Indian community funds, and gave preference to secular priests over friars from the regular orders.

This last effect was vividly demonstrated by the expulsion of the entire Jesuit order from Spanish America in 1767. The expulsion of the Jesuits affected Central America only slightly because the order had not been deeply involved there. It was, however, a clear signal for the entire Indies about who was in charge. The Bourbons, it became apparent, would not tolerate ecclesiastical power closely tied to the Vatican and the aggressive, doctrinaire Church of the Counter-Reformation.

Colonial fiscal reform was also high on the list of Bourbon priorities. The Bourbons instituted new taxes and royal monopolies on tobacco and some types of alcohol, revived old taxes, and collected taxes directly instead of contracting with private individuals to act as collectors. As a result, colonial tax revenues in Central America grew and changed in composition to the point that Indian tribute constituted less than half of the fiscal revenue during the eighteenth century rather than the three-quarters or more of tax collections typical during the previous century. The shift of some of the tax burden onto Spanish settlers was not popular among the colonists.

Increased tax yields and the Bourbon policy of repatriating less of the revenue to Spain meant that substantially more governmental resources were available for use within Central America. A good portion of the increased government expenditures in Central America went to defense. Spain was associated with England's enemies, especially France, in the series of eighteenth-century wars—the War of Spanish Succession (1701–1712), the War of Jenkins' Ear (or the War of Austrian Succession, 1739–1749), the French and Indian War (or the Seven Years' War, 1756–1763), U.S. independence (1776–1783), and the early years of the Napoleonic Wars (1793–1815).

As far as England was concerned, Central America was the possession of a hostile nation, and English merchants could ignore Spanish trade prohibitions and penetrate Central American markets without violating English law. U.S. merchants and shippers also benefited greatly from the Napoleonic Wars. As citizens of a neutral nation, they were allowed to trade with Central America, and many of their wares were English goods.

Even with the uncertainties of war, however, Spain's control of the Caribbean coast by the last quarter of the eighteenth century was more secure than it had been for 200 years. Spain's success there resulted from two Bourbon policies: an aggressive campaign to build up the area's military defenses and a more conciliatory attitude toward the rights of English log cutters and merchants operating in Belize.

Spanish policy also provided for the use of fiscal resources to augment and improve government bureaucracy, public works (e.g., roads), and tropical agriculture and commerce. The Bourbon reforms are often described as an expression of "enlightened despotism." The principal point, though, is that they reoriented Spanish colonial policy towards mercantile colonialism. That is, the Bourbons recognized that the imperial center could benefit more from its colonies by means other than the acquisition of gold and silver through tribute—virtually the exclusive emphasis of Hapsburg policies. In Central America, this meant stimulating the production of tropical produce to be sold to the rest of Europe, and by judicious use of franchises, taxes, and controls, a significant share of the merchants' profits and general colonial economic growth could be tapped to benefit Spain in both material and political terms.

The Bourbons reduced restrictions on trade and expanded the number of merchant guilds (consulados) in Spanish America beyond the two—in

Mexico and Lima—that had been set up in the sixteenth century. In 1790 they granted consulado status to the merchants of Guatemala. The Guatemalan merchants, no longer under the Mexican consulado, legally monopolized all (and especially foreign) commerce and operated their own civil court system to adjudicate commercial disputes. Expanding the number of consulados from two to ten was not liberalization. To the contrary, it strengthened and made more effective the private monopolization and government control of commerce. This was progrowth mercantilism, not to be confused with free market capitalism.

The Spanish Bourbon approach to colonies was similar to English mercantile policy in its Caribbean islands, where African slaves produced sugar. But within England, the eighteenth-century Industrial Revolution was creating a new economic order that was leading to the transformation of domestic social relations and of the technology, organization, and composition of production. England, along with a handful of other western European economies that had begun to progress into the competitive phase of industrial capitalism, needed raw materials as inputs for its growing industrial sector, food for its rapidly expanding urban populations, and markets for its industrial output. Colonies were to serve these functions, roles markedly different from what mercantile empires required of colonies.

The importance of the sugar islands to English economic growth and to the politically powerful in England was rapidly waning. In contrast, Spain was already a backward nation in Europe by the beginning of the eighteenth century. As noted in Chapter 1, Spain's colonial adventure was so successful in material terms that it had strengthened a powerful centralized state and parasitical seignorial order and retarded the internal transformations necessary for creating a modern economy and society.

The international market forces generated by the emerging industrial economies of northern Europe directly affected Central America. Cotton textiles were one of the most important branches of machine manufacture in the European industrial revolution, and the expansion of textile production created new opportunities for Central Americans to export indigo dye and to import cotton textiles. The export of indigo was one of the three major sources of economic growth in eighteenth-century Central America. Before discussing indigo, however, it is necessary to describe the expansion of silver production, which preceded large-scale indigo exports and contributed to their development.

Honduran Silver

The discovery of new and relatively rich silver veins in western Honduras during the early eighteenth century created considerable excitement and led to substantial migration to the area, some voluntary and some forced, as in the case of Indian repartimiento workers and African slaves. Prospectors found new silver deposits, opened new mines, and once again began washing for gold. The Spanish Crown encouraged Honduran silver mining by dropping the quinto tax from 20 to 10 percent and by opening the first Central American mint—in Guatemala in 1733.

The production of monetized metals has a dual economic character. The economic importance of Honduran mineral production for the region was more than the commodity value of the silver and gold extracted and of the other types of production directly and indirectly stimulated by increased mining activity. The greater availability of gold and silver enabled the monetization of the regional economy, which was being reduced to barter exchanges in the seventeenth century. Because gold and silver functioned as money (medium of exchange, store of value, and unit of account), it supported the expansion of production by lubricating transactions of all sorts, eliminating the commercial straitjacket of bilateral swapping of commodities, and facilitating the development of regional credit markets. Many of the mine operators' financing needs were supplied by Guatemalan merchants, who were rapidly displacing the Church as the principal source of credit.

The Indigo Cycle

The third source of economic growth in eighteenth-century Central America was indigo. After the 1740s, the expansion of western European economies, especially the English textile industry, increased the demand for the blue dye and stimulated indigo production in Central America, 100 years after the initial optimism about indigo. Even though El Salvador accounted for the vast majority of indigo production, the stimulus was sufficiently strong to affect almost the entire region. The plains and fertile valleys of Guatemala, Honduras, and Nicaragua were drawn on to supply food, cloth, and meat for indigo workers, and the level of regional economic integration and interdependence was greater than had ever been achieved.

Most indigo cultivation occurred on small and medium-sized farms located in El Salvador. Debt peonage and wage labor initially supplemented the repartimiento as means to mobilize the seasonal, unskilled labor needed for indigo production. By the end of the eighteenth century, though, the newer labor systems were beginning to replace the repartimiento. In Central America, the repartimiento had never been important outside of Guatemala and El Salvador, and by the end of the eighteenth century it was in decline in Guatemala and had virtually disappeared in El Salvador. These changes took place despite Bourbon policies that had abolished earlier prohibitions, making repartimiento labor in the indigo dye works legal for castas (people of mixed races) and Indians.

This pattern of individual employment was encouraged by the 1747 decree that obliged Indians to pay tribute in specie rather than commodities. This forced some Indian communities, especially those in the highlands of northern Guatemala, into the market for the first time. At the same time, wage labor in indigo areas was very much in demand. Individual employment was further supported by ladino indigo farmers' encroachment on, and occasional appropriation of, Indian lands. When people do not have access to the means of production (in the case of the Indians' access to land), they are forced to work for wages in order to pay taxes and to buy subsistence goods they are no longer able to produce.

The commercial elites in Guatemala were the major beneficiaries of the indigo boom in the second half of the eighteenth century. As in the case of Honduran miners, the merchants had replaced the Church as the principal source of credit for indigo producers. Moreover, Guatemalan merchants benefited significantly when the Bourbons formally made them a consulado. This status gave them legal backing for their dominance in indigo markets, a dominance already based on transportation and credit networks, which forced growers to sell their indigo to an agent of a Guatemalan merchant in El Salvador or at the annual auction in Guatemala City. The Guatemalan merchants were therefore able to coordinate effective market power over the indigo growers, the largest of which produced but a small proportion of the total indigo output. Through their position as sole creditors and sole purchasers, these merchants manipulated selling prices for credit and buying prices for indigo to their advantage.

The Guatemalan merchants' use of market power on indigo producers certainly increased regional antagonism, but there were also important divisions among the most powerful merchants in Guatemala. In the early eighteenth century, there had been an influx of Spanish immigrants with the means and abilities to become important merchants in Guatemala City. Although these newcomers married into the older elite, which was mostly criollo (Spaniards born in the New World), the peninsular Spaniards' connections with Spain and their aggressiveness enabled them to dominate long-distance trade and to establish themselves as the leading mercantile force in the consulado and the colony.

In addition to the social tension created by these successful interlopers, Bourbon reforms stimulated exports; they also encouraged imports that created some serious economic difficulties. When the Bourbons relaxed some restrictions on foreign trade, Guatemalan merchants were able to import cheap English cotton textiles, the leading product line of the Industrial Revolution and the factory system. These coarse cotton textiles from English factories were "wage goods" (that is, commodities bought by working-class families), and their importation through Belize threatened the livelihoods of Guatemalan and other colonial merchants who dealt in the regional trade of locally produced cotton textiles for working-class consumers. Merchants dealing in locally traded goods were smaller and had less influence in the consulado than long-distance traders, and they were unable to prevent the consulado policies that worked to their disadvantage.

But these imports had consequences that were more important than the effect on small merchants. The flood of cheap, imported cotton textiles ruined many local Guatemalan cotton farmers and textile producers. The importation of luxury goods did not constitute a threat of the same magnitude. Because luxury imports were still made under artisanal conditions rather than in factories, these European products were not as apt to undersell locally made goods. But this was not the most important effect. Almost by definition, luxury goods were produced mostly by Spanish, German, and especially French artisans. Locally made commodities were looked down upon by Central American consumers of luxury products. Relaxing trade restrictions, therefore, lowered the prices of luxury imports in Central America. Nevertheless, as in the rest of Spanish America, imports of luxury goods did not compete with local production nearly as much as those of wage goods did.

On the Eve of Central American Independence

The division among the Guatemalan criollos, based on economic activity, was graphically illustrated in the struggle over the relocation of the capital city. There was a series of severe earthquakes in Guatemala City in the third quarter of the eighteenth century, culminating in three very destructive quakes within six months in 1773. Bourbon officials decided to move the capital to a new, safer location twenty-five miles away, decreeing that the old capital be abandoned.

The long-distance merchants, many of whom were relatively new to the city and whose operations were mobile, did not seriously resist the move. Many of the older merchants, however, had substantial landholdings in and around the old capital (now called Antigua) and depended on local trade networks. The latter fought the decision; they were joined by other landholders, inhabitants of neighboring Indian villages, a good number of other residents of the old capital, and Church leaders, who realized that Church mortgages held on lands in the capital and surrounding area would become worthless. After seven years of arguments, petitions, and litigation, the move was made. Although there were some compromises, the authority of the Bourbon bureaucracy and their merchant allies over the older elite and Church was thus confirmed. The real losers were the Indian repartimiento laborers who had to build the new city.

The undisputed primacy of the capital city within Guatemala was unique in Central America; in the other four provinces, at least two or more cities vied for predominance. But by the end of the eighteenth century, economic growth and the Bourbon reforms had shifted political and economic power toward what is now the current capital city except in Nicaragua, where León and Granada continued to fluctuate in relative importance.

All together, the economic and political changes in the eighteenth century created a new society. In the 1790s, indigo exports peaked, both in volume and value, and Spanish control and internal political coherence were probably at their height. Despite this apparent prosperity and stability, however, both the economic and political structure of colonial Central America disintegrated within twenty years. We will return to this apparent anomaly after describing the major factors in that disintegration.

The decline of indigo markets after the turn of the nineteenth century contributed to the dissolution of the Spanish empire in Central America. The slump in indigo sales resulted in part from increased competition, especially from India, which the English had recently taken over as a colony, and from Venezuela. Moreover, there were recurring problems with locusts in the Salvadoran fields, and transportation posed persistent and costly difficulties.

The principal cause of falling indigo prices, however, did not result from changes in supply conditions but rather from changes in demand conditions. The Napoleonic Wars, which pitted England and other counterrevolutionary powers against revolutionary France, with which Spain was initially allied, reduced English demand for indigo and interrupted transport across the Atlantic. But with the success of Napoleon's Continental Blockade against English goods, a large portion of available English cotton textiles was sent to Spanish America by means of whatever shipping was available. Between 1809 and 1811, Latin America bought 35 percent of England's total exports, and English merchants inundated Central America with cheap cotton textiles.

The importation of these wage goods into Spanish America during the last half of the eighteenth century and the first two decades of the nineteenth century further damaged local manufacturing, both by artisans and in crude factories, throughout Spanish America. As a result, artisans and industrial workers were numerically important and a political force during the early years of the postindependence period only in the densely populated highland areas of Colombia, Mexico, and to a lesser extent in the highlands of Peru, Ecuador, northwestern Argentina (near the Bolivian mines), and northern Guatemala, where geography made transportation costs of imports from the coast prohibitive, thus providing some protection for local producers.

In Central America, then, the consequences of the depression in English textiles were double edged: poor markets for indigo, the most important export; and special efforts by English textile merchants to sell to Central America, competing with local cotton textile production. The previously achieved integration and interdependence of the Central American economy meant that the effects from the declines in indigo and local cotton textile production affected virtually every corner of Central America. The inability of producers to pay mortgages led to foreclosures by Guatemalan merchants, which heightened already existing hostilities between producers and merchants. Much of this hostility was expressed in regional terms—Salvadoran indigo farmers, Nicaraguan ranchers, Honduran miners, and others versus Guatemalan merchants.

In addition, the Bourbon fiscal reforms had created a tax structure that shifted some of the tax burden away from Indian tribute. The tribute was essentially a head tax insensitive to changes in levels of economic activity. The reforms that had placed increased taxes on criollos and their activities, however, were more sensitive to the volume of transactions and income. Fiscal receipts, therefore, plummeted in the first decades of the nineteenth century, and they did so at a time when both political unrest in Central America and defense costs in Spain were rising.

The Bourbon bureaucracy resorted to a series of emergency measures to raise needed revenues, and these measures alienated virtually every sector in Spanish America. For instance, the colonial state forced the wealthy to make loans to the government. It also decreed that all payments on mortgages owned by the Church would accrue to the government and that all mortgages would be entirely paid up within two to eight years, regardless of the time period originally set. The last measure resulted in forced sales at unfavorable terms, principally, but not exclusively, by owners of small and medium-sized landholdings who were unable to meet the accelerated payment schedules. The following example illustrates the burden of Spanish colonial taxes: It has been estimated that in the first two decades of the nineteenth century, tax rates in Mexico, as a percentage of income, were thirty-five times higher than the corresponding percentage levied by the English on the residents of the thirteen North American colonies. Had Spanish tax rates in colonial Central America been half those of Mexico, they still would have caused political disaffection.

All factions of the Central American criollos reacted sharply to these measures imposed by the Bourbon state. But in the early years of the nineteenth century, it was becoming difficult to find much of the Bourbon state in Central America. Although the Crown appointed some competent and active individuals to head affairs in Central America, the Bourbon presence in the region was substantially reduced. The Spanish Crown was not going to expend a significant share of its vastly reduced resources on the Central American backwater; other needs were far more pressing. The picture of political disarray was completed when the French turned against their Spanish ally in 1808, forcing the abdication of the Spanish Bourbon king in favor of Napoleon's brother, Joseph Bonaparte.

These events—war, changes in foreign production, toppled monarchs, and so on—had their origins outside of the region. But the consequences of these events for Central America were important only because of the internal social and political structures of colonial Central America through which these events reverberated. That is, even in this period one cannot accurately regard Central American social processes to have been determined by external forces. The effects of such forces were mediated by domestic contradictions and struggles, which determined whether a particular external event became an influence and if so how and to what extent. For our purposes, the principal development in this period was the independence of mainland Spanish America, including Central America, from Spain.

The Nature of Spanish American Independence

To understand Central American independence, it is important to begin at the hemispheric level and to recognize that Spanish American independence from colonial control was qualitatively different from the independence of, say, India, Indonesia, and Ghana after World War II. These African and Asian struggles for independence were conducted and won by a subjugated, colonized people. In Spanish America, however, it was the Spanish settlers who fought for and achieved independence from Spain. In other words, Spanish American independence was the project of those doing the subjugating and colonizing, not by the subjugated and colonized. Independence in Spanish America, then, had more in common with that of the United States of America and of the Union of South Africa than with post–World War II national liberation movements.

The struggle, then, was between the criollos and the Spanish Crown and its agents in the New World. The Central American criollos' complaints about the colonial order were similar to those heard throughout the Indies. Spanish colonial policy obstructed the translation of landownership into social and political power, restricted the exploitation of the indigenous population and of African slaves, and burdened commodity markets with restrictions, regulations, taxes, and monopolies. Altogether, many and perhaps most criollos had difficulty in maintaining an urban upper-class life based on land and servile labor.

An additional source of criollo dissatisfaction was the Spanish Crown's overt discrimination against criollos in granting titles of nobility and appointments to positions in the upper reaches of the political, military, and ecclesiastical bureaucracies. It is clear that the Bourbons simply did not trust the criollos. The consulados were dominated by the Spanish-born, and the colonial social and economic structure offered few opportunities for independent professionals and discouraged industrial entrepreneurship more effectively than did prohibitions.

Insult was added to injury by the mythology of criollo "racial" inferiority circulating among Spaniards, a belief that included elements frequently used to rationalize the subordination of other social groups: early maturation and decline, laziness, dishonesty, tendency to dissoluteness, and so forth. The difference between criollo and Spanish-born peninsulare is a matter of slight degree when compared to the differences between either of them and Indians and people of African descent. Nevertheless, it offers a clear example of the social construction of race.[2] That criollos are genetically identical to the Spaniards graphically illustrates the social meaning attached to "race differences." Even when there existed superficial physical differences, as in the case of Indians and Africans, the significance attached to these differences was not a biological phenomenon; it was socially determined. And in the case of the criollos, the significance managed to exist in spite of an absence of biological differences. Much of the same argument can be made in respect to cultural differences; certainly there were differences, but the significance attached to these did not grow out of a source independent of, or prior to, social relationships.

As a result of Bourbon reforms, the criollos did find some new opportunities as low-level bureaucrats. And prosperity in other areas of Spanish America, which did not generally experience the severe depression felt in Central America in the early decades of the nineteenth century, benefited criollos economically. Nevertheless, Bourbon reforms also centralized colonial political authority, reducing the voice of the criollos in local affairs, and raised the effective rate of taxation on criollo income and wealth. Spanish American prosperity and the growth of opportunities in the bureaucracy also attracted large numbers of Spanish immigrants whose privileges and beliefs in their innate superiority were resented by criollos.

The livelihoods of many criollos actually depended on colonial economic restrictions, and trade liberalization and economic reforms put criollos into competition with producers in other areas and were disadvantageous to them. But even in the most favorable cases, increased returns from economic growth were not only from higher prices for a given output but also from the greater volume of goods marketed in response to the higher prices. In the colonial setting of static labor productivity, increased volumes of marketed products came from the suppression of consumption levels and/or the intensification of the labor of workers already involved in the colonial economy or, alternatively, incorporating new groups into the circuit of production.

Both alternatives brought employers up against colonial labor policies and against the Church as protector of the Indians, competing producer, and mortgage holder. Even though both labor protections and the Church were weakened in the eighteenth century, the increased value of produce from the land stimulated production to the point that those restraints remaining were more confining.

The criollo complaints described here are conventional fare in studies of the Spanish American independence movements. Although they are neither wrong nor irrelevant, an exclusive focus on the relationships between criollos and Spaniards is inadequate to understand the pace of and regional variations in the wars of independence. Although the wars of Spanish American independence were fought between the criollos and peninsular Spaniards, this struggle can be understood only by appreciating that the entire scenario was conditioned by the core relationship between producing and nonproducing classes.

When one looks closely at the position of criollos with respect to Indians, castas, and African slaves, crucial elements of reciprocity between the criollos and the Spanish colonial administration are clear. The criollos, as employers and property owners, enjoyed substantial advantages under Spanish rule, and these advantages effectively bound them to the empire for three centuries. The Crown and its representatives protected criollo privilege in the Indies by guaranteeing a social order that freed criollos from work by enabling them to benefit from the work of others. All the disadvantages of Spanish rule experienced by the criollos were disadvantages because, and only because, the criollos lived off the work of the producing classes, composed principally of indigenous workers, castas, and African slaves. Criollos fought the wars of independence to preserve this relationship.[3]

In the second half of the eighteenth century and early nineteenth century, increased pressure on producers for more output led to serious unrest. Riots in Mexico City and Quito, recurring Andean rebellions, Venezuelan slave revolts, the Haitian slave revolution, the jacquerie by the followers of Father Hidalgo in central Mexico, and Indian uprisings in Guatemala served as vivid reminders to the criollos that colonial society in the late eighteenth and early nineteenth centuries was being threatened from below. Moreover, England's seizure of Cuba in the 1760s and Trinidad in the 1790s and the English raids on Buenos Aires and Montevideo in 1806 and 1807 similarly kept alive fears of a foreign invasion that would not be to the criollos' advantage. In each of these cases, the criollos and Spanish authorities united to put down a common enemy.

Spain's ability to protect the criollos militarily from internal and external assaults diminished sharply at the end of the eighteenth century. The eclipse of the Church and Napoleon's replacement of the Spanish king with his brother Joseph in 1808 were severe blows to two powerful, unifying symbols to all layers of colonial society. Even in these circumstances, however, Spanish American criollos as a group were reluctant to break with Spain.

The removal of the royal capstone from the centralized Spanish colonial administration resulted in the chaotic disintegration of the Spanish American empire, leaving small, local warring components, some desiring independence, some reluctantly accepting the fiction of Ferdinand VII's abdication in favor of Joseph Bonaparte, and some remaining loyal to Ferdinand VII, who was still the symbol of resistance for Spaniards struggling against French domination. The Spanish resistance was led by republicans; they wrote the republican Constitution of 1812, which provided for a constitutional monarchy, a more decentralized political organization with broad franchise even in the colonies (but excluding women and people of African descent), and generally more liberal market institutions.

When France was in retreat and Ferdinand was restored as king of Spain in 1814, he quickly repudiated the Constitution of 1812. Spain successfully reasserted its imperial authority in the New World (except in Argentina) between 1814 and 1816. Spanish colonial policy, however, continued to fluctuate, depending on the outcome of the struggle between the republicans and monarchists in Spain. Nevertheless, it was evident to all that the Spanish government was too weak to protect criollo interests, and even its intentions could not be trusted if and when the republicans regained power. Thus between 1815 and 1824, Spanish American criollos fought the wars of independence in a relatively well-organized manner, complete with heroes, and the mainland Spanish colonies became independent nations.

What had been, for the most part, a quid pro quo relationship between the criollos and Spanish colonial authorities turned against the criollos in the eighteenth and early nineteenth centuries. Although it might have been possible to sustain the unequal relationship over considerable periods of time, as in the even more unequal relationship of the criollos vis-à-vis Indians and African slaves, the very conditions that caused the terms of prevailing arrangements to turn against the criollos testified to Spain's inability to supply the necessary force and deception to maintain these arrangements. That is, the same inability of the Spanish Crown and its New World agents to protect the criollos against revolt from below also assured the success of criollo separatist movements.

This general framework helps to explain why the centers of the Spanish American independence movements were in areas where labor was mobilized in relatively noncoercive ways and where open class conflict was least apparent: The Crown's presence in these places was felt increasingly more as the tax collector rather than a guarantor of the social order. On the plains of Venezuela, in and around Buenos Aires, and in central Colombia and Chile, Spanish control was of minimal importance to the criollos. The major function of the Spanish presence in the outlying areas was to hold frontiers against raids by nomadic Indians, and even this responsibility was increasingly assumed by colonial militia and private armies.

In Peru, however, criollo welfare depended directly on sustaining a variety of coercive mechanisms similar to those in Central America to control the work and products of the large indigenous population in the highlands and the African slaves on the coastal plantations. The primary concern in Peru was internal control and stability. This concern became an obsession after the Indian revolts of the 1770s and 1780s reached a climax in the massive Indian rebellion led by Tupac Amaru II.[4] The role of the Spanish colonial administration in maintaining the criollos' positions was tangible and highly visible. Although Spanish weakness stimulated some criollo agitation for independence, the risks involved in such a move were so clear that the Peruvian criollos were too divided for an effective separatist effort. Peru essentially had to be conquered by the forces of San Martín and Admiral Thomas Cochrane from the south and of Simón Bolívar from the north in order to achieve political independence from Spain.

Indian uprisings, particularly the terrifying revolt led by Father Hidalgo in 1810, put the criollos of Mexico and Central America under pressures analogous to those felt by their counterparts in Peru. Considerable agitation and confusion were created by the ambiguous changes in Spanish internal politics after Ferdinand's restoration, but the resurgence of Spanish republican forces in 1820 presented too serious a challenge to the criollos. In 1821, the Mexican criollos broke with Spain and attempted to set up an independent Bourbon monarchy, similar to the political arrangement in Brazil. The criollo leaders first invited Ferdinand VII to accept the Mexican throne, but he refused, as did other Bourbon princes who were approached. The Mexican criollos then turned to one of their own, and General Augustín Iturbide became the emperor of Mexico.

Finally, it is instructive to look at the Spanish islands in the Caribbean, where African slaves outnumbered Europeans by large margins. The bloody and successful Haitian slave revolution of 1791 gave stark meaning to these arithmetic ratios, and no strong independence movement emerged anywhere in the Spanish Antilles until decades later.

These were the patterns and forces that defined the Spanish American wars of independence. When understood in this fashion, the dissolution of the Spanish American empire on the New World mainland, after the Bourbon reforms seemed to have succeeded in tying it more tightly to Spain, is not the anomaly that it seems to those whose views of society are based on notions of social equilibrium and harmony.

The bases of Bourbon colonial success were the more centralized, effective administrative apparatus, colonial prosperity, and greater economic integration. These successes became, in themselves, sources of discontent among colonists, fueling the drive for independence. Greater administrative efficiency reduced the latitude of colonial residents, who often were stymied in their attempts to avoid the restrictions and exactions of the colonial state. The centralization of administrative authority meant that the removal of the Crown paralyzed institutionalized political power. The organization and structure of the colony that lay behind colonial prosperity restricted economic growth to a type that necessarily exacerbated conflicts along class, regional, and sectoral lines. And the heightened social and economic integration of the colony meant that troubles arising from conflicts in a particular sector or region could not be isolated or contained. In the end, processes that seemingly led to greater colonial security actually increased internal contradictions, transforming the pillars of the colonial order into their opposites: sources of separatism.

Central American Independence

The dialectic that changed support into opposition was evident in Central America. The events in Central America leading up to independence occurred, in large part, in Guatemala. This is not surprising because the province of Guatemala contained both the political capital of colonial Central America and, as Table 2.1 shows, almost half of the population of the entire region on the eve of independence. Moreover, as noted in the last chapter, because of the position of the Guatemalan merchant consulado in export, import, and credit markets, the concentration of economic power in the province was greater than its proportion of population and production.

From Table 2.1, it is clear that Honduras, Nicaragua, and Costa Rica were almost empty provinces in the early nineteenth century. In addition, production in Guatemala depended on forced labor from a large, subordinate, and unassimilated Indian population to an extent greater than elsewhere in Central America. Much of the burden of five decades of

TABLE 2.1 Estimated Population and Population Densities, 1820 and 1860 (population in thousands, per 1,000 square miles)

		1820		1860	
	National Area	Estimated Population	Density (per sq. mi.)	Estimated Population	Density (per sq. mi.)
Guatemala	42.0	595	14.2	951	22.6
Honduras	43.3	135	3.1	230	5.3
El Salvador	8.1	248	30.6	424	52.3
Nicaragua	57.1	186	3.3	230	4.0
Costa Rica	19.6	63	3.2	115	5.9

Source: R. L. Woodward, Jr., "Central America from Independence to c. 1870," in L. Bethell (ed.), *The Cambridge History of Latin America, Volume 3: From Independence to c. 1870* (New York: Cambridge University Press, 1986), p. 478.

economic growth in the late eighteenth century, followed by two decades of decline in the early nineteenth century, had been passed on to the Indian communities. In the entire colonial history of the region, however, there were no Indian rebellions that rivaled those led by Tupac Amaru in Peru or Hidalgo in Mexico. Nevertheless, there were obvious signs of dissatisfaction among the Indians, including a serious Indian uprising in 1820. In addition, the rapidly growing population of castas was a constant source of criollo unease.

The criollo aristocracy in Guatemala cautiously sat out the rapid changes occurring in Spain and in the New World between 1808 and 1820. In El Salvador, Honduras, and Nicaragua there was some agitation for independence led by criollos in 1811 and 1812, but these protests were directed as much against Guatemalan merchants as against Spanish colonial authority. In 1813, there was a small criollo rebellion in Guatemala as well, but like the others, it was easily put down under the leadership of José Bustamante y Guerra, the able Spanish captain general of Central America between 1811 and 1818.

In general, Central America criollos, led by the uncompromising monarchist captain general, stayed loyal to Ferdinand VII through the years of Joseph Napoleon's reign as king of Spain. For the last couple of years of that period, this loyalty meant accepting the Constitution of 1812, which Bustamante reluctantly and selectively implemented. The resulting local and regional elections and new political institutions allowed active participation by criollo men (roughly 2 percent of the population).

When Ferdinand was restored to the throne in 1814, he abrogated the Spanish constitution. Bustamante then rapidly dismantled the tentative participatory institutions in Central America. This action alienated some of the criollo elite in spite of the fact that their assemblies seemed to have had little in the way of a political agenda that differed from Bustamante's. When the republicans regained power in Spain in 1820, however, they brought back the Constitution of 1812, with every intention to implement it in full. The Central American assemblies again formed, and this time there was a substantive issue: how to react to the events in Mexico, where Iturbide was leading a successful independence struggle.

On September 15, 1821, the "assembly of notables" in Guatemala, with representatives from all provinces, voted to sever the colonial relationship with Spain and subsequently to join the Mexican empire. The decision was predicated on the desire of the criollos to protect themselves from the republicans in Spain while retaining a monarchical form of government that explicitly guaranteed elite privileges. This was clearly expressed in the very first statement of the formal declaration of independence, which explained that independence had been declared "to prevent the consequences that would be fearful in the event that the people should proclaim it."[5] The decision to join the Mexican empire was also influenced by Iturbide's dispatch of Mexican troops to Central America to help them make the right choice.

Those making the decision in Guatemala thought, as usual, that they were deciding for the whole of Central America, but the Constitution of 1812 had required the establishment of municipal councils, and these voted on the independence issue in Central America. The results were varied among provinces and even within provinces. Even before Guatemala, Chiapas opted for independence from Spain and for joining Mexico, and after Guatemala's declaration, El Salvador chose independence from Spain and from Mexico and Guatemala as well. And various cities in Nicaragua, Honduras, and Costa Rica expressed different combinations of preferences.

El Salvador's opposition to the union with Mexico and Guatemala was the least ambiguous. Salvadoran troops successfully fought off Guatemalan troops, and the criollos applied for admission as a state in the United States. They lost in 1823 to a combined force of Guatemalan and Mexican troops who sacked San Salvador while they were there. But conquering El Salvador had little importance for the Mexican empire. The Mexican monarchy collapsed in a few weeks and Iturbide was later executed.

In July 1823, Central American criollos declared their independence from Mexico and pronounced themselves citizens of the independent United Provinces of Central America. But the criollos of Chiapas, encouraged by Mexican troops, chose to remain part of Mexico. Central American independence did not involve the bloody and destructive wars common in other parts of Spanish America. Nevertheless, Central American independence was similar to other Spanish American movements in that the criollos conducted it on two fronts: to free themselves from Spanish control and to contain Indian and ladino restiveness. Breaking with Spain was as much a social counterrevolution as it was a political independence movement.

From 1823, then, Central American criollos, along with their counterparts throughout Spanish America, struggled to create national political entities that were not dynasties. This new type of political organization had few precedents, and the effort put them on the frontier of political experimentation. As a consequence, the examples of the United States and of revolutionary France were important models.

Because the conservative criollos had seriously damaged their political credibility by joining Central America to the fiasco of the Mexican empire, the new constitution and political order were created under the auspices of the more liberal factions of criollo. That is, Central American politics began primarily to express the patterns of class forces that were competing for institutionalization in the political life of the new nations and not the dictates of an imperial power outside the region. As such, it is important to look more closely at the nature of the project undertaken by the criollos and the content of the conservative and liberal political positions that were eventually formalized in Conservative parties and Liberal parties. These parties became the principal organizations through which the criollos throughout newly independent Spanish America fought out their disagreements with each other.

Liberalism, Conservatism, and State Formation in Spanish America

The criollos' primary project in the newly independent states of Spanish America was to forge a class that would be sufficiently unified and powerful to give the new nations a geographical definition and political structure capable of containing the producing classes within a national political system. This was no simple feat. Spanish authority had actively promoted vertical economic and political linkages within colonial society while discouraging the development of horizontal integration, but Central American criollos had a definite advantage over their counterparts in other new Spanish American nations in creating a new political order. Their region had not experienced a war of independence that destroyed much of the physical means of production (for instance, in mining and herding), made criollo property vulnerable to appropriation by armed groups, shattered existing labor control mechanisms, or weakened racial patterns of control by enabling gifted but nonwhite military leaders to rise to political and economic prominence. Nevertheless, in regard to the

United Provinces of Central America, the criollos failed dramatically. The result was bloodshed and chaos that contrasted sharply with the peaceful transition to independence.

These events will be better understood within a general framework, or model, to aid our thinking about postindependence convulsions in Spanish America in general and Central America in particular in a more systematic fashion. Let us begin by recognizing that the disputes that wracked the new nations concerned, first and foremost, the political forms most appropriate for class rule.[6] Hierarchically ordered class societies are not a product of nature, and considerable human effort and struggle are necessary to create and maintain a system in which some people do the work from which others derive the benefits. This political endeavor in Spanish America was hampered by the colonial heritage, poor transportation and communication, and disruptive acts of nature. However, the primary obstacle was the highly varied conditions of production from which different elites drew their strength and class position. This variety was so great that different factions of elites required distinct and often contradictory forms of political organization.

In many of the new nations of Spanish America, including Central America, it was painfully clear that agreement among different groups of the upper class was to be reached at only the most general level: establishment of a political system that had the capacity to protect the class system as a whole while at the same time having minimum independent likelihood of threatening the system or important segments within it. These qualities, however, are internally contradictory. When a powerful state is necessary to protect a given class system, the state itself can be capable of acting against upper-class hegemony.

The political doctrines and practices of separation of powers ("checks and balances"), such as those of the United States, are an attempt to achieve protection for the class system while minimizing threats to it from the protector. Nevertheless, elites in the new Spanish American nations had to make definite decisions concerning which aspect of the political system was to be stressed at the expense of the other. Whenever present, the danger of having the class system overturned by assaults from below was always the overriding consideration, taking precedence over fears of possible encroachments by a powerful state. The manner in which different elites controlled the working classes conditioned their respective positions on the type of political structure preferred for the new states.

In those areas of Spanish America in which the class system was in complete disarray or where it was obviously vulnerable to assaults from mobilized producing classes, the type of political authority desired by the upper class was one maintained by the clear and constant threat of naked force, including frequent use of private paramilitary forces. Fearful upper classes tolerated, even promoted, this system but never liked it. First of all, it was expensive in the use of resources. In addition, it was risky, not only because such control in the early nineteenth century was uncertain and inefficient but because it made the possessing classes dependent on people and groups of people who might turn out to be unreliable guardians of upper-class interests. Thus in this view, as in the liberal view of politics, governance by overt force did symbolize failure, but a failure of upper-class power and organization rather than of morality, goodwill, and liberty.

In most of the new nations, the upper classes were not under such extreme pressure. The preferred means of class rule that emerged embodied two distinct (and European) conceptions of the ideal political order, conceptions that corresponded to the programs of Conservative and Liberal parties in their formative years and differed in matters of degree rather than kind. The Conservative vision resembled the colonial polity with its system of explicit social control. The major institutions formed a powerful, centralized state apparatus (in its extreme version buttressed by the symbolism of a monarchy) that carefully regulated social and economic life through an extensive bureaucracy and a strong military.

The second major pillar was the established church, whose moral authority was strengthened by a monopoly on education and on birth, marriage, and death rituals and by the possession of extensive political and economic power. Although this political system exercised social control directly and was envisioned as a means to preserve class society for the benefit of the possessing classes, it had the marked drawback that upper-class political power was indirect. Political power was vested in entrenched institutions that were at least potentially impervious to influence by even the most influential.

The European and Spanish American Liberal ideal of political organization was more conducive to direct class rule, but its method of social control was considerably more indirect. Social control was to work through an articulated structure of decentralized primary and secondary institutions—property and contract relations, disestablished church, public schools, formal and informal associations, family, and so on—and these exerted the economic, social, and ideological pressure necessary to sustain class society. Although violence still had an important role, it was exercised chiefly at lower levels of social organization by policemen, foremen, teachers, parents, and the like to contain what was seen to be dissidence by individuals. These mechanisms were monitored by local elites, and only when the basic structure was threatened were centralized instruments of violence such as the army utilized by those at the higher levels in national government.

In the Liberal model, as long as decentralized institutions effectively defined any challenge to the structure of class privilege and power as lying outside the range of legitimate political activity, the political system's ability to appear open, competitive, and flexible was in itself an important contribution to stability. With greater confidence in the effectiveness of decentralized institutions of control, the franchise could be broadened and electoral manipulation reduced. Central government was presided over by an executive in office for a short term and by a bureaucracy in which personnel in the top positions changed with the executive, thus guarding against entrenchment and insulation from influence.

In many of the newly independent Spanish American nations, of course, the distinctions between the Conservative and Liberal programs were not as sharp as those described previously, but the differences were still substantial and reflected the judgments of different sectors of the elite about how much direct pressure was necessary to keep the producing classes working for them and about whether the pressure could be adequately exerted at the point of production or required application at a systemic level. Plantation owners using slave labor and the merchants involved in credit and marketing of plantation products, for instance, favored direct coercion from a central authority. Landowners engaged in market production with a weak and divided labor force, along with merchant allies, generally favored a looser and more malleable political system that required considerably less tax support. In Central America, Salvadoran indigo producers exemplified this form of production and were the most adamant Liberals in the region.

An extreme point in this continuum was the large haciendas, generally in the interior, that had no labor control problems and slight, if any, connection with the market. The bosses of these primitive, largely self-sufficient units were often antagonistic to any type of national government that might impinge on their authority over personal fiefs.

This statement of alternative political ideals is not meant to suggest a linearly deterministic scheme nor to impugn the motives of individuals who espoused one form or another. It simply recognizes that the upper classes, in spite of differences over particulars, were sufficiently powerful as a group to veto any set of political arrangements incompatible with the interests of the class as a whole. This set definite limits on what was possible in practice and influenced the ascendance of certain ideas at particular times. The stream of political thinking from which the ideas came—Spanish and European (including Anglo-American) intellectual and cultural traditions—had its own history, not independent of material developments but with considerable integrity of its own.

Attention to the social and material spheres, however, makes more intelligible the nature of Spanish American Conservative and Liberal policies. The Conservatives were not, for instance, economic reactionaries, and postindependence Conservative regimes, such as those in Venezuela and Ecuador, were often distinguished by active programs of public works and reconstruction and promotion of local manufacturing, albeit under strict institutional controls. Moreover, the Liberals' political and economic radicalism was strongly conservative in social terms.

Political Turmoil in Postindependence Central America

The effort by Central American Conservatives to create a postcolonial state along Conservative lines, complete with a Mexican monarch, failed so completely that they were discredited, and many Conservative leaders were exiled. This gave Liberal criollos a relatively free hand in creating the institutional structure of the United Provinces of Central America. In this effort, they were helped by Salvadoran troops that occasionally entered Guatemala to contain the Conservatives.

The Liberal constitution of 1824 created a federation of five provinces, and local, provincial, and federal offices were filled by complex indirect election procedures. Although the franchise was still withheld from women, men of African ancestry were enfranchised. After considerable intrigue and dubious manipulation, the tiny constituency elected Manuel José de Arce the first president of the United Provinces. Arce was a Liberal Salvadoran firebrand, but upon becoming president he found new and compelling arguments for the Conservative cause, especially when articulated by the aristocratic Guatemalan merchants.

The federal government was very weak, however, and the provinces essentially went their own ways unless obliged to do otherwise by federal troops. One of the most troublesome provincial governments was that of Guatemala, which was more radically Liberal than the federal Liberal government and consistently critical of what it saw as an increasing accommodation to Conservative views and interests. By 1826, a vicious civil war that lasted for three years broke out in Guatemala. In several respects, this war and subsequent struggles resembled contemporary convulsions in Mexico. One striking common characteristic was the manner in which Conservatives borrowed heavily from the Church to finance their campaigns and that Liberals confiscated Church properties whenever they had the opportunity. In either case, the Church lost. Although it had been a target of Bourbon suspicion and outright anticlericism, it was still a powerful political and economic force in Central America. By one estimate, the Church owned over 900 haciendas and sugar mills in Central America at the time of independence. It had the capacity to lose for quite a while.

By 1829, Francisco Morazán, a Liberal Honduran general, emerged as the leader of the victorious side. He became president of the federation in 1830 and dominated federal politics for the next decade. The Liberal victory enabled the enactment of an ambitious set of Liberal policies. The government prohibited special privileges and titles for members of such elite institutions as the Church, merchant guilds, military, and university. It also implemented several anticlerical policies, including civil marriage, divorce, secular education, the right of children of clergy to inherit Church property, reduction of the number of religious holidays, frequent expulsion of the clergy, suppression of the tithe, and outright confiscation of Church property.

The Liberal assault on Church lands, however, did not stem exclusively from anticlericism or even from desire for Church properties, usually distributed to political favorites. The Liberals profoundly believed that the creation of a capitalist economy along Anglo-American lines was a necessary condition for material progress. This conviction indicted virtually all Hispanic institutions as archaic and antiprogressive. The faith in the efficacy of private ownership of the means of production meant that land held by the "dead hand" of the Church was seen as unproductive and wasteful. This Liberal criticism of nonprogressive ownership and use was not limited to Church lands and Hispanic institutions. Even though criollos avoided applying these principles to equally inefficient private haciendas, they did so to lands held in common by Indian communities, which thus became prey to governmental appropriation and criollo greed.

In the same spirit, with an additional incentive supplied by the Guatemalan consulado's strongly Conservative bent, the Liberals moved against restrictions on trade. This included abolishing the consulado in 1829. Although the Guatemalan consulado supported free trade, in the sense that there should be no restraints on the international movement of goods and capital, its members were certainly not in favor of losing their domestic monopoly over that trade. However, as has been noted, local producers of goods that competed with imports, especially producers and merchants of domestic cotton textiles, were badly hurt by the freeing of international commerce, although in general all producers and merchants involved in domestic commerce welcomed breaking the consulado's hold.

Free trade was indeed an issue in Central America, but it was a policy issue that cut across Conservative-Liberal lines drawn over the political organization of social power. Although free trade is usually identified with liberalism, it concerns market relations of commodities rather than social relationships of production. It thereby stood apart from more fundamental aspects of social and political organization. Two nineteenth-century examples of the neutrality of free trade in this respect were the high tariffs of the liberal United States and the free trade feudalism of southeastern Europe. Serious conflicts developed over free trade throughout Spanish America only after the class order had been secured within a political system.

Consistent with the promotion of competitive capitalism, characterized by "free" wage labor, Central American Liberals abolished slavery at this time. The abolition was not politically difficult, because slave owners were neither politically nor economically very important. The abolition of slavery, then, was inexpensive and ideologically consistent. Moreover, it damaged a source of Conservative support, eliminated the threat to social stability posed by slave revolts, and stopped the importation of Africans, whom many criollos feared, whether slaves or free. In its prompt granting of manumission, Central America was similar to other areas with few slaves (for instance, Chile and Mexico). In places where slavery was economically important, such as Uruguay, inland Argentina, Colombia, Peru, and Venezuela, slavery was not abolished until the 1840s and 1850s. It lasted until the 1880s in Cuba and Brazil, where it was critical in the production of sugar and coffee.

Judicial reforms were also important, but for our purposes here one more example of the Liberals' sense of progressive policy is sufficient. Central American Liberals made a serious effort to promote immigration from northern Europe, much like the policy of Domingo Sarmiento, the Argentine president who was the quintessential Latin American Liberal of the postcolonial period.[7] Their purpose was to increase output of the land, but perhaps more important, they hoped that the Hispanic and Indian cultures would be changed for the better by hard-working, disciplined, and frugal Protestants from northern Europe.

It is safe to say that some Central American criollos disapproved of all of these Liberal measures and all disapproved of some. The reforms provoked strong reactions from many different groups of criollos. Consequently, Morazán had to suppress continual revolts. In 1837, he moved the federal capital from Guatemala City to San Salvador, in part to benefit from the greater protection offered by the ardent criollo Liberals of El Salvador.

The decisive reaction to the Liberal program came from below. In 1837, some Indians of northern and western Guatemala revolted, but this event paled in comparison to the massive uprising of Indians and ladinos in southern and eastern Guatemala (the Montaña) led by a mestizo swineherd named José Rafael Carrera, an energetic and brilliant military commander. Liberals and Conservatives closed ranks against the common enemy, but Carrera and his informal army swept away the provincial troops and entered triumphantly into Guatemala City in the first weeks of 1838. An English diplomat who was an eyewitness to the entry of Carrera and his troops into Guatemala described it as follows:

> Awhile after came the hordes of barbarians headed by Carrera. Only think what a sight—You would have thought there was a return to the age of Alaric, when he invaded Rome—the sight was awful and horrible—to witness 4,000 barbarians, rude, half-naked, drunk and elated, vociferating with all their might "long live Religion and death to all foreigners"—some had only staves, others Muskets . . . at the hour of "oracion" they all knelt down in the [central] square and sang the Sanctus Deus and Ave Maria.[8]

It seemed as though the criollos' most terrifying nightmare had finally come true, and Central America was witnessing Hidalgo and Tupac Amaru rolled into one crude leader with a massive following of the rural poor, unwashed and unwhite. The revolution had come. But it was not so. Carrera and his followers had not revolted against criollo oppression in general but rather were fighting against the specifics of Liberal policies. As the preceding quotation suggests, there was a strong current of xenophobia in Carrera's movement, directed especially at the arrival of northern European immigrants. The antipathy toward foreigners was probably heightened by a recent cholera epidemic, which had originated in Belize and New York and had hit the Montaña region hard.

The immigrants were not only foreigners; they were Protestants. Thus the movement was animated by extremely strong religious (specifically Catholic) convictions in reaction primarily to the anticlericism of the Liberals. Local clergy had been instrumental in focusing that feeling into armed political action.

The political content of Carrera's movement, then, was narrowly conservative. As soon as the Guatemalan criollo elite realized this and overcame their personal distaste for having to deal with the likes of Carrera, the Conservatives broke from the anti-Carrera alliance with the Liberals and began to court him. They were successful, and the movement's conservative populism became Conservative with a capital C. Carrera returned with his troops to the Montaña with the promise that the Liberal reforms would be rescinded and replaced by a Conservative program. One account adds that Carrera also was given 1,000 pesos for himself and 10,000 pesos for his followers, along with 1,000 muskets with ammunition.

At one level, the pattern seems puzzling. Why would poor Indians and ladinos revolt against Liberal policies that, despite some cynicism in their application, were still predicated on the doctrine that Indians and ladinos were fully human individuals deserving to be free, and why would they demand that these measures be replaced by Conservative ones whose vision explicitly relegated Indians and ladinos to an an inferior position in a tightly controlled social and political order?

Liberal social theory cannot be axiomatically equated with freedom, liberty, or liberation; the vision of freedom embodied in liberalism is basically negative. The less free and the more unequal the society to which its permissive tenets are applied, the more readily can the most powerful exploit others without restraint. Even though many criollo Conservatives appeared to have serious doubts about whether Indians were truly human, their conception of the social order contained a clear place for Indian villages, lands, and ways of life. The Liberal vision, though based on putative convictions about human equality, saw Indians as undesirable atavisms and obstacles to progress.

In Central America, this attitude was evident in the alienation of communal land to private ownership, the promotion of individually negotiated contracts as the sole regulator of relations between workers and owners, and the weakening of the Church, which among other things often did attempt to protect the Indians and rural poor from predatory criollos. The severe damage to Indian communities wrought by the Mexican Liberal constitution of 1857, promulgated by Benito Juárez—Mexico's first full-blooded Indian president—is the obvious comparison.

Later in 1838, Carrera threatened to return to Guatemala City because the promises made to him were not being honored. Morazán brought federal troops from San Salvador to prevent this. By 1840, however, Carrera was the undisputed military master of Guatemala. Morazán escaped to exile but was executed when he returned two years later. Carrera and his followers re-created many colonial policies and institutions, including the merchant consulado in Guatemala, Church control of marriage and education, prohibition of divorce, reconciliation with the Vatican, and so on.

In July 1838, the federal assembly formally dissolved the United Provinces of Central America. Despite a shell of a federation that lasted until 1847, the five provinces became independent nations. This action was merely a formal acknowledgment of what had been a fact for several years. The federal government had never possessed the legitimacy or power to create a tax system capable of generating revenues sufficient to fund its operations. The federal government's finances depended primarily on sporadic foreign loans at extravagant prices (but uniformly defaulted) and occasional levies on local groups, who therefore joined the opposition. Although the federal government passed legislation and circulated decrees, these could be ignored with impunity or implemented selectively by provincial and municipal governments, except when federal troops that remained loyal to the federal government were called in.

This does not mean that provincial governments were much more effective. None had a tax base that produced the resources necessary for real authority. The entire political system was essentially run by a series of local strongmen (*caudillos*), who made and broke alliances with and subjugated or ignored each other and in some general way identified with the Conservative Party. Since the programmatic differences between the Conservative and Liberal parties were becoming harder to discern—they were becoming more alike in what earlier would have been seen to be Liberal terms, except on Church-related issues—the caudillos' preference for the Conservative Party may have been only to avoid a confrontation with Carrera, the most important caudillo in Central America. But even Carrera wielded little authority outside areas occupied by his troops. Until his death in 1865, he frequently did control most of Guatemala, El Salvador, and Honduras and occasionally invaded Nicaragua. Nevertheless, a caudillo's influence cannot be mistaken for strong government.

Although the new Central American national states were weak and inchoate during the first decades of independence, they were more open to international pressures as politically independent nations than they were as Spanish colonies. I have already noted how the activity of English merchants, who were selling, not buying, intensified as a result of the Napoleonic Wars. Although the English remained distant from the independence efforts, this trade pattern was sustained during the years of the post-Waterloo depression in Europe.

Indigo exports continued to be weak even after the European depression because of the destructiveness of the postindependence wars between Guatemala and El Salvador, occasional natural disasters, and increasing competition from producers in India and other parts of Latin America. Cochineal, raised in central and eastern Guatemala, replaced Salvadoran indigo as the leading regional export.

A second major change in international commerce was brought about by the completion of the railroad across the isthmus of Panama in 1855. This brought the Pacific coast of Central America much closer to the markets of Europe and the eastern United States and reoriented a significant proportion of international commerce in Central America toward its Pacific coast ports at the expense of Belize. But the reorientation was not of expanding exports of dyestuffs. The discovery of an inexpensive way to produce fast blue dyes from coal tar in the 1850s sharply reduced the demand for Central American indigo. During the same time, however, it must have helped a bit to export indigo through the Pacific ports to the newly opened Levi Strauss & Co. of San Francisco to dye cotton denim material a distinctive blue.

But the importance of international processes to Central America was not limited to exports and imports. In the postindependence years, the English strengthened their hold on the Caribbean coast of Nicaragua (the "Miskito coast") with an eye on the potential value of an interoceanic passage through Nicaragua. And that value rose with the discovery of gold in California in 1848 and the consequent gold rush. It also brought the first substantial U.S. involvement in the isthmus.[9]

Cornelius Vanderbilt used the passage through Nicaragua for his extensive and profitable business of transporting goods and about 130,000 people between 1840 and 1860 back and forth between the U.S. eastern seaboard and California. This movement increased tensions between the United States and Great Britain. As a result, the two nations agreed, in the Clayton-Bulwer Treaty of 1850, that they would control and protect jointly any canal through Nicaragua and that neither side would engage in any military activity in the area. While Nicaraguan opinions were neither solicited nor heard during the negotiations, and although the British presence in Nicaragua violated the Monroe Doctrine of 1823, this formal recognition of mutual interests in Nicaragua smoothed the way for eventual British withdrawal from the Miskito coast at the end of the century and the consolidation of their hold on Belize.

During the time that Great Britain and the United States were settling their differences over Nicaragua, quarrels among Nicaraguans were heating up. Although the struggles were between the Liberals of León and the Conservatives of Granada, there were so many shifting alliances and such a high level of opportunism that the lines of the disputes, much less the issues, were difficult to define clearly. In any case, the Liberals believed that they were being persecuted. They appealed to the U.S. government for help in their fight against the Conservatives, who, with Carrera's aid and British approval, controlled national politics.

The news of the request percolated down to a complex and highly educated lawyer and journalist named William Walker, who at that time was living in San Francisco and had recently participated in a foray to Baja California in Mexico. He recruited a small group of soldiers of fortune, many of them veterans of the Mexican American War, and they landed on the Pacific coast of Nicaragua in 1855. With the help of Liberal troops, Walker and his irregulars captured Granada and set up a Liberal as president. Shortly thereafter, Walker declared himself president. In spite of his earlier abolitionist record, he apparently initiated overtures for the admission of Nicaragua to the United States as a slave state. His activities also raised hopes among conservative antislavery politicians in the United States who were fashioning "colonization" schemes to rid the United States of freed slaves by sending them to Central America rather than to Liberia in western Africa. In addition, Walker made a series of bizarre proclamations, which included declaring English to be the official language of Nicaragua.

An army of the other four Central American nations finally defeated his forces (the "National War"), and Walker surrendered to the captain of a U.S. naval vessel in 1857. In a subsequent "filibustering" expedition, this time into Honduras, he was captured by the British and turned over to Honduran authorities, who executed him in 1860.

In addition to the death and destruction it caused, the Walker episode, which in the United States had definite comic opera qualities, discredited the Nicaraguan Liberals and laid a solid foundation for anti-U.S. sentiment in Nicaragua.

Patterns of State Making

As should be clear from this chapter, the decades following independence from Spain were not especially bright ones for the new nations of Central America. Neither the region as a whole nor its individual nations possessed the socioeconomic structure necessary to create a stable politics. Cacao, indigo, cochineal, mining, and cattle had not produced the upper-class coherence and political institutions necessary for the new nations of the Central American isthmus to form durable state systems.

Indigo production in the second half of the eighteenth century had come closest to being the economic basis of a social formation capable of a regularized politics, but cochineal exports had not been strong enough to offset the decline of indigo in the early nineteenth century. Nevertheless, the eighteenth-century indigo boom, in the way in which its production was organized and the consequent development of transportation and credit systems, had left a strong legacy of institutional development in El Salvador, where its production was the base of Salvadoran liberalism, and in Guatemala, where the commercial monopoly supported Conservative politics. The effect of indigo was considerably less in Honduras, Nicaragua, and Costa Rica in spite of the widespread stimulus for production that indigo exports exerted.

The center of Central America in all respects remained El Salvador and Guatemala. El Salvador was on its way to creating a wage labor force and an aggressive stratum of commercial farmers, but these farmers had not become sufficiently organized to constitute a coherent governing class.

Guatemala was several steps ahead of El Salvador in respect to effective political institutions. Guatemala also had experienced considerable economic growth and institutional development, and in the nineteenth century it clearly held the lead in economic diversification, including foodstuffs, cochineal, textiles, and commerce—especially credit and transportation. Although there were serious dissensions among members of the Guatemalan upper class, they were economically more powerful and culturally more coherent than their counterparts in El Salvador, in part because they were a Europeanized minority among an Indian majority.

So even though it lagged behind El Salvador in regard to the beginnings of an individualistic, market-oriented capitalism, Guatemala had been the colonial capital and thus the site of the best-developed political institutions, and the need to contain large populations outside the Hispanic cultural orbit while utilizing them as a work force united the upper classes and gave them the incentive to develop a strong state system. Even in Guatemala, however, criollos were not all that successful in doing so, and state development was rudimentary and politics were, by and large, determined by the loyalties of different armed groups. Carrera's exceptional ability to sustain the necessary loyalties gave Guatemala a political stability that belied the weakness of its political institutions.

The process of national consolidation and state formation did not really get under way until the midnineteenth-century development of large-scale agricultural exports of coffee and bananas. Coffee proved capable of generating a governing class, but this was far from a uniform process in the isthmus.

Notes

1. See the essays by John Lynch, Timothy Anna, and Tulio Halperín Donghi in L. Bethell (ed.), *The Cambridge History of Latin America, Vol. 3: From Independence to c. 1870* (New York: Cambridge University Press, 1985), for general background on the eighteenth-century Bourbon reforms, the early nineteenth-century independence movements, and subsequent turmoil throughout Latin America. Good comparative treatments of the eras are Mario Rodríguez, *The Cádiz Experiment in Central America, 1808–1826* (Berkeley: University of California Press, 1978); Robert S. Smith, "Financing the Central American Federation, 1821–1838," *Hispanic American Historical Review* 43, no. 4 (1963); Ralph Woodward, "The Aftermath of Independence, 1821–c. 1870," in L. Bethell (ed.), *Central America Since Independence* (Cambridge: Cambridge University Press, 1991), pp. 1–36; and especially Miles L. Wortman, *Government and Society in Central America, 1680–1840* (New York: Columbia University Press, 1982). For studies of more specific aspects, see E. Bradford Burns, *Patriarch and Folk: The Emergence of Nicaragua, 1798–1858* (Cambridge: Harvard University Press, 1991); Keith Miceli, "Rafael Carrera: Defender and Promoter of Peasant Interests in Guatemala, 1837–1848," *The Americas* 31, no. 1 (1974); and Ralph L. Woodward, *Class Privilege and Economic Development: The Consulado de Comercio of Guatemala, 1793–1871* (Chapel Hill: University of North Carolina Press, 1966).

2. Robert Miles, *Racism* (New York: Routledge, 1989), is an interesting, recent study of racism that emphasizes the socially constructed nature of the phenomenon. On the origins of racial thought in Latin America and the early debates over what constituted "humanness," see Anthony Pagden, *The Fall of Natural Man: The American Indian and the Origins of Comparative Ethnology* (New York: Cambridge University Press, 1986).

3. In addition to the citations on the wars of independence in note 1, see Timothy E. Anna, *Spain and the Loss of America* (Lincoln: University of Nebraska Press, 1983), for the other side, as it were.

4. Leon G. Campbell, "Recent Research on Andean Peasant Revolts, 1750–1820," *Latin American Research Review* 14, no. 1 (1979), pp. 3–50, is a thorough survey of the scholarship on the eighteenth-century Andean revolts.

5. Quoted in Louis E. Baumgartner, *José de Valle of Central America* (Durham: University of North Carolina Press, 1963), p. 147. This biography gives considerable insight into the Central American independence movement.

6. See Frederick S. Weaver, *Class, State, and Industrial Structure: The Historical Process of South American Industrial Growth* (Westport, CT, and London: Greenwood Press, 1980), pp. 59–78, for a more extended form of this argument about Spanish American independence movements.

7. The classic statement is Domingo Sarmiento, *Life in the Argentine Republic in the Days of the Tyrants, or Civilization and Barbarism* (New York: Collier Books, 1966). W. J. Griffeth, *Empires in the Wilderness* (Chapel Hill: University of North Carolina Press, 1966), contains material on Guatemalan population policy.

8. Quoted in Miles L. Wortman, *Government and Society in Central America, 1680–1840* (New York: Columbia University Press, 1982), p. 264.

9. In solidarity with Mexico, which was losing one-third of its national territory to the United States in the Mexican American War, Honduras declared war against the United States in 1847. Not enough came out of this event, however, to count as serious U.S. involvement in Central America.

3

The Export Economies: Coffee, Bananas, and Social Structure, 1850 to 1930

During the colonial era, politics was in command. The power of the colonizer, Spain, structured the life of the region, including its economic activities. There were definite limits to the reach of the Spanish authorities, and economic interests and various forms of social power developed within the interstices of life of the colony. Nevertheless, it was primarily Spanish rule that determined who was to exercise authority within the colony and benefit from the work of others.

After independence, this changed. The authority of colonial rule was not replaced by other types of authority. Although there was an economic elite from the colonial era, the criollo elite's economic base was insufficient to create a powerful ruling class in Central America. The government of Carrera brought new support and energy to Conservatism by involving the peasantry, but the coalition was very precarious. As a consequence, the region frequently dissolved into warring factions, and the innovation did not survive Carrera's presidency.

During the later nineteenth and early twentieth centuries, however, international commodity and financial markets became the source of new and vital economic activities in Central America. This process served to strengthen and unify the propertied classes in three of the nations and profoundly affected the meaning of nationhood in the two with less coherent upper classes.

As mentioned in the previous chapter, the initial integration of the new nations into nineteenth-century world markets was on the import side. Throughout Spanish America, the most active foreign penetration in the years immediately following independence was by English merchants selling, not buying. But the purchase of imports requires foreign exchange, and without strong exports the availability of British pounds, U.S. dollars, German marks, and so on was limited. The new governments of

Central America found it difficult to obtain the foreign investment, either as loans or directly in production, that helped other new Spanish American governments to finance imports and, more generally, to supply fiscal resources that the new states were unable to obtain from a tax system.

After considerable effort, the government of the United Provinces of Central America managed to float a small loan on the London market in 1828. After the demise of the United Provinces, the defaulted loan was apportioned out among the five new republics. As repayment was to be in pounds sterling, export earnings were necessary if these bonds were ever going to be redeemed. Some scholars, including notables like Jean-Charles-Léonard Simonde de Sismondi, Tugan Baranowski, and Rosa Luxemburg, have argued that the loans to Spanish America (and to Egypt and Turkey) not only financed imports of British goods but that the debts became a bludgeon with which the new nations were forced into the world markets as exporters of primary products and importers of manufactured goods.

There is no question that England and the United States had definite interests in Central America, and they used defaulted loans as a lever to maintain a hold on a possible interoceanic canal through the isthmus. But the degree to which British and U.S. coercion actually influenced Central American participation in international markets was probably slight.

The economies of Latin America, including Central America, did indeed become integrated into the international division of labor, but not on a grand scale until the second half of the nineteenth century. Foreign demand for Latin American exports was stimulated by the economic growth on the European continent and in England, dramatic declines in freight costs as a result of innovations in ocean transport, and the U.S. Civil War. By the beginning of the twentieth century, most of the nations of Latin America were firmly enmeshed in an international division of labor. The role of Latin Americans in this global specialization was to export primary products (the products of fields, mines, forests, and seas) and with those earnings, minus interest payments and profit remittances to foreigners, to import manufactured goods and, especially in the case of Central America, foodstuffs. The pull of these lucrative opportunities in international markets, which were very attractive to portions of the local possessing classes eager to consolidate and extend their positions vis-à-vis domestic working classes and competing segments of elites, was more decisive than the push by the English.

Central America in the World Economy

In Central America, the export boom in the late nineteenth and early twentieth centuries was primarily but not exclusively in coffee and bananas. Tables 3.1 and 3.2 show that all the nations exported a range of goods. As background for the following discussion, Figure 3.1 displays the proportional value of exports in national production, and Figure 3.2 shows the per capita incomes of the Central American nations during the 1920s.

In the sixteenth century, the first bishop of Panama carried banana plants to his new diocese from the Canary Islands, where banana cultivation had arrived in the course of its slow journey from southeast Asia across south Asia and Africa. But it was not until toward the end of the nineteenth century that commercial banana cultivation became important along the Caribbean coasts of Costa Rica, Honduras, Guatemala, and, to a lesser extent, Nicaragua, under the auspices of foreign firms based principally in the United States.

Coffee was introduced into Central America considerably later than bananas were. By the eighteenth century, the French Caribbean islands of Martinique, Guadeloupe, and Haiti were exporting substantial volumes of coffee to Europe, where a taste had already been developed for the Middle Eastern beverage. Coffee had appeared in Guatemala and Costa Rica as well in the eighteenth century, and the Bourbons had promoted

TABLE 3.1 Percentage of Central American Exports by Commodity, 1913

	Guatemala	Honduras	El Salvador	Nicaragua	Costa Rica	Regional % Total	1,000 U.S.$ Total
Coffee	85.3	3.4	80.4	64.3	35.2	63.1	28,475
Bananas	5.7	50.8	--	5.5	50.7	18.1	8,164
Metals	--	26.3	16.1	13.7	10.0	9.9	4,467
Hides	3.2	4.7	1.0	4.2	1.3	2.6	1,171
Timber	1.7	0.4	--	4.1	1.4	1.6	722
Rubber	0.7	0.4	0.2	3.6	0.4	1.0	455
Sugar	2.4	--	0.8	0.4	--	1.0	454
Chicle	1.0	--	--	--	--	0.3	142
Balsam	--	--	1.0	--	--	0.2	89
Coconuts	--	6.5	--	--	--	0.5	220
Indigo	--	--	0.6	--	--	0.1	53
Cacao	--	--	--	0.5	1.0	0.3	145
Cattle	--	7.4	--	3.7	--	1.2	539
Percent Total	100.0	100.0	100.0	100.0	100.0	100.0	
1,000 U.S.$ Total	14,373	3,375	9,320	7,785	10,243		45,096

Source: Derived from Dana G. Munro, *The Five Republics of Central America: Their Political and Economic Development and Their Relations with the United States* (New York: Oxford University Press, 1918), p. 266.

Table 3.2 Percentage of Commodity Exports by Country, 1913

	Guatemala	Honduras	El Salvador	Nicaragua	Costa Rica	Regional % Total	1,000 U.S.$ Total
Coffee	43.0	0.4	26.3	17.6	12.7	100.0	28,475
Bananas	10.1	21.0	--	5.3	63.6	100.0	8,164
Metals	--	19.9	33.5	23.8	22.9	100.0	4,467
Hides	38.9	13.7	8.2	27.9	11.4	100.0	1,171
Timber	34.1	1.8	--	44.6	19.5	100.0	722
Rubber	22.0	3.1	4.0	61.3	9.7	100.0	455
Sugar	76.9	--	16.1	7.0	--	100.0	454
Chicle	100.0	--	--	--	--	100.0	142
Balsam	--	--	100.0	--	--	100.0	89
Coconuts	--	100.0	--	--	--	100.0	220
Indigo	--	--	100.0	--	--	100.0	53
Cacao	--	--	--	27.6	72.4	100.0	145
Cattle	--	46.6	--	53.4	--	100.0	539
Total	31.9	7.5	20.7	17.3	22.7	100.0	
1,000 U.S.$ Total	14,373	3,375	9,320	7,785	10,243		45,096

Source: Derived from Dana G. Munro, *The Five Republics of Central America: Their Political and Economic Development and Their Relations with the United States* (New York: Oxford University Press, 1918), p. 266.

its planting. At this time, however, its most important uses were as an ornamental shrub and to counteract drunkenness.

The demand in foreign markets for coffee led to its commercial cultivation as an export crop in Costa Rica during the third and fourth decades of the nineteenth century. It was not until the second half of the nineteenth century, however, that growers in Guatemala, El Salvador, and Nicaragua responded to the strong European demand by beginning systematic cultivation for export. Honduras's rugged topography made transporting coffee for export difficult and costly, and it was not until the 1940s that Honduran coffee entered the international market in substantial amounts. Unlike with banana production, coffee cultivation in all of Central America remained in the hands of residents.

Foreign conspiracies had little to do with the entry of Central America into the international economy. Domestic possessing classes, like those throughout Latin America, had been looking for the main chance to confirm and extend their positions in the new nation-states, and they were willing and eager to take advantage of world market opportunities that constituted that chance. The relative political stability of Central America in the late nineteenth and early twentieth centuries indicates that the strategy was rather successful.

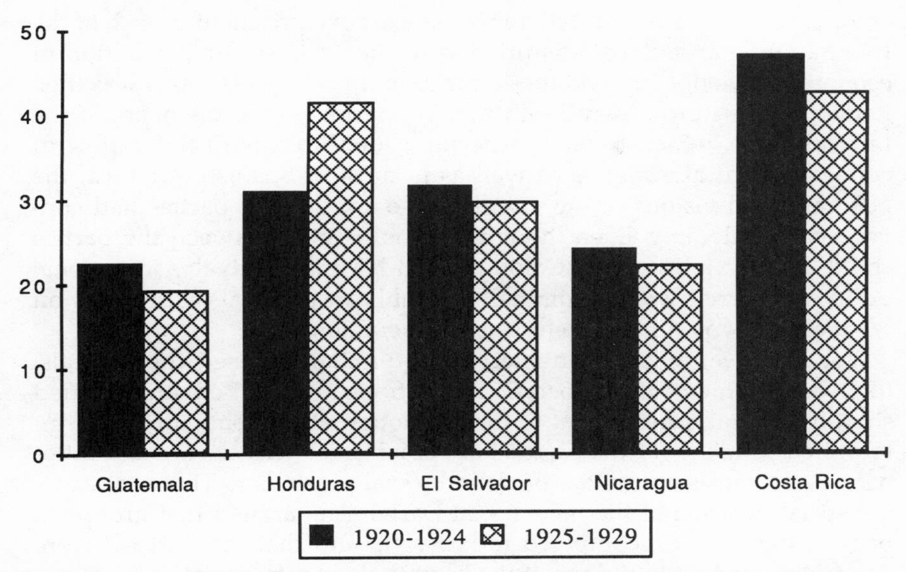

FIGURE 3.1 Exports as a percentage of gross domestic product, 1920–1929. *Source:* Adapted from Victor Bulmer-Thomas, *The Political Economy of Central America Since 1920* (New York: Cambridge University Press, 1987), pp. 312–313, 330–331.

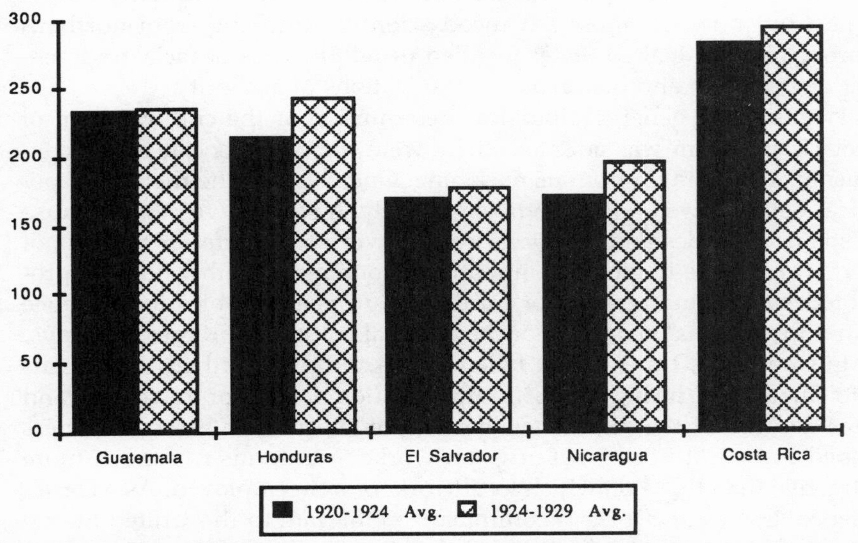

FIGURE 3.2 Per capita gross domestic product, 1920–1929 (1970 U.S.$). *Source:* Adapted from Victor Bulmer-Thomas, *The Political Economy of Central America Since 1920* (New York: Cambridge University Press, 1987), p. 312.

As a part of this process, there was at least one president in each of the five nations particularly identified with the enthusiastic promotion of economic development and modernization (or "progress," as it was then known). These progressives—in material terms—were members of the Liberal Party, which became especially identified with the export of coffee. In Central America as well as in most of Spanish America, the general social visions of the Conservative and Liberal parties had converged considerably. Even though the competition between the parties could still be violent, as in Colombia and Nicaragua, rivalry in national politics occurred within nominally republican political institutions on what earlier would have been seen as Liberal terms.

For instance, whereas anticlericism still characterized the Liberals, their commitment to democratic institutions and participation waned sharply. Liberal commitment to the promotion of economic progress, interpreted primarily as the product of applying modern science and rationality, was consistent with a profound social pessimism. The most exciting social doctrine of the time, social Darwinism, argued that groups of people, like species, competed for survival and that the "fittest" were those who made it to the top of the heap to dominate others.

This tautology, masquerading as a statement of causality, seemed to supply a scientific basis for the "inferiority" of indigenous peoples, those of African descent, all women, and any others not in the forefront of economic and scientific progress. This conclusion, so convenient for the elite, had been an integral part of Spanish American culture since colonial times, but now the most advanced scientific thinking from northern Europe and the United States justified usual practices of racial and gender degradation and hierarchical organizations of authority.

Whether the genetic (biological determinist) or the cultural form of social Darwinism was adopted, there were important social policy conclusions to be drawn from its reasoning. One was that the rhetoric of political equality was not to be taken literally. A second was that because Hispanic attitudes and practices were proving to be inferior to those of northern Europe in global competition, economic growth would be promoted by the immigration of northern European peoples to influence either the national gene pool or the national culture in progressive ways.

In Chapter 2, I mentioned failed efforts to bring northern Europeans into Guatemala during the 1830s. Immigration policies of the middle and later decades of the century were no more effective. In essence, leaders hoped to recruit northern European workers on terms not much more attractive than those on which local workers were employed. As a consequence, European workers continued to emigrate to the United States, Canada, Australia, and Argentina rather than to Central America.

But a good number of Europeans did emigrate to Central America. Instead of working-class immigrants, however, they were people who possessed some capital, business experience, and contacts, and many of them became very important in the development of the Central American coffee economies. Somewhat to the dismay of the Central American elites, these immigrant entrepreneurs, mostly from Spain, Germany, and Great Britain, established coffee plantations (*fincas*), merchant houses, and in many ways competed with the more established elements of Central American society.

The growth of coffee and banana exports between the middle of the nineteenth century and 1930 was impressive but not even and steady. Recessions in Europe and the United States in the 1880s, 1890s, and 1920 and 1921 were general setbacks, and banana exports from Honduras grew spectacularly during the 1920s while those from Costa Rica declined as a result of banana disease.

In addition, the large-scale entry of Brazilian coffee into world markets in the 1880s also significantly affected Central American exports. Brazilian coffee was grown on a moving frontier, and when soil fertility declined, the coffee fincas moved on to new lands. In contrast, Central American coffee was grown on permanent fincas, and the renewal of soil fertility was vitally important. Although Brazilian coffee was an inferior grade, the size of the Brazilian harvest still affected the market for the higher-quality Central American coffee. And Colombian coffee, which also entered the international market in this period, was more directly competitive.

Central American exporters near Pacific coast ports received a significant boost from the opening of the Panama Canal in 1914. It was much more important than the opening of the Panama railroad in 1855 because the customs duties levied by Colombia (of which Panama was a part) and the dangers of transshipment offset most cost savings. The canal, however, was much more successful.

Even though Nicaragua seemed to be the more feasible site, geographically and economically, for an interoceanic canal, negotiations with President José Santos Zelaya of Nicaragua broke down at the end of the century. Zelaya was unwilling to concede sovereignty over the proposed canal and its adjacent areas. Because of this impasse with Nicaragua, the U.S. government was attracted to the repeated offers to sell its works by a financially strapped French company that had been digging a canal through Panama.[1] But again, the deal was threatened by the unwillingness of the Colombian government to cede complete sovereignty over the proposed canal and surrounding zone in Panama. This problem was overcome by a well-organized Panamanian secessionist revolt against Colombia in 1903. There had been several Panamanian efforts to separate from Colombia since independence from Spain, but this one was encouraged and even partially financed by outsiders, perhaps by the U.S. government and certainly by the French canal company desperate to sell out to the U.S. government. The creation of an independent Panama was enthusiastically welcomed by the United States, which recognized the new nation and in two weeks closed the canal deal with the rebels and the French company.

The benefits of the canal's opening to Central American exporters was initially offset by World War I, which began that same year. The disruption of European markets and the shortage of shipping were serious problems, though they proved to be temporary and had no lasting effects on levels or organization of Central American exports. The major result of the war was to change the direction of Central American trade, which, like all Latin American trade, became much more strongly oriented to North American markets. Although European markets came back after the war, they never recovered their preeminence.

Central American entry into international markets produced far-reaching implications for the domestic social orders. To understand the multiple significance of the export-based economic expansion, it is necessary to use a framework that goes beyond the commodity and financial flows and connects export activity to the social and economic structures of the Central American nations.

Analytical Issues

There are major divisions of opinion about whether foreign trade and investment resulted in long-term benefits to peripheral areas incorporated into the European-dominated world economy. Among U.S. scholars, the principal division in the debate is between those working in the Anglo-American tradition of neoclassical economic theory and those identified with dependency theory. Dependency theory is a name used for a range of theoretical positions, and here I will use it narrowly to represent the position initially argued by the United Nations Economic Commission for Latin America and the Caribbean (or CEPAL, its Spanish acronym), the work of Andre Gunder Frank, and the "world system" approach pioneered by Immanuel Wallerstein. In Latin America, the term includes analyses that are much richer and more sophisticated than the narrow, economistic version, but because the latter is still alive and well among some U.S. writers and students, it is worth critically evaluating.[2]

Although neoclassical theory and the economistic style of dependency theory yield widely divergent conclusions, one of the most significant aspects of the debate is the uniform narrowness of their common premise: The growth-inducing or growth-retarding effects of foreign trade and investment in Central America (and elsewhere) resulted principally from the availability of economic resources. In the neoclassical tradition of economic analysis, the central conceptual framework guiding economic research on the relation between foreign trade and economic growth is the theory of comparative advantage (or comparative costs), first formulated by David Ricardo in the early nineteenth century. The theory's principal insight is that engaging in international commerce enables a nation to specialize in those commodities that it can produce relatively cheaply and exchange them on the international market at terms more advantageous than the technical trade-offs (or opportunity costs) of domestic production for commodities it produces relatively expensively. The result is that all participating nations can have higher value combinations of commodities available to them through international commerce and specialization. This insight is analytically identical to Adam Smith's argument about the advantages of the division of labor for individuals within a nation.

These gains are derived from the reallocation of a nation's productive resources (considered to be fixed in size and quality for the purposes of the argument) and the resulting changed composition of national commodity production. As such, the argument is static in that the gains are from a onetime reallocation of existing productive resources and a change in the composition of domestic production. In this form, it does not directly address the prospects of long-term economic growth, but scholars have made it into a more dynamic argument that does address the prospects for long-term growth.

The result is a logically coherent argument for the significant contribution that participation in the world economy can make to a poor nation's economic advance. But when it is pointed out that the optimistic neoclassical scenario has not been realized by the small poor nations who would be expected to gain the most from international trade and investment, neoclassical economists respond that the theory of comparative advantage can only indicate potentialities. If the nation squanders the benefits by simply increasing current consumption of domestic and foreign products, the theory cannot be faulted. This line of defense tacitly admits that the theoretical scope of orthodox economics is too narrow for a satisfactory accounting of the most important effects of international trade and investment. In other words, the availability of economic resources is of only secondary importance in explaining the materially progressive or nonprogressive effects of international trade.

In sharp contrast to the theory of comparative advantage, dependency models were formulated with the explicit purpose of explaining the failure of international trade and investment to bring about long-run, self-sustaining economic expansion to the poorest participants in the world economy. Although the ideas and assertions included in the category of dependency models are extremely varied and heterogeneous, early formulations of dependency theory had a common explanatory core that is still alive and well in North American scholarly circles. The common explanatory core is that the particular manner in which the nations of Latin America have been integrated into the world economy has adversely affected the level of benefits, in terms of economic resources, that those nations received from international trade and investment.

Albeit with some analytical diversity, dependency theorists of this type share the conviction that the principal obstacles to Latin American economic development have been, and continue to be, the flow of resources out of the nations as a result of the workings of the international economy. One mechanism frequently cited to account for the failure of the comparative advantage model to deliver its promised benefits is the repatriation of profits from foreign investment in Latin America to stockholders residing in the investing nations.

On the demand side, dependency theory emphasizes the disadvantages inherent in Latin America's place in the international division of labor because of long-run declines in the prices for Latin American primary product exports relative to the prices of manufactured imports from industrialized nations—declining "terms of trade." On the supply side, the theory contends that the production of primary products has not experienced the technological dynamism undergone by industrial production processes. Therefore, being trapped in an international division of labor supplying unprocessed agricultural and mining products and importing manufactured products condemns these nations to stagnation and poverty.

The dependency explanation turns attention away from national social structures and focuses on external, technical forces and implicitly absolves national elites from any blame for poor economic performance. This reasoning is clearly convenient for the wealthy and powerful classes within Latin America and for U.S. social scientists who are reluctant to address the issue of privilege. Although this perspective may make one suspicious about its popularity, it is not in itself a cogent criticism of dependency theory.

At best, dependency theory of this type offers some mild qualifications to the optimistic conclusions of comparative advantage thinking and at its extreme suffers from serious logical and empirical error. But the central problem with this whole approach is that even in the terms in which it is expressed, it is not an explanation for the failure of Latin American economic development; it is merely a description of it. The central question is why the nations of Latin America did not build upon and move beyond primary product lines that were disadvantageous for long-run economic growth, a transition made successfully by Germany and the United States in the nineteenth century and by Japan, Australia, Canada, and South Korea in the twentieth. To describe the situation in sectoral and productivity terms simply is not an explanation.

In many ways, then, this form of dependency theory is simply the mirror image of conventional conceptions of economic processes: Economic progressiveness and nonprogressiveness is seen to be governed by quantitative amounts of economic resources available to the nation, and international trade and investment are viewed as a source of loss for the less powerful nations. Moreover, both comparative advantage and dependency theory use nations as basic units of analysis and regard them as active agents that possess resources and that trade with and exploit each other. To consider nations to be homogeneous, internally harmonious entities is extremely problematic because this assumption obscures the way in which social structures mediate and condition the relation between external influences and domestic economic dynamism. Lacking in this approach is an understanding as to the ways in which international trade and investment affect the social organization of a nation and the implications of those effects. Which groups are strengthened and which weakened? What consequences do the resulting patterns of ascending and descending groups have for economic growth and development?

What is needed is a framework that relates foreign trade and investment to domestic class structure and then to economic development and underdevelopment without short-circuiting the analysis as do both neoclassical and dependency theory. That is, instead of deriving explanations about growth or its lack directly from the way the nation engages in international commerce, one must study the manner in which foreign trade and investment affect and are affected by the technical and social conditions of production. One can then explain the materially progressive or nonprogressive consequences of foreign penetration in Latin America.

A study of the way in which exports were produced is necessary to appreciate the ways in which domestic social structures mediated the connection between international commerce and national economic growth. This examination would cover both the technical conditions of production (the amounts and types of labor, capital equipment, technology, and other inputs and how they are combined) and the social conditions of production (the organization of power relationships among different groups within the process of export production).

Although the possibility of economic dynamism is governed by the social and technical conditions of production, the actual ways in which the expansion of export production stimulates other branches of domestic production (and thus affects national production as a whole) can be traced through the operation of three kinds of connections, or linkages. The first is the demand that export production creates for domestically produced inputs such as tools, raw materials, transport facilities, and financial services—"backward linkages." The second is the incentive to engage in additional processing of an export commodity, such as timber exports leading to pulp, paper, and furniture production for local as well as foreign markets—"forward linkages." And the third is the stimulus to expand local production of consumer goods serving the markets created by workers and others receiving income from export production—"income multiplier linkages."[3]

These categories are very crude, and one must be careful to respect the mutual interactions among the technical and social relations of production and the various linkages. Nevertheless, these categories can help sort out the effects of Central American export expansion by connecting export expansion to social structure and then to generalized economic growth and its absence.

The Organization of Export Production

Coffee and bananas were the principal exports in Central America, but there were important national differences in the way their production was organized. This was especially so in regard to the most important aspect: the mobilization of labor. In spite of the shared borders, small size, and common heritage of the nations, these differences resulted in societies with very distinct economic and political structures.

Costa Rica

The commercial cultivation of Central American coffee for export began in Costa Rica during the 1830s, and regular export began in 1843.[4] Costa Rican coffee exports rose rapidly and soon formed the economic backbone of the nation. The coffee economy developed in a distinctive social context. First, as has been noted several times, Costa Rica was an extremely poor, backward part of the isthmus with a small population and large stretches of empty but arable land. In the early nineteenth century, the population of Costa Rica was by and large of European origins, and there were no large pools of indigenous peoples capable of being forcibly molded into a servile labor force. While pre-coffee Costa Rica was certainly not an egalitarian society, the distance between those on top and those on the bottom was not very great in material terms, especially when compared with other parts of Central America (or Latin America, for that matter).

The scarcity of labor and availability of land meant that it was extremely difficult for a few to live on the work of others: Individuals could move rather easily out of unattractive work situations and set up their own small subsistence farms practically independent from the market. And labor scarcity was exacerbated in 1856 when a cholera epidemic killed close to 10 percent of an already small population.

When coffee cultivation began in earnest, therefore, it was produced by many small farmers using primarily family labor, and new lands were drawn principally from unused public lands. There were some larger fincas, but compared to Guatemala, El Salvador, and Brazil, even the largest were modest in size. The larger fincas did use wage labor, especially at harvesttime. A few of these wage laborers were landless rural workers, but most of the seasonal wage work force either worked some land of their own or were recruited from urban areas for the harvest. Wages in Costa Rica were very high by Central (and Latin) American standards.

It is important, however, to keep in mind the extent of social differentiation that existed prior to the introduction of coffee and which indelibly marked the coffee era. Members of elite families had accumulated sufficient resources from cacao, tobacco, and mining to be able to supply the credit necessary for small farmers to begin coffee production. Because coffee is grown on trees that need three to five years to reach maturity, entering into coffee production entails a significant period during which no income is generated by the land and labor used to nurture the coffee trees. As a consequence, small subsistence farmers found it difficult to leap into coffee production without access to substantial credit to tide them over the period of initial investment.

The importance to the Costa Rican elite of the control of credit was graphically demonstrated by its reaction to Juan Rafael Mora's attempt to establish a bank in 1858. Mora was president of Costa Rica and a powerful member of the coffee elite, but his effort to open a bank was perceived to be a threat to the control of credit by other members of the elite. The army removed him from office, and he was later executed when he headed an invasion from the Pacific coast in an effort to return.

Processing coffee for export also required a major investment. Processing plants called *beneficios* were built for this purpose, and there the outer pulp of the coffee berry was removed from the seed, followed by removal of the outer husk from the seed to expose the two coffee beans in the middle. Technology of this processing was increasingly mechanized and required the use of imported machinery, especially when more efficient use of water was introduced. Much of this stage of production was initially done in Chile, where the coffee, shipped through Costa Rica's Pacific port of Puntarenas, was en route to the markets of Europe and the east coast of the United States via the Straits of Magellan. The capacity for coffee processing, however, was increasingly established in Costa Rica by the largest growers and commercial houses, who could afford the necessary investment. The economic control exercised by the large commercial houses was formidable because they maintained an interlocking control of financing, processing, and marketing of coffee.

The development of transportation facilities was another important linkage for coffee exports. The most important breakthrough in transportation came in 1880, when the railway from the highlands to Limón on the Caribbean coast was opened. The rail connection to the Pacific was completed in 1910, and competition between the ports of Limón and Puntarenas, and among the steamship companies serving them, resulted in substantial declines in transportation costs to coffee sellers and buyers.

The construction of the Atlantic railway had widespread and unexpected ramifications far beyond that of a linked source of additional economic activity or even a more efficient way to transport coffee. Apparently believing that one should go for the best, the government of Tomás Guardia in 1871 granted the contract for constructing the railway to Henry Meiggs, a famous U.S. rail builder with a record of impressive achievements that included completing a railway through the Peruvian Andes. Meiggs subcontracted the work to two nephews, who thus received the large tracts of land that had been granted by the Costa Rican government as part of the payment. Even before the railway was completed, one of the nephews, Minor Cooper Keith, began to use the completed rail sections to Limón to transport bananas grown on some of the lands adjacent to the railway to finance the construction of the railroad. Keith sold the bananas in New Orleans, and because this sale proved profitable, he quickly increased plantings and shipments.

There had already been a casual, sporadic trade in bananas between the Caribbean area and the United States for fifteen or twenty years. One of the better-organized banana export enterprises had been operated since 1870 between Jamaica and Boston by a sea captain named Lorenzo Baker. In 1899, Keith and Baker merged their firms and established the new corporation's headquarters in Boston. Thus was born the United Fruit Company (or, as it came to be known in Central America, *el pulpo*—the octopus).

Banana exports from Costa Rica increased by more than ten times between 1883 and 1907, and although not strictly a forward linkage from coffee exporting, there was no question that the transportation network to serve coffee had resulted in another important economic (and export) activity. Although local banana growers contributed some to this export, the vast bulk of banana cultivation and all of banana transport and marketing were in the hands of the foreign firm. The Costa Rican government received tax revenues from banana exports, but bananas had no forward linkage effects in Costa Rica. In fact, the self-contained, enclave nature of the banana enterprise (discussed later in the chapter) reduced linkages with the rest of the national economy.

In keeping with the enclave character of activity, the labor force for the banana plantations was recruited from abroad, consisting primarily of workers of African descent from the Anglophone Caribbean. The Costa Rican government was not enthusiastic about this new population. Although the government continued to promote immigration to reduce labor shortages and high labor costs, earlier Costa Rican governments had explicitly prohibited immigration by Asians and Africans. In this case, however, they allowed the immigration of United Fruit Company workers but discouraged them from moving to or even traveling in the highlands.

Coffee production and the foreign exchange received from its export contributed to the use of metal tools (e.g., axes, rakes, hoes, machetes, plows, and so on) in coffee cultivation and probably in Costa Rican agriculture in general. But while there were technical advances in processing, cultivation techniques remained rather primitive. As a result, there was a marked deterioration in soil fertility.

The nature of forward linkages from coffee exports was not as complex as that of backward linkages. Coffee processing in beneficios represented a forward-linked activity, and the location of beneficios within the nation was not only an additional economic activity but was also an important means of control by a few. Further processing of coffee was done in the consuming nations rather than in the producing nation because raw coffee beans deteriorate very slowly when stored in good conditions but lose their flavor rapidly as soon as they are roasted.

One might expect that the income multiplier linkage from coffee exports would have been a powerful engine of economic growth. The widespread ownership of the land, with the resulting diffusion of economic power, meant that the prosperity from coffee was widely shared. Coffee exports resulted in tangible material benefits to virtually all involved in the production, processing, and transport of coffee, and the standards of living of even the poorest strata were substantially above those of their counterparts in Central America and Latin America. The per capita income indicators in Figure 3.2 thus represent general welfare better than those of other nations, where income was much less evenly distributed. The coffee industry therefore resulted in the development of a substantial internal consumer goods market that was not limited to luxury items.

The triumph of coffee exports, however, stimulated very little domestic production through the income multiplier linkage. First of all, the foreign exchange earnings from those exports could be used to buy relatively inexpensive imported goods, especially from England. And second, the changes in transport (e.g., steamships and railways) that lowered the costs of transportation of coffee exports from Costa Rica to Europe and North America, thus contributing to the success of coffee exports, at the same time facilitated low-cost transport of European and North American consumer goods to Costa Rican markets. To return empty railcars and ships to pick up more coffee was clearly not desirable.

So the very conditions that contributed to the success of the exports simultaneously undermined the income multiplier linkage. The hardest hit of the domestic industries were the cotton textile firms in and around Cartago, which lost the protection from foreign competition that had been afforded by the high cost of transporting goods. Luxury goods, with lower ratios of transport cost to final selling price, were always more feasible to import, even when transport costs were high.

Local food production for domestic markets was another Costa Rican economic activity that was negatively affected by coffee exports. The influx of cheap grains and meat from Argentina and the United States, along with the high returns from coffee cultivation, led to a decline in local food production for domestic markets. The high degree of economic specialization that ensued made Costa Rica vulnerable to food shortages in times of coffee market downturns.

In summary, coffee was successful and in some significant ways supported the expectations of the neoclassical comparative advantage model. But even in Costa Rica, coffee and banana exports were not the basis for a strong, durable, and self-sustaining national economic growth.

Guatemala

Large-scale commercial cultivation of coffee came to Guatemala later, and the Costa Rican example and advisers were important for Guatemalan entry into the world coffee market. But the organization of coffee production and the consequences of the coffee boom in Guatemala, where the majority of the population lived in Indian communities, were very different from those in Costa Rica.[5]

From the very beginning of coffee cultivation in Guatemala, the differences were obvious. The Carrera government encouraged coffee exports in the 1840s by guaranteeing prices for producers. But there were entrenched forces that resisted establishing the conditions Guatemalan coffee finca owners (*finqueros*) considered necessary for success. For instance, because many of these finqueros were urban or foreign entrepreneurs and new entrants into Guatemalan agricultural production, they were outside the network of Carrera's most important political constituencies—the consulado, small and medium-sized farmers, and the Indian communities. The consulado in Guatemala was interested in promoting coffee exports, of course. With its legal monopoly over long-distance trade and control of agricultural credit, the consulado was in a position to benefit significantly from a new and lucrative trade. Coffee finqueros, in contrast, saw the consulado's ability to manipulate prices through its monopoly on trade to be an obstacle.

The decline in cochineal production in the middle of the nineteenth century coincided with the "cotton famine"—an international shortage of cotton resulting from the U.S. Civil War—which led to a temporary rise of Guatemalan cotton exports in the mid-1860s. Both of these factors helped loosen local political and economic restraints, and the death of Carrera and the weakness of his Conservative successor gave coffee producers a political opening. A group associated with coffee production overthrew the Conservative regime in 1871 and put a Liberal administration in power. The new president was rather ineffective, but he did decisively terminate the consulado before 1873, when he was replaced by Justo Rufino Barrios, a coffee finquero and one of the leaders of the initial Liberal coup.

Barrios ruled Guatemala with an iron hand until he was killed in 1885. He is credited with laying the social and political bases of the coffee export economy, which flourished in part because of his efforts. Barrios's policies included the usual Liberal anticlerical suppression of the tithe; confiscation of Church lands; expulsion of clergy; and state appropriation of education and of marriage, birth, and death rituals. More important, however, he moved against Indian community lands and set up a rigorous scheme of forced labor. To implement these policies, Barrios expanded the army, opened a national military academy, and created a centralized military command structure.

In Guatemala, there was less unclaimed land suitable for growing coffee than in Costa Rica. Barrios, therefore, moved against the Church and Indian communities to make their lands available for coffee growing. Barrios's 1877 law removed any special legal status for Indian community lands and resulted in some Indian community lands being bought, stolen, or otherwise taken over by private individuals or by the Liberal state and sold to aspiring coffee finqueros.

The loss of land no doubt forced some people to work on the coffee plantations, but the principal effort to create a supply of labor available for the coffee harvests was a series of policies implemented in the 1870s explicitly designed to mobilize labor for coffee production. One set reactivated labor conscription institutions very much like the colonial repartimiento. The repartimiento had been revived earlier, but cochineal production did not call for large numbers of unskilled labor and, in any case, the Conservative government was wary about putting pressure on the Indian communities, one of Carrera's major supports.

Between the 1870s and 1930s, however, the new policy enabled quotas of eligible workers to be rounded up and employed, for a low, fixed wage, on public works (roads and buildings, for instance) or on private plantations. Military conscription operated in a similar manner. A rigorous law against "vagrancy" was an attempt to ensure that all Indians were "gainfully employed" for a stipulated number of days each year.

These land and labor policies did supply Indians to public and private work sites on a temporary basis. There were also the *colonos,* landless workers who were permanent residents on a finca. The finquero usually gave them a small piece of land for a hut and subsistence cropping, and on exceptional fincas, some access to medical and educational services. Colonos were subject to year-round demands for work, and although they enjoyed security of a sort, only the most desperate families became colonos.

But the greatest demand for labor was seasonal, during the harvest times from October to December (with some complementarity with the corn cycle). Because a large number of Indian communities were located in (or had retreated to) the highlands, which at elevations of over 3,000 feet were too cold for coffee cultivation, the major effect of the directly coercive devices, such as land alienation, conscription for work and military service, and the general threat of the vagrancy law, was to force people to work on the fincas through debt peonage, which became the main mechanism of labor mobilization. Workers who could prove that they were in debt and were working the required number of days in repayment (always partial) of the debt were exempted from conscripted labor, military service, and punishment as a vagrant. Other avenues of exemption, such as substantial property holdings and payment of fees, were closed to the majority of rural people.

Workers incurred debts by accepting advance payments, and these were recorded in booklets that the workers were required to carry. An extensive network of labor contractors, working for individual finqueros or as independents, made their livings by getting people to accept monetary advances and to sign work contracts. Armed with cash, alcohol, and threats, they were constantly scouring the countryside for prospective recruits, especially during feast days. Once into the system, there was little likelihood that these workers would ever get out of debt, nor was there much incentive to do so. The low pay, fines for contrived offenses, and employer cheating ensured the continuation of indebtedness. In any case, being out of debt made one prey to even less desirable possibilities, and at least there were the cash advances. After a couple of rounds, the amount of the debt was meaningless and workers simply looked forward to the advances.

Although the inheritance of debt responsibilities was prohibited by law, because debtors' property was used as collateral, wives, children, and other relatives often had to assume a deceased worker's debt to avoid losing everything. And men often accepted and signed work contracts for their wives and children, forcing them into the debt system.

Although the system was operated at the local level by private individuals, it did so within the context of direct and immediate state coercion. In addition to severely structuring workers' alternatives to make debt peonage preferable, debt contracts had the force of law and were enforced by officials. Nevertheless, workers were not entirely powerless. Many fled, sometimes across the border to Mexico or Belize, or to another region where they could hide or start the cycle afresh, thus continuing a "culture of refuge."

Even those in the system could, within limits, play one finquero off against another (even accepting advances from more than one employer), petition and bribe officials, sue finqueros and labor contractors for unfair practices, or, in extreme situations, use individual or collective violence against the especially brutal. These avenues of resistance did serve to set limits to the system's practice. The system was extremely unfair and harsh, and the work was hard and frequently led to death and impairment resulting from exhaustion, disease, and accident. But generally the system was not gratuitously vicious. After all, since finqueros primarily wanted work done at a low cost, wanton cruelty was not in their interests either. The steady growth of the Indian population in the late nineteenth and early twentieth centuries is one crude indicator that the system was not completely murderous.

Moreover, although the labor mobilization system battered Indians and their communities, at the same time it also contributed to the preservation of these communities. For instance, the allocation of workers to a public construction project or to the military was often done by the communities' internal political structures, thus strengthening them. And because the alienation of communal lands reduced the margin of Indian communities' subsistence, especially since many communities were beginning to feel pressure from population increases, external sources of earning were increasingly necessary to keep the communities intact. The preservation of Indian communities as a reserve of seasonal labor was vitally important for the finqueros because the communities supported the workers during the months that the finqueros had no use for them. As such, the state occasionally supported the communities and their land claims against the interest of an individual finquero but in the interests of all finqueros.

While these considerations are important and interesting, the most important pillars on which the entire labor mobilization system rested were (1) the continued threat and exercise of official violence and (2) extreme rural poverty (which also was a product of the system). Without these two pillars, the system would have crumbled immediately. As it was, both conditions lasted for almost sixty years, and it was successful in terms of durability and underwriting the steady expansion of export agriculture.

The coffee finqueros were not simply traditional landowners who began to grow coffee in response to new market opportunities. Traditional landowners, including the Church, which was prohibited from owning land after 1871, were supplanted to a large extent by politicians and military officers connected to the Liberal Party, urban-based entrepreneurs, and others. Traditional landowners had few market connections or else produced foodstuffs and dyes in a casual, inefficient manner.

Foreigners were also important in establishing the Guatemalan export economy. Spaniards and Germans, especially, were active in import trade, and German finqueros were prominent in coffee production. In the late nineteenth century, German-owned coffee fincas constituted about 10 percent of the total but produced as much as 40 percent of Guatemala's coffee exports. The German finqueros, located primarily in Alta Verapaz, far from the social and political center of Guatemala, remained aloof from Guatemalan national politics but eagerly took advantage of all governmental policies favorable to coffee cultivation and marketing.

The most extensive foreign economic penetration in this period, however, was by the United Fruit Company. Soon after its formation in 1899, it began operating in Guatemala. As in Costa Rica, the United Fruit Company established banana plantations along the tropical coast of the Caribbean and three decades later on the Pacific coast, recruited labor primarily from the Caribbean and El Salvador, and operated the plantations as self-contained entities. The Guatemalan government did not impose an export tax on bananas until 1928, but even then, the rate charged was less than a fourth of the corresponding tax on coffee and the government had already relinquished its right to inspect the company's books.

The United Fruit Company's principal effect on the nation in the early twentieth century was through its control of the transportation network. As in Costa Rica, the rise of coffee as an export crop required the backward-linked development of a transportation system capable of efficiently handling bulk cargo. Dyes, especially cochineal, were the principal exports of Guatemala before the advent of coffee, and they were of very high value per bulk. Coffee, however, was a crop with relatively low value per bulk, and tens of thousands of tons of it were moved from the fincas to the ports. Although cart roads were improved, the consensus was that the nation badly needed railways, which were both a symbol of progress and a necessary key to a modern transportation system.

The Guatemalan government began building a 200-mile railway between Guatemala City and the Caribbean port of Puerto Barrios during the 1880s. Over the years, the government poured millions of dollars into it, but the combination of financial and technical problems prevented the line's completion. Although there were only sixty or so miles needed to finish the railway by 1897, it then lay dormant so long that some of it had to be completely reconstructed. This was the situation when the United Fruit Company stepped in. Under the direction of Minor Cooper Keith (the vice-president of the United Fruit Company and head of operations in Guatemala), the railway was completed. In payment, the Estrada Cabrera government gave the United Fruit Company the entire line, a monopoly franchise for all rail traffic to the Caribbean, a pledge never to intervene in company affairs, the port facilities of Puerto Barrios, nearly 500,000 acres of land alongside the track, and a ninety-nine–year exemption on all taxes except on coffee exports.

In 1912, the United Fruit Company acquired the 600 miles of track in western Guatemala and monopolized all rail traffic in the nation. In addition, the United Fruit Company's shipping company (the "Great White Fleet") monopolized all Guatemalan shipping in the Caribbean. So while the banana plantations were enclave operations, the entire United Fruit Company operations in Guatemala certainly were not.

The social and economic organization of Guatemalan export production enabled large amounts of coffee and bananas to be produced, but, as I will discuss later in the chapter, it was not a social and economic structure conducive to general economic development.

El Salvador

There are some definite parallels between the development of the coffee export economy in El Salvador and Guatemala. First, coffee replaced an already existing strong agricultural export crop—indigo in the case of El Salvador. Second, the creation of an export economy based on bulky coffee required the large-scale development of transportation facilities that had not been as necessary for indigo, with its much higher value per physical unit. And third, although substantial amounts of coffee were produced on small farms in the early years of export growth, by the last third of the nineteenth century large fincas dominated coffee production in El Salvador as well as in Guatemala. Landholding in El Salvador, however, was considerably more highly concentrated.[6]

Moreover, as in Guatemala, many if not most of the coffee entrepreneurs were from outside the agrarian economy, and prominent coffee entrepreneurs included considerable numbers of recent European and North American immigrants. But here the differences begin, and they are significant. Foreign coffee entrepreneurs married into and merged with the existing upper class, including families whose wealth had been based on indigo. In addition, there were no banana exports from El Salvador, and there was very little foreign investment of any kind in El Salvador in this period, a situation that lasted until the 1960s.

The most important difference between El Salvador and Guatemala, however, was that the best coffee lands were those that were initially the most densely populated. The development of large-scale coffee production thus meant the dispossession of a large proportion, perhaps a majority, of the rural population, both ladinos and the remnants of Indian communities.

Rafael Zaldívar, president from 1876 to 1883, was a Liberal reformer who sponsored the legislation that turned all landed properties into private property and led the assault on communal lands. Within a few decades, the vast majority of the rural population either lived on someone else's land as tenants or were part of the migrant labor force whose existence was marginal, to say the least. In contrast to other parts of Central America, El Salvador was densely populated and the dispossession of the rural majority from the land forced them to work for others. As a consequence, wages were low, and conditions for both tenants and temporary laborers were extremely harsh.

So in El Salvador, as opposed to Guatemala, the national state was not directly involved in mobilizing labor because workers were in a position sufficiently disadvantageous that the "free market" could regulate the flows of labor needed for coffee cultivation, processing, and transportation. Although legislation was handed down by the national government that mandated private property in land, established a series of "vagrancy" laws similar to those in Guatemala, and generally created the necessary conditions for a coffee export economy, once the system was securely established, direct central government intervention was only minimally necessary.

Despite the absence of direct government interference with the economy, late nineteenth- and early twentieth-century El Salvador was no liberal paradise, with individuals making free choices, determining their destinies, and operating in a harmonious social system. Sharp resistance to the alienation of the lands constantly required the suppression of revolts by desperate workers. Direct, continuing, and brutal mechanisms of social control were indeed vital, and these functions were performed by a specialized rural police, not unlike the infamous *rurales* of prerevolutionary Mexico. But the rural police in El Salvador did not constitute a national army. Rather, they were administered at the local level by the landlords, who directed police and judicial operations through minions immediately beholden to them.

Nevertheless, the production of coffee in El Salvador occurred under conditions that were more like a capitalist market system than anywhere in Central America. Although the politics of the system in the early decades of the twentieth century were increasingly competitive in urban areas, and more so than in the other Central American nations, there was only slight economic growth outside of export and export-related activities. The linkages to commerce, finance, and transportation were significant and underwrote a thriving urban life and the beginnings of a middle class. But the extreme concentration of wealth and economic power in a few hands severely impaired the development of income multiplier linkages and the promotion of general economic development through public policy.

Nicaragua

Nicaragua entered the international coffee economy in the third quarter of the nineteenth century. Coffee became the most important export crop in Nicaragua by the end of the century, but, as shown in Table 3.1, it did not achieve the level of economic dominance seen in Costa Rica, Guatemala, and El Salvador. Mining in the north and east, and cattle and sugar in the southern plains, were not completely eclipsed by the coffee boom, and the elites who were based on these activities continued to be politically powerful. This was the case especially with the ranchers and sugar producers around Granada in the south—the bastion of the Conservative Party that continued to struggle for national dominance with the coffee finqueros and allied merchants of the north, based in León.[7]

U.S. fruit company activity penetrated the Caribbean coast of Nicaragua around the turn of the twentieth century, but banana production never grew to much. The eastern half of Nicaragua, populated mainly by Miskito, Suma, and other indigenous peoples and English-speaking peoples of African descent, remained thinly populated and of only marginal importance to the 90 or more percent of the population who lived in the western half of Nicaragua and spoke Spanish.

Despite the political struggles among contending elites, coffee quickly became of such national significance that even Conservative governments had to support its development. As throughout most of Central America, the expansion of coffee production was impeded by chronic labor shortages. Although the Conservative regimes implemented the usual policies of mobilizing workers through the alienation of communal lands, vagrancy laws, debt peonage, and other coercive devices, these efforts were not as effective as in Guatemala and El Salvador. Nicaragua was very sparsely populated, mostly with ladinos but with a few small communities of indigenous peoples. Strong pressures on workers simply led to their fleeing to unutilized lands farther away. The pressures also led to a major rebellion by the Indians in 1881, when they "liberated" a large part of the region around Matagalpa. The War of the Comuneros was concluded when 9,000 Indians (more than a quarter of the total) were killed and the rest beaten into submission by national troops armed with modern weapons.

Labor and transportation problems impeded the development of coffee production, and its rise did not succeed in consolidating the economic and political elites of the nation. Coffee was grown on the slopes of the northern and western mountains of Nicaragua and formed a new economic base for the Liberals of León, who were still recovering from the disgrace of having invited William Walker to help them in their continuing fights with the Conservatives.

José Santos Zelaya, a Managuan Liberal, became president in 1893 in a compromise with the Conservatives, and the coffee growers found their champion in him. Zelaya ruled Nicaragua between 1893 and 1906, vigorously promoting the expansion of coffee production by the use of state resources to build transportation, storage, and port facilities and to strengthen and enforce coercive labor laws. The extent of these activities exacerbated the tension with Granadian Conservatives, whose cattle activities required little in the way of state support. The inability of the most powerful elements of Nicaraguan economic life to forge an effective alliance is the reason that the history of Nicaraguan political economy in this period is not principally about economics. The effects of political forces, including international politics, were considerably stronger determinants of the Nicaraguan social order than were economic developments.

Honduras

In the last third of the nineteenth century, silver and gold mining again revived in Honduras, this time around Tegucigalpa. By the end of the century, mining was dominated by one firm, Rosario Mining Company, a foreign firm whose owner, Valentine Rosario, had close connections with Honduran society and politics. As in most Central American endeavors of this era, an adequate supply of cheap labor was a problem, and efforts of the Honduran state to coerce men on behalf of the company incurred the resentment of neighboring landowners, who did not want anyone competing for their workers.[8]

For a while, minerals were important exports and a source of revenue for the chronically strapped state, but the scale of mining was never so large that it had widespread effects. It is doubtful that the Rosario firm ever employed more than 1,000 workers.

The broken terrain of Honduras prevented the development of a large-scale coffee industry in the nineteenth and early twentieth centuries.

Much of the land was worked by peasants with only tenuous connections to any local markets, much less to national or international ones. Although land was plentiful in the thinly populated nation, there were some landlords with substantial holdings on which they produced cattle, timber, and tobacco for markets. But while these landlords, together with the few larger merchants in the cities, were an elite, they did not constitute a coherent, powerful social class on the national scene. The scope of their influence was limited to local and regional affairs, and Honduras as a nation remained a formal rather than actual political entity during the nineteenth century.

In significant ways this situation changed with the advent of large-scale banana exports. During the late nineteenth century, bananas were produced by local landholders who sold them to international fruit companies. The companies controlled finance, refrigerated transportation, and access to foreign markets and were thus able to deal advantageously with domestic producers.

As advantageous as this arrangement was, however, the fruit companies sought greater profits in the early decades of the twentieth century by directly producing bananas in Honduras. They initially obtained land for their plantations through generous land grants from the government for railroad construction—or, rather, for promises of railroad construction. In Honduras, several foreign rail contractors had failed to achieve anything other than financial gain, and often not even that. And the banana companies were no exception. The companies built only those rail lines that were immediately useful for transporting bananas, and Tegucigalpa, the capital city, still has no rail connection. Nonetheless, by the beginning of World War I, the three banana companies operating in the country had acquired almost a million acres of prime banana land on or near the northern coast of Honduras by means of these grants. Although their holdings increased through the 1920s, expansion was chiefly a result of purchase and lease from local landowners.

The largest and most powerful banana company was the United Fruit Company, although the Cuyamel Fruit Company, run by the colorful "Sam the Banana Man" Zemurray, offered stiff competition. This competition came to a definite halt in 1929, however, when Zemurray sold out to the United Fruit Company, subsequently becoming the president of the enlarged United Fruit Company. The third important banana company, Vaccaro Brothers (or Standard Fruit Company), was considerably smaller than the other two.

Banana cultivation, even more than mining, was an enclave activity. The fruit companies grew bananas on Honduran soil, but for all intents and purposes the plantations were not a part of national territory. The fruit companies recruited workers from the West Indies principally, although the plantation work force included Garifuna people of African descent, who lived in the northern coast of Honduras, as well as Salvadorans. These individuals were year-round wage workers, cultivating and harvesting bananas, which, unlike coffee, were not a perennial, orchard crop.

The workers were paid with U.S. dollars, which were declared legal tender by the Honduran government in 1918. The employees spent most of their wages on imported goods sold at company stores, and the companies used little in the way of local goods in their operations. Transportation and storage were fully in company hands, and because there was no further processing of the fruit before shipment and consumption, there were no forward linkages with the domestic economy. The plantations' principal economic link with Honduras was through low and ineffectively enforced taxation. In any case, because the companies "sold" their bananas to their own wholly owned shipping and distributing subsidiaries, the price was simply an administered price established by company officials.

This does not mean that banana production and export had little effect on Honduras, but again, as in the case of Nicaragua, the major impact was not directly through the organization and social relations of production.

The State

The variety of ways in which export production was organized in Central America was reflected in a similar variety of politics. The dynamic expansion of the export sectors in the five Central American nations under discussion substantially affected the political organization of social power, and those effects were manifested in different ways.

Costa Rica

Figure 3.3 shows the contribution of government expenditures to gross domestic product; therefore it shows primarily governmental wage and salary expenditures and not the entire budget (the amount of economic resources controlled by the state) as a percentage of gross domestic product (GDP). Its comparisons are useful, and the figure shows that the Costa Rican state apparatus remained modest in size, in good part because the direct exercise of violence was not necessary to expand the export economy or preserve the social order. For instance, there were no coercive labor codes, a situation that reflected the land tenure patterns, free and scarce labor, and high wages. Market domination rather than overt coercion was the principal lever of power.

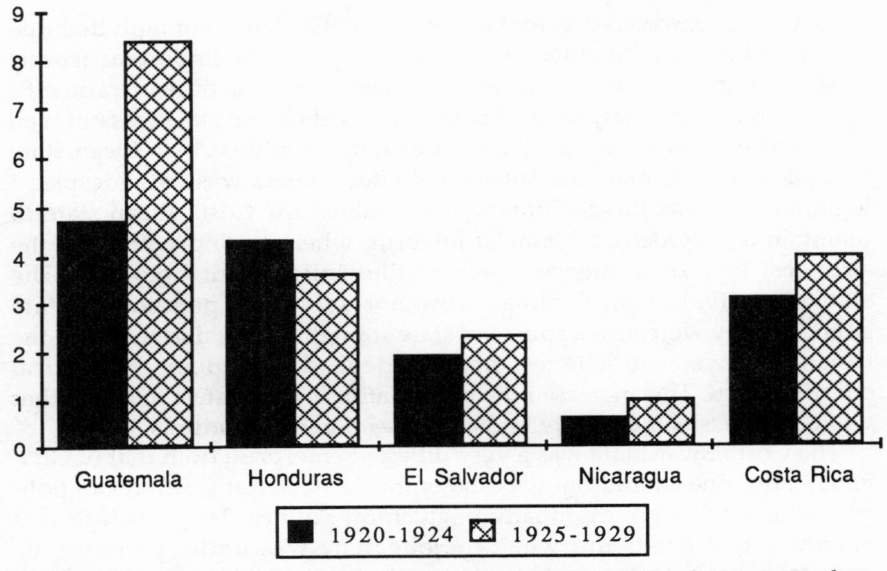

FIGURE 3.3 "General government" as a percentage of gross domestic product, 1920–1929. *Source:* Adapted from Victor Bulmer-Thomas, *The Political Economy of Central America Since 1920* (New York: Cambridge University Press, 1987), pp. 308, 324.

Costa Rican national politics was solidly in the hands of the oligarchy who controlled the financing and processing of coffee production and export, and extremely high proportions of the presidents and political leaders came from their ranks. This political eminence was not translated into omnipotent power, however, because even the most powerful had to pay attention to the large number of small landowners.

In response to popular pressures, the state promoted a number of social services that sharply distinguished Costa Rica from other republics in Central America. Public education was one such policy area. The Church had never been as strong in Costa Rica as elsewhere in the isthmus, so there was little entrenched opposition to the establishment of the region's leading public schooling system. Over three-quarters of the Costa Rican population was literate by 1927, almost twice the proportion of El Salvador, the second most literate nation of Central America, and close to four times the proportion in Guatemala, the nation with the lowest literacy rate. Somewhat anomalous in light of this interest in education is the fact that the national university, the country's only university, was closed in 1880 and not reopened until 1940.

The stability of the social structure, whose maintenance did not require the continuing administration of violence, and the way in which the state was embedded in that society, gave the state a strength that distinguished it from the other nations in the region. The important aspects of state strength were not in terms of armaments or bureaucratic efficiency, a fortunate circumstance in that the Costa Rican state was not well endowed in either respect. Rather, the strength of the Costa Rican state that allowed it to maintain substantial effectiveness was its widespread legitimacy. It was this legitimacy that enabled the Costa Rican state to maintain a surprising amount of integrity when dealing with even the strongest foreign influences, such as the United Fruit Company. The state's relatively firm dealings were not only an expression of state strength; they were also a source of state strength. Taxes derived from the banana enclave were state resources not dependent on domestic political constituencies. This increased the policy latitude of the state in a way that will be discussed more fully in the later section on Honduras.

The Costa Rican state was a very different enterprise from that of Guatemala, but one should not wax too enthusiastic about Costa Rican politics, which still were essentially oligarchical politics. The franchise was narrowly restricted, and when the oligarchy was under pressure, its political behavior was more like that of its counterparts in Central America than the Costa Rican democratic myth would suggest. For instance, when unstable coffee markets seemed to threaten the economic elite's control, the elite sponsored the dictatorship of Tomás Guardia (1870–1882).

The disruption of trade during World War I is another example of the Costa Rican oligarchy's willingness to contravene even the appearance of democracy. When the government initiated income and land taxes and the supervision of banking in response to the crisis, the oligarchy countered by encouraging a military coup led by General Federico Tinoco in 1917. Once in power, however, and to the chagrin of the oligarchy, Tinoco decided not to relinquish the presidency, and he reimposed the taxes. Although a favorite of the United Fruit Company, Tinoco antagonized the Woodrow Wilson administration in the United States, which refused to recognize his presidency. He was ousted in 1919 through the combined effort of the Costa Rican oligarchy and the U.S. ambassador. The oligarchy again resumed direct control of the state, and having learned a lesson, it proceeded to reduce governmental expenditures and taxes by virtually dismantling the military establishment.

The U.S. role in the overthrow of Tinoco, however, offended members of the urban middle and working classes and contributed to their politicization. The mobilization included newly organized unions of artisans (or craftspeople), such as of shoemakers, carpenters, and bakers, that succeeded in winning the eight-hour workday for urban workers through a general strike in 1920. Beyond the immediate goals, the successful grassroots political mobilization was a clear signal that oligarchical control of Costa Rican politics was contingent on the consent of others.

Guatemala

The state system of Guatemala necessary to maintain the social order based on coerced labor was larger and more powerful and authoritarian than that of Costa Rica. (See Figure 3.3.) The army was an essential and active component of social control, and political participation was strictly limited. At least two administrations—those of Justo Rufino Barrios (1873–1885) and Manuel Estrada Cabrera (1898–1920)—were outright dictatorships with only nominal democratic trappings. While there is no question that governmental policies usually benefited the finquero elite, the finqueros themselves did not govern. The coffee aristocracy obviously agreed on general approaches to the development of coffee, including land and labor policies. But the infusion of foreigners into the ranks of the finqueros during the early days of coffee growth reduced their coherence. The state remained in the hands of professional politicians and military men, who headed a state apparatus that had considerable power in its own right. The Guatemalan state's dealings with the United Fruit Company is an excellent example of its latitude.

As described earlier in this chapter, the United Fruit Company and its two transportation subsidiaries blatantly manipulated prices for maximum returns, squeezing Guatemalan coffee growers and merchants as well as virtually everyone else in reach. Even after the overthrow of Estrada Cabrera in 1920, the Guatemalan government continued to make deals with the United Fruit Company on terms that consistently and strongly favored the company.

Why did the Guatemalan government so obviously favor the United Fruit Company over the interests of finqueros? Or to phrase it differently, why was the Guatemalan state, which was more centralized, militarized, and powerful than that of Costa Rica, seemingly less able to resist the United Fruit Company?

First of all, the United Fruit Company was an agent of progress as defined by governmental leaders. A national goal had long been to develop the poor, unhealthful, isolated, and sparsely populated Caribbean coast, and the United Fruit Company operations there did make real improvements in all these ways. In addition, a modern transportation network in Guatemala had been difficult to construct and operate, and the United Fruit Company did both rather effectively. The costs, however, were daunting. The United Fruit Company banana plantations in the Caribbean area created an enclave with virtually no linkages to the national economy. And the transportation system in United Fruit Company hands was a means to extort and strangle the national economy.

In addition, although coffee and bananas were not precisely strategic materials, the United Fruit Company had the diplomatic and military backing of the U.S. government (except for short periods during the Woodrow Wilson and Franklin Roosevelt administrations). This factor was not insignificant for a small country dependent on international product and credit markets. Finally, the importance of the venality of top governmental officials cannot be underestimated. It is clear that successive presidents, ministers, and other top governmental officials benefited substantially from their dealings with the United Fruit Company.

This brings us back to the internal balances of political power that enabled the government to inflict these costs on even the most powerful domestic economic interests. First of all, the policies were not completely incompatible with finquero interests. Although the price discrimination that the United Fruit Company practiced on rail cargo cut into planters' and merchants' profits, rail transport was still cheaper, faster, and more secure than transporting the coffee by carts on bad roads. But even so, repeatedly generous concessions by the government to the United Fruit Company hurt domestic planters and merchants, who often complained loudly.

In order for the coffee economy to function along Guatemalan lines, a powerful central state was necessary to organize and maintain the labor mobilization and social control mechanisms crucial for the coffee economy's operation. The power of the Guatemalan state that was necessary for the very existence of the finquero class also limited finqueros' direct influence over the state. Those in charge of the political apparatus had the capacity, within limits, to contravene the interests of even the most powerful when those political leaders believed that doing so was in the greater national interest or in their individual, personal interests.

This does not mean that political leaders were omnipotent; when the limits were violated, the fragmented finquero class could mount formidable political leverage. The fall of Estrada Cabrera in 1920, for instance, resulted in part from planters' dissatisfaction with his dealings with the United Fruit Company. Concessions by subsequent administrations to the United Fruit Company were a source of continuing unrest among the Guatemalan elite. Toward the end of the 1920s, the finqueros were joined by urban groups, especially in Guatemala City, which had a population of 100,000 that included a sizable corps of professional and other middle-class elements. The activities of this group, along with the bloody labor strikes in the 1920s, indicated that Guatemalan political life was beginning to become more complex.

El Salvador

The extreme concentration of wealth and power in El Salvador has been inscribed in legend that depicts the nation as owned and operated by the

"Fourteen Families." This depiction is an exaggeration, but probably sixty-five or seventy families did indeed possess the power attributed to the fabled fourteen. With the means of production and of violence tightly and effectively monopolized at the local level, the national state managed to look somewhat like a relatively open, competitive liberal polity, tending toward laissez-faire policies. Figure 3.3 shows that compared to Guatemala, the El Salvadoran government's contribution to the GDP (mostly through wages and salaries) was small.

Politics in El Salvador operated more like that in Costa Rica than in Guatemala: The presidency passed among members of the elite families. Even though direct rule was exercised by the economically most powerful, the elite was not a homogeneous group. One division was sectoral. The economic base of some families was landownership and coffee cultivation, whereas others were active in processing, finance, and commerce. And these sectoral divisions were crosscut by personal antagonisms and rivalries. The result was political competition among different branches and individuals of the oligarchy, thus creating the possibility of new forces entering national politics.

El Salvador was the most economically integrated of the five nations by the early years of the twentieth century, and this integration, along with direct pressure by employers and lack of indigenous communities, was conducive to political organization by agricultural workers. In urban areas, especially San Salvador, which had become the unchallenged center of national power, culture, and elite residence, craft workers also founded formal associations, with the help of Mexican union organizers, to promote their interests. The competition within the oligarchy, then, motivated politically ambitious individuals from the leading families who were cautiously enlisting support from other constituencies for their candidacies and interests by incorporating reform elements into their platforms.

This pattern was more evident in the cities than in the countryside. Whereas a multitude of political programs were allowed to flourish within the urban areas in the first decades of the twentieth century, agrarian workers' organizations, viewed as much more threatening, were often brutally repressed. But Salvadoran politics had to be conducted with the political potential of rural workers constantly in mind.

This pattern led to a rather open style of politics with an ideologically broad spectrum of ideas and organizations, including a Communist Party. As a consequence, various oligarchical administrations during the 1920s, pushed by occasional popular demonstrations, implemented a series of reforms designed to improve urban work and life. This pattern, which did not threaten the economic and political position of the oligarchy, culminated in the election of 1930, which was, perhaps, the freest election in Salvadoran history. Arturo Araujo, the head of the Workers'

Party and not a member of an elite family, was elected on a strongly reformist platform. He served for less than a year, when the entire trajectory of Salvadoran political history was suddenly and completely reversed by the depression of the 1930s and the response to political unrest.

Nicaragua

José Santos Zelaya, president from 1893 to 1906, was an archetypical Liberal president of the era. He was thoroughly committed to "progress" as defined at that time, which essentially was to use the powers of the state to promote the production and export of coffee. In the process of doing so, he created a strong state system, but he also pursued a strongly nationalist program that distinguished him from his progressive Liberal counterparts in Guatemala, El Salvador, and Costa Rica. But neither his coffee policy nor his brand of nationalism endeared him to the Conservatives, who continued to look for ways to unseat him.

In conducting international relations, Zelaya was not simply indifferent to the opinion of the U.S. government; he was downright hostile. This left him vulnerable to attacks by his domestic opponents. Although the presence of U.S. banana companies in Nicaragua was negligible, as was U.S. investment of any kind, the potential for an interoceanic canal through Nicaragua loomed large. Negotiations with Zelaya broke down in the late nineteenth century, when Zelaya was unwilling to concede sovereignty over the canal and adjacent areas.

Even after the consummation of the deal among the U.S. government, the bankrupt French canal company, and newly independent Panama, the U.S. government continued to worry that someone else might put a canal through Nicaragua and compete with a U.S. monopoly. The rumor that Zelaya was opening negotiations with European nations and possibly with Japan for the construction of a Nicaraguan canal, and Zelaya's general lack of deference to U.S. wishes and interests, made him a candidate for the application of Theodore Roosevelt's "big stick" diplomacy. The so-called Roosevelt corollary to the Monroe Doctrine was that the United States had the right, even the duty, to ensure political stability in Latin America to protect the area from European incursions. The strategic importance of the entire region to the canal, and Zelaya's 1906 invasion of Honduras in an effort to reduce Estrada Cabrera's influence, triggered direct U.S. intervention in Nicaragua.

Although I am not for a moment questioning the self-serving arrogance behind U.S. policy in Central America, the fact remains that the magnitude of U.S. stakes in Nicaragua during the first decade of the twentieth century was minimal. Yes, there was the canal to protect. Yes, there was a debt. Yes, there were the United Fruit Company and other U.S.-based fruit companies' plantations operating in Costa Rica and rapidly expanding in Guatemala and Honduras. Although one might list several additional economic and political interests that Zelaya's Nicaragua might have threatened, they still fail to add up to convincing material or strategic reasons for the U.S. government to send in the marines. Nevertheless, the marines landed on the Caribbean coast of Nicaragua in 1909, occupied the town of Bluefields, and supported the overthrow of Zelaya by the Conservative troops based in Bluefields.

To understand U.S. actions, one needs to add to the equation the sell job done on U.S. diplomats and politicians by representatives of the Nicaraguan Conservative Party, led by Adolofo Díaz, Emiliano Chamorro, and Juan Estrada, who were eager to replace Zelaya with a Conservative president. This certainly was not the last time that Central American partisans would manipulate the U.S. government into believing that it had a substantial stake in some domestic dispute in order to have it intervene to protect those fictitious interests.

Once installed under U.S. tutelage, the Conservative government of Díaz was as supine as promised, but when the U.S. marines withdrew from the Atlantic coast, the new government was attacked by Liberal troops. In 1912, the U.S. marines returned to restore the Conservatives to office, but not to political power. This time the marines occupied Managua, the U.S. government directly supervised the client government's affairs, and U.S. banks looted Nicaraguan governmental finances. Two years later, the infamous Bryan-Chamorro Treaty was signed, pledging the United States sole rights, in perpetuity, to build a canal across Nicaragua, to a naval base in the Gulf of Fonseca, and to a long lease of the Corn Islands off the Caribbean coast. The Central American Court of Justice, which earlier had been established at U.S. behest to restrain Zelaya, ruled this treaty to be illegal—a violation of national territorial rights. The United States and Nicaragua ignored the ruling and thereby destroyed the court.

After trying several combinations of personnel, the U.S. ambassador and military commander believed that they had established a workable and cooperative government in Nicaragua, and the U.S. troops were withdrawn in 1925. The Liberals, with Mexican military aid, quickly reopened the civil war, and the Conservatives again petitioned for the return of the U.S. marines. Over a thousand of them came in 1926. By 1927, the Conservatives, Liberals, and the United States had hammered out a compromise to which all subscribed except one minor Liberal "general" named Augusto César Sandino. For six years, Sandino and a small band, based in the northern mountains, waged a courageous and skillful guerrilla war against several thousand U.S. marines and members of the Nicaraguan National Guard, which had been created by the U.S. military. Sandino's struggle was celebrated by anti-imperialist groups throughout the world; for instance, a brigade of the Guo Min Dang in China was named after him.

Sandino accepted support from the Communist Third International, and for several years during the struggle Farabundo Martí, a Salvadoran Communist, was his assistant. But Sandino was no socialist, or even a radical reformer; his social platform was mild and general. Sandino was first and foremost a nationalist. His goal was to rid Nicaragua of the U.S. troops, and when they were finally withdrawn in 1933, he readily negotiated with the Nicaraguan government that those same troops had installed. The treaty to which he finally agreed stipulated no social or even political reforms, but in any case the treaty was moot. Sandino was murdered in early 1934 on the orders of Anastacio Somoza García, the head of the National Guard, and the remnants of Sandino's troops were killed or dispersed by the Guard.

Honduras

The enclave character of Honduras's export production, both minerals and bananas, meant that the most dynamic productive activity of the nation was contained in relatively watertight units with very little impact on the rest of the nation. This is the usual understanding of enclave export production, and it is accurate as far as it goes. But it misses the fact that enclave production of exports can become the basis for a powerful state.

No matter how cut off an export enclave is from the rest of the society, it is likely that it will pay taxes to the state of the host nation. If these taxes are substantial, and especially if the enclave is foreign owned, the state has access to resources produced from an economic activity that is the basis of no domestic possessing class. This revenue, then, is a source of resources that does not depend on the consent of any domestic constituency and thereby may be used to develop state power unencumbered by interest groups in civil society. I have already noted some tendency in this direction in Costa Rica, and other examples from Latin America of fiscally remunerative exports produced in enclave conditions include Peruvian guano in the middle of the nineteenth century and Venezuelan petroleum and Bolivian tin in the early twentieth century.

Experiences in Honduras with mineral exports and then with bananas are related to this model of state building, albeit as a poor cousin. Although corruption and opportunism by individual politicians played an important part in the Honduran state's willingness to make generous concessions to the U.S. fruit companies, there were also other factors. The Honduran state had been badly cheated by foreign railroad contractors, who had left behind nothing but a sizable foreign debt. In this bleak situation, then, the fruit companies appeared to offer a real opportunity to establish productive activities in the northern coast and to secure a railroad network. Honduran governments were therefore generous in granting land and tax concessions to the foreign fruit companies. Even when banana company exports became subject to taxation, the government depended on the companies to record their tax liabilities, and the tax was low—between 1 and 2 percent of the value of banana exports. Moreover, attempts to raise the tax could result in strong resistance. In 1919, the U.S. ambassador secured the resignation of the Honduran president who had suggested that the export tax on bananas be raised one-half cent a stalk. For decades, the U.S. government, for all intents and purposes, acted as an agent for the fruit companies in Honduras.

The Honduran state was kept poor and the U.S. government and fruit companies meddled incessantly in Honduran politics. U.S. marines landed at La Ceiba in the first decade of the twentieth century and occupied Tegucigalpa in the 1920s as part of U.S. supervision of Honduran affairs. In general, Zemurray's Cuyamel Fruit Company supported the Liberal Party and the United Fruit Company backed the conservative National Party, and occasionally the rivalry led to the ludicrous situation of different fruit companies arming competing Honduran groups to fight civil wars eventually arbitrated by the U.S. government. The competition between the two major fruit companies ended in 1929, when Zemurray sold out to the United Fruit Company.

As if this were not enough, Honduras was vulnerable to invasions by neighboring states as well, and there were perpetual coups, countercoups, conspiracies to overthrow the government, and rumors of conspiracies. Honduras was ruled by eighteen different presidents in the first thirty years of the twentieth century.

The political instability in Honduras in the early twentieth century was similar to that experienced by all five Central American nations during the early decades of independence; Honduras seemed to have become frozen in the earlier pattern of Central American politics that the other nations had left behind. The reason is that Honduras's export economy, unlike those in Costa Rica, Guatemala, and El Salvador, did not generate a powerful domestic possessing class that constituted the structure for a system of national politics. It was even different from Nicaragua, where strong national elites were so deeply divided that the U.S. marines eventually imposed a political stability of sorts. In Honduras, there was no domestic oligarchy capable of taking charge of national affairs. There were numerous examples of a Honduran president and sometimes the legislature simply refusing to take orders from the U.S. government and fruit companies, but it is clear that the Honduran state was deeply and consistently influenced by the U.S. government and fruit companies, even if it was not completely a client of those interests.

So far, the description certainly does not sound like the powerful, centralized, autonomous state that export enclaves were supposed to be capable of supporting. But the enclave model of state building is relevant for understanding the nature of the Honduran state. Figure 3.3 indicates that the Honduran state did indeed have some resources. And in spite of banana workers' increasingly effective organizations and strikes, the Honduran state did have considerable autonomy in respect to any domestic constituencies. These features made it an attractive target, a prize for political entrepreneurs. The state system was not beholden to domestic groups that would crush any attempt to wrest the state away from them and their minions. There were regular fiscal revenues, and there were significant opportunities for bribes. The state was a coveted source of income, especially because there was but little other high income activity outside of the export enclaves. Political control in Honduras was a major source of economic power, whereas in the rest of Central America, political control (or at least influence) was an expression of economic power. This was both the strength and the weakness of the Honduran state.

Economic Growth Without Development

The decades marked by the vigorous expansion of export production significantly affected the character of the five Central American nations, giving social and economic content to what had been virtually empty political categories containing loose congeries of diverse groups and aspirations. Nevertheless, the specialized production of exports for international markets did not transform the nations into materially progressive economies capable of self-sustaining economic growth. This economic weakness did not mean that the international economy pumped economic resources out of the region, even though the United Fruit Company made every effort to do so. On the contrary, there is good reason to believe that mobilizing domestic factors to produce exports for foreign markets did increase the total economic resources available to the "nation."

The reason for the quotation marks around "nation" is that, as noted earlier, the use of the nation as a unit of analysis in both liberal and dependency models obscures the way in which export production created a wide variety of social formations (including economic relations and political structures in this umbrella term). And it is to those social formations, not international commodity and financial flows, that one must look for an understanding of the failure of dynamic export production growth to create materially progressive capitalism in Central America.

Any definition of capitalism must include the production of commodities (that is, goods and services for sale on markets rather than for direct use), the private ownership of the means of production, and the predominance of wage labor. The last characteristic refers to situations in which the majority of the population have no control over the means of production, such as land and capital equipment. Thus workers were a proletariat, with no way to make a living other than by selling their only productive resource—labor service—to those who do control the means of production. The classical way to form a proletariat is by forcibly dispossessing people, separating them from the means of production. The coercion resulting from an absence of alternatives is then represented as a natural feature of social life, indeed as freedom. This process in England was described by Marx in characteristically vivid terms:

> [The working class was being formed as] a mass which was free in a double sense, free from the old relations of clientship, bondage and servitude, and secondly free of all belongings and possessions, and of every objective, material form of being, free of all property; dependent on the sale of its labor capacity or on begging, vagabondage and robbery as its only source of income. It is a matter of historic record that they tried the latter first, but were driven off this road by gallows, stocks and whippings, onto the narrow path to the labor market.[9]

For capitalism to operate effectively, this basic inequality in respect to the ownership of the means of production must be institutionalized and the attendant definition of freedom accepted. After this is accomplished, it is then possible to have an apparently smoothly operating, seemingly impersonal and equitable labor market that does not require the direct and continuing use of violence by a centralized state. This is the liberal capitalist ideal.

But in addition to institutionalizing capitalist social relations, a vigorous capitalism is materially progressive—that is, it results in economic growth because of increased productivity of human labor rather than because of an expanded work force or intensified work done by a given number of workers. Again, the ideal is a setting of strong market competition in which owners of the means of production must constantly improve the organization and technology of production so as to lower the costs of production. The continued lowering of costs for a firm in a competitive market is imperative if that firm is to keep product prices as low as those of other firms. Only in this way can firms in a competitive market avoid being undersold and thus driven out of business by competitors who are continually innovating to cut costs. The continuing effort to produce more efficiently, and thus cheaply, raises the productivity of workers. It is precisely this materially progressive characteristic of capitalism, which seemed to Adam Smith, Karl Marx, and other theorists of capitalism to flow ineluctably from capitalist organization, that has distinguished capitalism as the materially progressive mode of production.

When we look now at Central America, it is clear that there was indeed significant production for markets and private ownership of the means of production (land being the most important). But Central America fell far short of achieving even the institutional ideal of capitalism during the late nineteenth and early twentieth centuries. Contrary to the expectations of observers from many different ideological perspectives, the proletarianization of the work force was not an automatic consequence of producing for sale on product markets.

Although there were definite pressures and tendencies in that direction, commodity production in Costa Rica, Guatemala, and Nicaragua did not quickly create the predominance of wage relationships. Guatemala is a good example of the compatibility of vigorous market production over an extended period with unfree labor, and Costa Rica illustrates that small proprietorships may be a very tenacious form of production, resisting the tendency to transform all workers into proletarians. In El Salvador, the dispossession of the workers went further than in the rest of Central America, but under an extreme concentration of economic power. In Honduras, Guatemala, and Costa Rica, the export production of bananas was done with wage labor, but in enclave conditions that severely inhibited the generalization of capitalist relations of production.

In addition to the weakness of the wage labor system, the competitive market conditions for classical capitalist growth were also muted. Although prices for the export commodities (especially coffee) fluctuated widely, local costs of production had little influence on those prices. In addition to the effects of weather, diseases, and other factors always present in agriculture, the magnitude of the effects of international demand and supply conditions (for instance, consumer prosperity in Europe and the United States and the size of Brazil's coffee exports, respectively) completely swamped the influence of local costs of production on local growers' profits. And in the case of bananas, the extent to which the large fruit companies controlled the market reduced the competitive imperative of constant cost reduction for profitability.

Improvements were made in the processing of coffee and in the transport and distribution of both coffee and bananas, but very little effort was put into increasing the productivity of labor in growing and harvesting. Both the relations of production and the market conditions for coffee and bananas made depressing wages and intensifying work seem the most rational way to increase profits.

The competitive capitalist model of growth and development outlined previously is derived principally from eighteenth- and nineteenth-century English experience, and it is this model that informs both neoclassical and Marxian approaches to the subject. But by the end of the nineteenth century, there was another materially successful historical experience with economic development that posed a very different dynamic from that of the highly individualistic, market-oriented growth of England. This was the economic development of Germany, whose rise as a world economic power demonstrated that a strong central state guiding large financial institutions could establish a vigorous industrial economy by underwriting large-scale enterprises producing capital equipment, armaments, and intermediate products (e.g., steel and chemicals) for use by other firms rather than consumer products. In the process, market forces were all but suspended by government purchases and government-sponsored cartels, and widespread national economic development was compatible with large proportions of the German work force not involved in a wage labor system but working as peasants, serfs, and independent artisans.

The German model, therefore, emphasizes the role of the state rather than pervasive wage labor and market competition. The stunted capitalism in Central America formed by the export boom was not materially progressive, nor did it support the liberal capitalist ideal of stable, democratic political systems that is the political counterpart of the competitive market. Although the variety of Central American production modes generated an equal variety of political formations, there was an important common element, with considerable variation in local detail, visible throughout the region. The export economies not only produced coffee and bananas, but they also produced powerful elites who exercised preponderant political influence, often to the point of functioning as an oligarchy. As a consequence, even a state system as developed as Guatemala's did not have the political wherewithal to be the driving force of economic development. The central reason for this was that general economic growth for the nation was not necessarily in the interests of those whose fortunes and positions were dependent on exports.

At the simplest level, widespread economic development encouraged by strong backward, forward, and income multiplier linkages would have meant new employment opportunities and therefore increased competition for labor, with consequent increases in wages in the export sector. That growth would have had to be promoted by state policy, requiring higher taxes. Moreover, the development of new branches of production would constitute new sources of social and political power. Emerging elites based on the new activities would press for governmental policies favorable to their interests, which might conflict with the needs of the export economy. And the mobilization of new groups of organized workers would further dilute export producers' political control and strengthen the impetus for reform. In the early decades of the twentieth century, the Mexican revolution (1910) and the Russian Revolution (1917) graphically demonstrated to Central American elites the dangers of social and political change. Finally, exporters had no interest in expanding local markets for commodities; the demand for their products depended on foreign markets.

The development of export production created the Central American export elites' power, which in turn ensured the veto of any initiative likely to generate widespread, self-sustaining national development in the early decades of the twentieth century. In considering the contradictory way in which export-led economic growth prevented more thoroughgoing economic development, it is important to remember that the national domicile of capital is not a central issue. The principle that general economic development in a nation can threaten those tied to local production for foreign markets holds whether those controlling the export sector are citizens of the exporting nation or foreign investors. The nationality of capital makes less difference to capital's interests and behavior than nationalist rhetoric would lead one to expect.

The result of the export boom in Central America, then, was growth without development of either the English or German variety. The significant growth that occurred resulted from either the use of more land and labor, the intensification of work, or the rise in export prices that increased the market value of a given quantity of output.

The growth did not result from increasing the productivity of human labor. All Central American nations experienced considerable economic change, but none managed to achieve the economic and political transformations necessary for a vibrant, competitive capitalism or a state-sponsored form of sustained economic development. This is the reason that export expansion failed to stimulate continuing economic growth in Central America, not some putative net loss of economic resources resulting from international trade and investment. It is likely that additional resources from exports would have done little more than strengthen, and increase the durability of, the nonprogressive political and economic systems.

Although not materially progressive, the social formations established in the late nineteenth and early twentieth centuries depended on the continuing profitability of export production. As a result of the Great Depression of the 1930s, World War II, and the immediate postwar period, those social orders were called into question. Many features of the old social orders had to change quickly for their basic structures not to change.

Notes

1. A good source on this history is Walter LaFeber, *The Panama Canal: The Crisis in Historical Perspective,* updated edition (New York: Oxford University Press, 1989).

2. Andre Gunder Frank, *Capitalism and Underdevelopment in Latin America* (New York: Monthly Review Press, 1967), and Immanuel Wallerstein's essays in his *The Capitalist World Economy* (Cambridge: Cambridge University Press, 1979), are good statements of the narrow form of dependency theory that captured the imagination of many North American scholars. The more broadly conceived versions that emphasize social structure, such as Fernando Henrique Cardoso and Enzo Falleto, *Dependency and Development in Latin America* (Berkeley and Los Angeles: University of California Press, 1974), are substantially more interesting. For critical appraisals of dependency theory and the issues addressed by dependency theory, see Diana Hunt, *Economic Theories of Development: Analyses of Competing Paradigms* (Savage, MD: Barnes and Noble, 1989); Ronald H. Chilcote and Joel C. Edelstein, *Latin America: Capitalist and Socialist Perspectives of Development and Underdevelopment* (Boulder, CO: Westview Press, 1986); Cristóbal Kay, *Latin American Theories of Development and Underdevelopment* (New York: Routledge, 1989); and especially Anthony Brewer, *Marxist Theories of Imperialism: A Critical Survey,* 2d ed. (London and New York: Routledge, Chapman and Hall, 1990).

3. The concept of linkages is described and applied in Frederick S. Weaver, *Class, State, and Industrial Development: The Historical Process of South American Industrial Growth* (Westport, CT: Greenwood Press, 1980), pp. 79–96. A good survey of the period, with an excellent bibliography, is Ciro Cardoso, "The Liberal Era, c. 1870–1930," in L. Bethell, *Central America Since Independence* (Cambridge: Cambridge University Press, 1991), pp. 37–68. Also valuable are the relevant sections of Victor Bulmer-Thomas, *The Political Economy of Central America Since 1920* (New York: Cambridge University Press, 1987); and James Dunkerley, *Power in the Isthmus: A Political History of Modern Central America* (London and New York: Verso, 1988).

4. See Ciro F. S. Cardoso, "Formation of the Coffee Estate in Nineteenth-Century Costa Rica," in K. Duncan and I. Butledge (eds.), *Land and Labour in Latin America: Essays on the Development of Agrarian Capitalism in the Nineteenth and Twentieth Centuries* (New York: Cambridge University Press, 1977); and Lowell Gudmundson, *Costa Rica Before Coffee: Society and Economy on the Eve of the Export Boom* (Baton Rouge: Louisiana State University Press, 1986).

5. See the following for Guatemala: J. C. Cambranes, *Coffee and Peasants: The Origins of the Modern Plantation Economy in Guatemala, 1853–1897* (Stockholm: Institute of Latin American Studies, Monograph No. 10, 1985); David McCreery, "Coffee and Class: The Structure of Development in Liberal Guatemala," *Hispanic American Historical Review* 56, no. 3 (1976), and "Debt Servitude in Rural Guatemala, 1876–1936," *Hispanic American Historical Review* 63, no. 4 (1983); Jim Handy, *Gift of the Devil: A History of Guatemala* (Boston: South End Press, 1984); Carol Smith (ed.), *Guatemalan Indians and the State* (Austin: University of Texas Press, 1990); and Paul J. Dosal, "The Political Economy of Guatemalan

Industrialization, 1871–1948: The Career of Carlos F. Novella," *Hispanic American Historical Review* 68, no. 2 (1988).

6. Good sources on El Salvador are David Browning, *El Salvador, Landscape and Society* (Oxford: Oxford University Press, 1971); Hector Lindo-Fuentes, *Weak Foundations: The Economy of El Salvador in the Nineteenth Century* (Berkeley and Los Angeles: University of California Press, 1990); and E. Bradford Burns's two articles, "The Modernization of Underdevelopment: El Salvador, 1858–1931," *Journal of Developing Areas* 18 (1984), and "The Intellectual Infrastructure of Modernization in El Salvador," *Americas* 41, no. 3 (1985).

7. E. Bradford Burns, *Patriarch and Folk: The Emergence of Nicaragua, 1798–1858* (Cambridge: Harvard University Press, 1991); Jaime Wheelock, *Imperialismo y dictadura: Crisis de una formación social* (México: Siglo Veintiuno, 1975); Donald C. Hodges, *The Intellectual Foundations of the Nicaraguan Revolution* (Austin: University of Texas Press, 1986); and C. L. Stansifer, "José Santos Zelaya: A New Look at Nicaragua's 'Liberal' Dictator," *Revista/Review Interamericana* 7 (1977).

8. For Honduras, see Charles Kepner, *Social Aspects of the Banana Industry* (New York: Columbia University Press, 1936); Mario Posas and Rafael Del Cid, *La construcción del sector público y del estado nacional en Honduras 1870–1979* (Ciudad Universitaria Rodrigo Facio, CR: Editorial Universitaria Centroamerica, 1981); and K. V. Finney, "Rosario and the Election of 1887: The Political Economy of Mining in Honduras," *Hispanic American Historical Review* 59, no. 1 (1979).

9. Karl Marx, *Grundrisse,* edited and translated by M. Nicolous (New York: McGraw-Hill, 1974), p. 507.

4

Economic Decline, War, and the Ascent of the State, 1930 to the 1950s

The decade of the 1930s is defined by the Great Depression, which swept through the capitalist world from the October 1929 stock market crash in the United States until World War II began in 1939. Even though the 1920s was a period of unprecedented export expansion in Central America, there had already been some signs of export weakness in Central America before the worldwide economic collapse. Nevertheless, the severity and length of the depression in the 1930s called into question the very existence of the Central American social and political orders, which rested on the export economies.

Coffee and bananas are not essential foodstuffs, and as such the market demand for them is quite sensitive to changes in income. The sharply reduced incomes of consumers in Europe and the United States, therefore, meant substantial declines in the quantities of coffee and bananas desired at any given price. The effects of the depressed markets for coffee and bananas, however, were quite different. A large part of the cost of producing coffee, an orchard crop, is sunk into planting the trees and in the three to five years of nurturing before they produce to capacity. The cost of weeding, harvesting, processing, and transporting a particular year's crop is thus a much smaller proportion of total cost than in the case of bananas, which are grown on plants that are more like annuals.

As these considerations suggest, the decline in the demand for coffee in the 1930s had little effect on the quantity produced and exported from Central America. The full impact of declining demand for coffee, therefore, fell on price adjustments, and in the early 1930s coffee prices fell to about one-third of their high in the previous decade. Figure 4.1 traces the precipitous declines in the U.S. dollar value of exports from the Central American coffee-exporting nations during the early 1930s. The general economic effect of this decline can be seen in Figure 4.2, which shows that

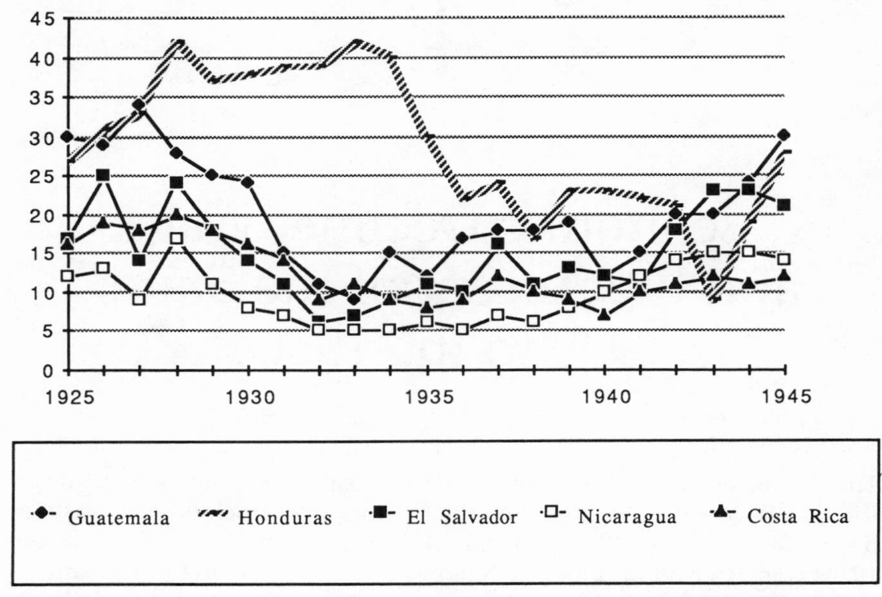

FIGURE 4.1 Value of Central American exports, 1925–1945 (U.S.$ millions). *Source:* Adapted from Victor Bulmer-Thomas, *The Political Economy of Central America Since 1920* (New York: Cambridge University Press, 1987), p. 326.

gross domestic product declined during the first five years of the decade throughout Central America.

Figure 4.1 also shows that the experience of Honduras was different from that of the rest of Central America: Its export earnings did not fall nearly as precipitously after 1928 or 1929. First of all, the price of bananas fell considerably less than that of coffee. The recorded price of banana exports from the exporting country was an administered price, not a market price. It was the price set by United Fruit Company policy, and most of the recorded sales at those prices were sales from one part of the United Fruit Company to another—from a producing subsidiary to a transportation subsidiary. Even when that administered price represented how much the United Fruit Company paid independent producers, it still was an administered price, and it changed only slowly, even though the demand for bananas was falling.

Even final market prices, as opposed to those recorded at export points, held up better for bananas because of the market power of the United Fruit Company, which could affect final selling price by adjusting production levels. The United Fruit Company had the choice, therefore, of absorbing some of the diminished demand through reducing the quantities sold rather than through reducing prices and through switching more production to their low-cost Honduran operations. But in any case, much of the quantity reductions resulted from disease, not corporate strategy. As banana diseases spread along the coast from Costa Rica to Nicaraguan and Honduran plantations, output levels fell. In the 1930s the Nicaraguan plantations were closed completely and they did not reopen for forty years.

Honduran exports also held up longer than those from the other Central American nations because when the leading European and North American economies abandoned the international gold standard, the price of gold rose. This in turn increased the value of gold (and subsequently silver) exports and increased the incentive for greater mining output. When the full force of the depression hit Honduras, however, it hit harder than in the four other nations. This is suggested in Figure 4.2, but in more explicit terms, Honduran per capita income, which in 1920 was the second lowest among the five nations, was by far the lowest in the early 1940s and did not recover its predepression levels until the late 1960s, more than a decade later than Nicaragua, which experienced the next slowest recovery.

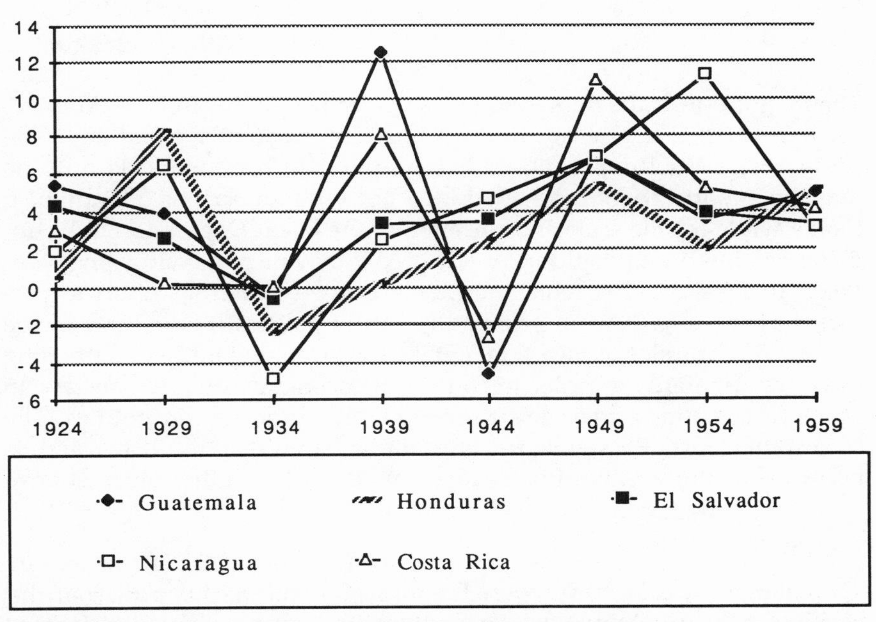

FIGURE 4.2 Average rates of GDP growth, 1924–1959 (five-year averages). *Source:* Adapted from Victor Bulmer-Thomas, *The Political Economy of Central America Since 1920* (New York: Cambridge University Press, 1987), p. 308.

Because of the steeper decline in banana production, the depression tended to result in more unemployment among banana workers than among coffee workers. Wage and job losses in the export sector, however, were only the most immediate effects of the depression. The governments' fiscal revenues, derived primarily from export and import taxes, dropped precipitously; the wealth and power of the wealthiest and most powerful of national elites were threatened; the livelihoods of all those working in commerce, finance, and transportation depended on healthy exports; and so on. That is, all the linkages were working with negative signs.

The dramatic expansion of the export economies during the late nineteenth and early twentieth centuries had failed to propel the nations of Central America into self-sustaining, dynamic economic development, and exports still formed the economic base of those social orders. The resources flowing into the nations through the sale of exports, and more specifically, the resources flowing into the hands of specific groups within the nations, had created the social orders and were essential for their reproduction through time. With severely weakened export sectors, the continued existence of these social orders required actively interventionist state policies designed to shore them up.

Political Reorganization

The magnitude of the depression was not immediately obvious. After all, the export sectors had not uniformly and consistently expanded. The post–World War I depression, for example, had been a shock, but one that the export economies had ridden out without serious alteration. It took a while for the scale and duration of the Great Depression to be appreciated, but once people acknowledged it they moved swiftly and resolutely to preserve that which suddenly needed conscious effort to preserve. These moves were principally in the political realm, and in the nations of Central America they entailed centralizing and strengthening the state apparatus in order to control the economy and civil society. In four of the nations, this meant an explicitly authoritarian politics. The closest that Costa Rica came to authoritarianism was in the 1940s, and its political content was vastly different from that of the other four nations.

El Salvador

The changes in El Salvador were the most dramatic and brutal. The 1930 election of Arturo Araujo was the culmination of an extended process of political organization and competition.[1] At the time of the election, there was considerable enthusiasm by the urban middle and working classes, especially in San Salvador, for Araujo and his reformist platform. This support quickly eroded, however, when the new president seemed unable to respond to the exigencies of the depression in a constructive manner. The rapidly rising agitation and restiveness by rural workers, along with a three-month delay in paying the military, precipitated a revolt by young army officers in 1931. After taking power, however, these officers, who had no connection with the oligarchy and initially had considerable popular support, were uncertain about what to do. They soon turned the presidency over to Araujo's vice-president, General Maximiliano Hernández Martínez, even though he was distrusted by the elite because of his modest origins, previous use of populist rhetoric, and personal idiosyncrasies.

During a period of confusion, including a struggle over new elections, the urban and rural working classes launched a poorly coordinated revolt in 1932. The government learned of the revolt in advance, and Farabundo Martí—the most important figure in the Salvadoran Communist Party and urban revolutionary politics—and other leaders were promptly arrested and executed prior to the revolt. Nevertheless, the desperate rural and urban working classes went ahead with the insurrection. In the countryside, the revolt had an explicitly Indian character that frightened some urban ladinos who might have sympathized with their demands.

Expected support for the revolt by factions of the army failed to materialize, and the revolt was so easily crushed that Martínez did not need to draw on the help offered by the U.S. and Canadian naval vessels off the Salvadoran coast. It was the aftermath of the revolt that is especially important. In revenge, army and civilian squads killed thousands of Salvadorans within a few weeks. The estimates are that in this period, known as La Matanza, between 10,000 and 40,000 people were killed—perhaps as many as 7 or 8 for every 100 people in the population. Wearing Indian dress and ornaments made one especially vulnerable to attack by the death squads, and thus was hastened the disappearance of visible signs of Indian culture from El Salvador.

This insurrection marked the end of populist and reformist politics in El Salvador for decades. The potential of the uprising and Hernández Martínez's brutal effectiveness in suppressing it convinced the oligarchy that it needed a more centralized, militarized state and that it could trust Hernández Martínez, as strange as he was, to run it on their behalf. The oligarchy, therefore, turned over the job of directly ruling El Salvador in exchange for assurance that its social and economic positions would be protected. For twelve years more, Hernández Martínez ran El Salvador with an iron hand in the name of order and anticommunism. In this, he was supported by the forces of reaction and by the quiescence of the middle classes, who also had been frightened by the lower-class and Indian uprising.

Guatemala

Even though Martínez of El Salvador and Jorge Ubico, president of Guatemala, apparently had little regard for each other, their presidencies were similar in many respects. They both were presidents from 1931 to 1944, and they were both military men with political experience and ambitions with an earlier interest in vaguely populist reforms. Ubico was also a wealthy landowner, and he had an impressive reputation for honesty and administrative skill.[2] Shortly after assuming office in 1931, winning an election in which he was the only candidate, he reorganized the bureaucracy and mounted an extensive anticorruption campaign. But Ubico's nationalist and reformist tendencies, prominent in his forays into national politics in the 1920s, had disappeared by the 1930s. As president, he was a loyal supporter of the United Fruit Company and brutally suppressed internal dissent. His approach to working-class issues was clearly demonstrated by his transferring the Department of Labor from the Development Ministry to the National Police. Ubico also organized an extensive network of police informers and was constantly, to the point of paranoia, alert to any challenge to his power. His most frequently quoted remark is, "I have no friends, only domesticated enemies."[3]

Again unlike Martínez, Ubico initiated an important change in the organization of production. He dissolved the debt peonage system and replaced it with very stringent vagrancy legislation. Under the new system, all adults who did not own at least seven acres of land had to prove that they worked for wages 100 to 150 days a year. With this new mechanism of coercive labor mobilization, finqueros were relieved of the debt peonage system's requirement to give workers advances in their wages. The vagrancy law was significantly different from the debt peonage legislation in that it was enforced directly by the national state through appointed district military commanders rather than by finqueros and local government officials. In another major change, Ubico replaced elections for local mayors with appointed officials, further centralizing political power in national government.

Honduras

Tiburcio Carías Andino, a third authoritarian figure in the 1930s, was president of Honduras from 1932 to 1948. As an unsuccessful United Fruit Company candidate for president in the 1920s, he had demonstrated that he possessed impeccable credentials as a United Fruit Company loyalist.[4] With the United Fruit Company's purchase of Cuyamel

Fruit Company in 1929, intercorporate competition no longer offered Honduran politics the ability to play one large company off another. (Standard Fruit was not powerful enough for this purpose.) Although Carías was from humble origins and refrained from moving aggressively against banana strikers in 1932, he did not hesitate to crush another strike two years later. From that point, he never deviated from the United Fruit Company line. The weakness of internal social and economic structures, the ability of some workers to resort to subsistence agriculture in the sparsely populated countryside, and the power of the United Fruit Company that neutralized internal political opposition allowed Carías's years in office to be less violent than those of his authoritarian counterparts in El Salvador and Guatemala.

Nicaragua

When the U.S. marines withdrew from Nicaragua in 1933, they left behind a new national government. Even though the president was elected with U.S. supervision, he was a Liberal and not what the U.S. representatives preferred.[5] But the marines also left Anastacio Somoza García in control of the National Guard. Somoza was a nephew of the new president, was fluent in English, and had ingratiated himself into the U.S. military and diplomatic community. After Somoza had Sandino murdered in 1934, his path to the presidency was clear. Playing on popular dissatisfaction with the ineffective government, Somoza supported a general strike against the government, mediated a settlement, suppressed the left wing of the unions involved, and removed the president by coup. With the support of the National Guard, he easily won the presidential election against an exiled opponent. This formally established the Somoza dynasty, which ruled Nicaragua until the revolution of 1979.

The U.S. occupying forces established the National Guard in the hope that it would be a nonpartisan keeper of order, ending the long history of Conservative-Liberal strife in Nicaragua. Given the setting, this hope was naive, but in regard to the nonpartisan aspiration it worked out better than most thought possible. Even though Somoza was formally a Liberal, the National Guard, under his leadership, favored neither political party. Its support was essential for Somoza's personal rule, and the Guard, as an institution, was a full partner in the plundering of Nicaragua, which was conducted in a nonpartisan manner. By the 1940s, the responsibilities of the National Guard had been augmented so that in addition to all military and police functions, the Guard was in charge of communications, health, tax collections, and the railroads.

The "exceptionalism" of Nicaragua and Somoza can easily be overdrawn. Although the U.S. occupation set the stage for Somoza's takeover of the state, he still needed domestic political support. Somoza quickly devalued the Nicaraguan currency, suppressed political dissidents, attended assiduously to the welfare of the National Guard, and in general made every effort to curry the favor of politically significant individuals and groups. The policies and functions of the Nicaraguan state, and thus domestic political support at this time, were closer to that of Ubico's Guatemala and Hernández Martínez's El Salvador than often is recognized.

Costa Rica

In spite of the need to suspend civil rights to suppress strikes and demonstrations in 1932, Costa Rican politics was essentially business as usual during the 1930s.[6] Two regularly elected presidents continued the tradition of rotation among members of the Costa Rican oligarchy. The government of Ricardo Jiménez (1932–1936) experimented with some mild reforms (for instance, price guarantees for coffee and nationalizing the insurance industry), supported the workers' demands in the 1934 banana strike (which were agreed to but not honored by the United Fruit Company), and at the same time vigorously suppressed any radical politics, which in Costa Rica were confined to the Caribbean banana zone. The second administration in the 1930s, that of León Cortes Castro (1936–1940), represented a conservative backlash, and the reforms were halted. A more significant reformist period of Costa Rican politics was the 1940s, and the constituency patterns were very unusual.

New Patterns in State Policies and Power

All four of the strongmen presidents who presided over governments in El Salvador, Honduras, Guatemala, and Nicaragua assumed and maintained power by means that were hardly constitutional. In the first years of the 1930s, the United States disapproved of their governments, in spite of their trenchantly anti-Communist and status quo stances. By the mid-1930s, however, the United States recognized the de facto regimes, clearing the way for Somoza's presidency as well as the irregular methods by which all four presidents stayed in power. President Franklin Roosevelt's celebrated Good Neighbor policy was in effect during this period. The essence of that policy was to honor the principle of nonintervention and thus support dictatorial regimes without getting too close to them. This policy was not without tensions in the United States, particularly over the obvious fascist sympathies of Martínez, Ubico, and Somoza. Ubico had strong reservations about Hitler, but all three were strongly attracted to the Italian fascism of Mussolini. Moreover, individual Central American states distinguished themselves among the world's nations by giving prompt diplomatic recognition to Franco's Spain and the Japanese puppet regime in Manchuria. The fascist sympathies were tolerated by the U.S. government in the 1930s as long as they did not get in the way of their functioning to maintain societies that were stable and safe from the viewpoint of U.S. interests.[7]

Although there was considerable variety among the five nations' governments in the 1930s, reflecting their divergent patterns of social development, their policy goals were, for all intents and purposes, identical. All five governments worked strenuously to preserve the social formations based on export economies, which were severely weakened by the depression. At the most obvious level, this meant containing any forces that might lead to social and political disruption and unfavorable change. All five of the national governments were quite effective in destroying political initiatives by rural and urban workers.

In addition to beating down direct challenges to the social order, the governments worked to raise the profitability of the export sector. Extensive programs to promote economic recovery and the welfare of those hurt by the depression were precluded by adherence to strictly orthodox fiscal principles in all of the governments except that of Costa Rica. That is, the four governments made valiant efforts to reduce public expenditures in line with their shrinking revenues. Despite this constraint, however, all five governments deliberately influenced national economic activity in a systematic manner that contrasted with previous less interventionist practices.

The type and scope of such economic policies differed by nation. The more extensive development of the Guatemalan state apparatus allowed Ubico, alone among the five, to alter the fundamentals of the labor mobilization system in favor of finqueros. But enforcing reductions in the wages of export-sector workers and reducing or eliminating export taxes were policies taken by all the governments. Devaluing the national currency in respect to the U.S. dollar was another policy response, used by the governments of El Salvador, Costa Rica, and, after 1936, Nicaragua. The devaluations increased the price of the U.S. dollar in terms of the local currency. This meant that the dollars received from export sales would be converted into more units of the national currency. Because the costs of producing exports were incurred in the national currency, the devaluations meant that exporters' profits in terms of the national currency increased.

But it also meant that in terms of local currency, the prices of imports were higher, thus discouraging the purchase of imports and helping to maintain the external balance of payments. Therefore, even workers whose wages did not fall but who depended on imported foods experienced a decline in the real value (purchasing power) of their wages.

Devaluation also caused the local costs of paying the foreign-held debt to rise, but this was offset by governments' defaulting that debt. These defaults gave more room for imports, including the machinery and materials necessary for export production, and it relieved some pressure on government budgets. Costa Rica's repurchase of some of its defaulted external debt at highly discounted prices was innovative.

The international debt moratorium (default) sometimes, as in El Salvador and Costa Rica, was extended to domestic private debt and interest rate reductions. This was done to give coffee finqueros relief from creditors and, in the case of Costa Rica, to protect small holders from foreclosure. Neither devaluation nor debt default was feasible for the Carías government in Honduras, however, because the U.S. dollar circulated as legal tender in Honduras and the client status of the Honduran government in respect to the United States discouraged defaulting debt held in the United States.

In the governments' efforts to keep expenditures down, they cut and frequently deferred the wages of public employees. (They treated the military more cautiously.) Budgetary deficits were hard to avoid, however, and governments borrowed to cover fiscal deficits. Because defaulted international loans made international credit difficult to obtain, most of the borrowing was from domestic sources. In a small way, deficit-financed government activity probably did stimulate domestic demand and income and thus in itself contributed to mitigating the effect of the economic downturn for those producing for domestic markets.

The policies pursued by national governments, used in different combinations in different places, succeeded in keeping coffee production and exportation profitable through the 1930s, albeit at lower levels than in the 1920s. And the United Fruit Company declared stock dividends every year through the 1930s, indicating profitability. The impact of government policies, however, was uneven, and large growers prospered more than small ones. This pattern led to greater concentrations of coffee land in Guatemala, El Salvador, and Costa Rica, despite efforts to protect small growers in Costa Rica. But while the holdings of coffee land became more concentrated, finqueros quit expanding the amount of land devoted to coffee, thus reducing the dispossession of small holders.

These directly defensive actions were not, however, the sole policy ventures of the Central American governments during the depression. The governments of both Costa Rica and Guatemala encouraged the United Fruit Company's expansion of Pacific coast banana plantations in order to escape from diseases. All of the governments also launched road construction projects, which were especially ambitious in Guatemala and Costa Rica. In Guatemala, this work was done with unpaid, conscripted labor, so there were no direct increases of income and demand resulting from it, although it lowered the cost of transporting exports, imports, and domestic products for domestic markets. The improved roads also facilitated the movement of troops from one area to another, increasing social control. In Costa Rica, in contrast, the purpose of the road-building program was at least in part to have been an effort to relieve unemployment, and its cost contributed to Costa Rica's fiscal problems that became chronic during the decade.

The depression and the attendant political forces propelled powerful individuals to the forefront of national histories, and in El Salvador and Nicaragua these individuals broke the pattern of presidents recruited from the economic elites. Ubico represented a change for Guatemala because he *was* a member of the landed elite, but his administration was not an exception to the new Central American pattern of an expanded state run by professional politicians, including military officers. Moreover, these individuals' idiosyncrasies indelibly colored the era. It was the peculiar circumstances of the period that led to Martínez's ardent convictions about theosophy, Ubico's obsession with Napoleon, and Somoza's voracious greed to be historically significant.

The importance of individual presidents indicated the threat of social dissolution resulting from the depression's effects on the export sector. These individuals were pushed up to unify and lead a weakened elite and at the same time were imposed on the elites by circumstances. Their prominence also indicated a more fundamental change of the decade: the clear tendency in all of the nations for the state to grow in size and authority. By the end of the 1930s, all of the states had developed greater capacity to intervene directly into matters of production and finance. These interventions were necessary for the state to preserve the export sectors and the social formations based on them. Nevertheless, the political changes continued to express the diversity of national patterns, which, as I argued in Chapter 3, primarily reflected differences in the organization of export production.

The Guatemalan state of the early twentieth century, needed to monitor the coercive labor mobilization of large Indian communities, was the most developed. Honduras possessed a small, ineffective state and a weak military because the control of labor was done in the foreign-owned export sector with little public control necessary. The strength of the Salvadoran propertied class at the site of production also required a rather small state, although it did require a substantial militarized police force. The U.S. occupation of Nicaragua in the second and third decades of the twentieth century meant that state power was not in local hands. Before they left, the occupying forces had created a military that became an instrument of personal rather than class rule. Finally, the Costa Rican state was dominated by a wealthy oligarchy, but the relatively broad base of landownership and political participation led to its responding to a wider range of citizen concerns. Moreover, the state and military had never been needed to enforce coercive labor mobilization systems, and the Tinoco administration had demonstrated that the military could be used against the interests of the elite. After Tinoco was overthrown in 1919, the military was deliberately weakened.

These patterns were manifested in the scope and effectiveness of the states' policies that reacted to the imperatives of the depression. For instance, the relatively undeveloped character of predepression state policy in El Salvador meant that violence was one of the few instruments available in its repertoire of social control measures, and the same was true for Honduras, though there was less need for it. The policies of these states, then, contrasted with the more sophisticated responses in Guatemala and Costa Rica. The last two governments certainly did employ violence, but they did not need to rely so exclusively on it.

The exigencies brought upon by the depression, though they varied considerably in their urgency, forced all of the Central American states to implement policies that represented a definite break with the more laissez-faire, noninterventionist nature of state policy during the late nineteenth and early twentieth centuries. It is important, however, to recognize that even the ideal of laissez-faire in liberal political and economic theory never conceived of a state that did not have an economic role.

For instance, the liberal state needed to conduct international relations, regulate credit and monetary issue, and maintain a legal and judicial system capable of enforcing private contracts. This last function, expressed here in conventionally abstract, sanitized language, meant that the state protected private property in production from threats posed by those without property, thus maintaining the fundamental inequality underlying a wage system. So while the ideal state's judicial and legislative system was to be neutral in respect to conflicts among individuals and segments of the propertied classes, it could not be neutral in respect to conflicts between propertied and nonpropertied classes. Only in Costa Rica was there even any pretense at neutrality in the sense of propertied versus nonpropertied.

The Central American governments worked hard and on the whole quite effectively to protect propertied interests in the export sector from the collapse of the world economy. The direct, unambiguous, and unqualified defense of the propertied by those governments distinguishes Central America from other Latin American nations. Although the depression precipitated immediate political crises in all Latin American export-oriented economies, populist leaders ended up as presidents in some nations.[8] Although populism in Latin America is at best an ambiguous concept, the fact remains that during the 1930s and early 1940s, leaders with significant support by the urban working class took political power in Brazil, Mexico, Chile, Colombia, and Argentina.

Even in nations where export interests took over political control, as initially in Argentina through the military, state policy had to incorporate the interests of the nonpropertied strata. Although Uruguay was the Latin American pioneer in creating a modern welfare state, governments in the economically most advanced nations of Latin America during the 1930s implemented such legislation as social insurance and income maintenance as well as labor codes that went beyond the punitive by recognizing the right to form unions and to strike. Formal labor codes, including those legislated in Central America during the 1940s and early 1950s, were another avenue of increased state power. Such codes transformed struggles between workers and employers from worksites to the national political arena. The state was explicitly established as the arbiter and mediator of strikes, which accordingly were directed at influencing the state rather than employers.

Although there were some weak gestures in the direction of ameliorative social policies by the Central American governments, they remained weak gestures. The small numbers of nonpropertied urban dwellers in Central America in the early years of the depression meant that, in contrast to Brazil, Colombia, and the nations of the southern cone of South America, keeping unemployed workers from rioting in city streets was not as great a concern. The same lack of significant urbanization, in which people are directly and immediately dependent on markets for survival, had very important economic consequences as well. It prevented the depression, which weakened the world market's influences, from stimulating the domestic production of previously imported manufactured goods ("import-substituting industrialization").

The growth of domestic, import-substituting production of manufactured goods in Central America was slight during the 1930s—limited to textiles, cement, and a handful of consumer goods—and the principal increase in import-substituting production occurred in agriculture. The decline of profitability of export agriculture made alternative crops more attractive. The contraction of the value of exports (and thus the availability of foreign exchange for purchasing imports) along with currency devaluations made food imports harder to obtain and more expensive in terms of local currency.

As a consequence, there was some increase in the production of foodstuffs for local markets and a decline in the importation of food. That is, Central American agriculture became less specialized in export crops, diversifying a bit to produce food for domestic consumption directly rather than indirectly—export earnings that financed the importation of food. Some of this increased production of food for local purchase came from switching from export production, but as noted earlier, the physical volumes of coffee did not decline. The rise in the domestic price of food induced some small holders to increase production for sale on local markets, a process that was supported by the expansion of roads, especially in Guatemala and Costa Rica, and increased the integration of the national economies. The increased opportunities for profitable sale of foodstuffs on the local markets, along with fewer encroachments on small landholdings by finqueros, probably increased the material welfare of the majority of campesinos in the coffee-exporting nations. But although land areas devoted to coffee cultivation did not expand, the concentration of coffee landholdings became greater.

Another form of agricultural diversification was initiating or expanding the production of export crops other than coffee and bananas. Cotton, tobacco, cattle, timber, and cacao are examples, but agricultural export diversification did not amount to much during the decade. More important export diversification came from mining rather than agriculture. The value of gold exports from Nicaragua, Honduras, and, to a lesser extent, El Salvador grew significantly during the 1930s. The largest mining companies in Nicaragua and Honduras were subsidiaries of U.S. firms.

The depression in Central America, then, was not a complete economic debacle. Coffee output was fairly stable, and there were some new types of production. Although none of the new lines of production was especially significant in itself, together they added up to less than economic catastrophe. There was very little alteration in the economic structure and the social order.

As already noted, however, there were some very important changes, especially in the character of the national state. I have emphasized the extent to which the five national states acted to preserve the economic structure and the social order. This effort is frequently observed, but what too often is missed is that in their performing of this function, the relationship between the state and society in Central America underwent a watershed change. To protect privilege and power in the Central American nations, the power and capacity of states to act effectively in a range of new policy areas grew considerably. If the state can successfully use violence to suppress the majority of a population, and if it can regulate economic life well enough to maintain the incomes of the propertied elite, it is an institution that potentially could be used against the privileged whom it was created to protect.

This takes us back to the discussion of state forms from the second chapter, where I compared the social and political visions of the Liberal and Conservative parties shortly after independence from Spain. The imperative to respond to the depression undermined the Liberal state that had been created in the export boom of the late nineteenth and early twentieth centuries. What replaced it was, in these very general terms, more like the early Conservative, even colonial, organization of political power, even though its purpose and social bases were different.

Moreover, the political institutions that connected the state to civil society, even if only to the very top of civil society, were drastically curtailed. To protect the existing structure of power and privilege, the power of the state was enhanced substantially and political institutions that linked the state to the upper reaches of civil society, especially political parties and competitive elections, were severely weakened or destroyed. For instance, the dictatorships of Martínez and Ubico eliminated the traditional political party systems of El Salvador and Guatemala, and the party system of Costa Rica would be greatly transformed by the end of the 1940s. Liberal and Conservative party labels were retained as empty shells under Somoza in Nicaragua, existing only to the extent that they served Somoza's political manipulation of domestic and foreign constituencies. Only in Honduras, the politically and economically most backward of the five nations, did the old Liberal Party and the conservative National Party survive.

Therefore, the access to militarized states and influence over state policy, even by those whose interests were being served by those states and their policies, became negotiable rather than automatic. Export elites remained the most powerful economic group in the nations and often functioned as potent veto groups. Neverthless, it is revealing that during the 1930s, coffee exporters, ranchers, mine owners, and other producer groups founded, for the first time, industry associations through which they coordinated their political lobbying. These industry associations did not reflect greater political power by export elites; instead, they were the institutionalized expression of the exporters' new political status as pressure groups that did not directly hold the reins of power.

The economic elites, therefore, who encouraged and benefited from the establishment of states capable of preserving the social order, were in danger of becoming dependent clients of those same states. That is, the very nature of the success posed dangers. This varied state by state, of course, and, as noted in Chapter 3, the Guatemalan state in the 1920s already contained some of these tendencies toward relative autonomy and detachment from even the most powerful in civil society. The depression, however, pushed all of the Central American state systems in that direction.

It was during the 1940s that some of this dialectical potential—a strong state created to protect propertied interests becoming a threat to those very interests—began to be realized.

The War and Political Reform

When Europe became engulfed by war in 1939, it was yet another blow to coffee exporters. During the 1930s, European markets for Central American coffee had risen in importance, and by the end of the 1930s Costa Rica was selling almost half of its exports to England and Germany. El Salvador, Guatemala, and Nicaragua also were sending around 10 percent of their exports to Europe. Because Germany was by far the largest European customer for Central American coffee, coffee prices were substantially depressed when exports to the Third Reich were curtailed. Problems from the closing of the German market were exacerbated by the shortage of ships, commandeered for the war effort. Figures 4.1 and 4.2 show the effects of the beginning of the war on exports and economic growth, which were hardest hit in Guatemala and Costa Rica.

The crisis for coffee exports in the first years of the war was quickly resolved. In 1940, an international coffee agreement signed with the United States established quotas of coffee to be shipped to the United States at a guaranteed price, and both the quotas and the price were generous. Banana exports, however, did not benefit from a comparable agreement, and the shortage of shipping also continued to hinder banana exports. The contraction of banana exports was to some extent offset during the war by the United Fruit Company's efforts, paid for by the U.S. government, to grow tropical strategic materials that were in short supply because of the Japanese occupation of southeastern Asia. Of the various materials tried, only Manila hemp and rubber were of much importance.

When the United States entered the war after Pearl Harbor, in late 1941, all five of the Central American republics responded quickly by declaring war on the Axis powers. Several Central American governments, as a sign of good faith, sent German nationals to the United States to be interned as enemy aliens. Because the United States embargoed all goods produced by German, Italian, and Japanese citizens wherever they resided, Central American exporters had to be able to assure the U.S. government that no enemy aliens had been involved in export production in order to continue to send coffee to the United States and receive the benefits of the coffee agreement.

There were a number of German nationals residing in Costa Rica and Nicaragua, and although there were German immigrants in El Salvador, they were much more likely to have become Salvadoran citizens. The German coffee fincas in Nicaragua posed no problem for government policy. Somoza, moving in ways that were becoming the hallmark of the dynasty, bought them (and some German-owned commercial firms) for his own. In that the alternative for the German owners was to have their property expropriated by the government, Somoza paid bargain prices. In Costa Rica, class allegiances were strong enough for Costa Rican landowners to help German nationals protect their property from the government of Rafael Calderón Guardia, which acted vigorously to confiscate German property.

Moving against the Germans in Guatemala posed a major problem for the government of Guatemala, where a large proportion of the coffee crop was grown on fincas owned and operated by German nationals. Although Ubico temporized sufficiently to assure access to U.S. markets, he was unwilling to give in to U.S. pressure to expropriate the fincas owned by German nationals. There is no evidence that he had any special regard for the German finqueros of Alta Verapaz. On the contrary, early in his military career he was the district commander in Alta Verapaz and had several disagreements with the German finqueros, who succeeded in having him reassigned to another district. His reluctance to move against large landed property was that he believed such expropriations smacked of communism, and as he was a wealthy landlord in his own right, he disliked establishing such a precedent. In any case, he eventually did expropriate the fincas and had them operated by state managers.

The coffee agreements and subsidized experiments in tropical agriculture conducted by the United Fruit Company were only two sources of U.S. public money for the region during the war. There were U.S. naval or air bases in all nations except Honduras, the construction of the Pan American highway went ahead with an infusion of U.S. funding, and the Lend Lease program enabled governments to buy armaments on favorable terms. Nicaragua's Somoza was at the head of that queue.

By 1943, economic activity in Central America had generally returned to predepression levels. Indeed, there were inflationary pressures that led to food price controls in some Central American countries, controls that probably discouraged domestic food production for local consumption. The major problem, of course, and the reason for the inflation, was that although export markets were adequate, the war effort precluded imports from Europe and the United States. The income generated from exports, then, could be used to purchase only domestic products, and the lack of imported machinery and materials discouraged domestic industrial production to grow enough to meet domestic demand and to substitute for imported goods. As a consequence, prices rose.

In this period, Central American governments piled up considerable amounts of foreign exchange (mostly U.S. dollars), because they could not be used to purchase imports. The Nicaraguan and Honduran governments, always eager to make a good impression on the U.S. government, paid back a large part of their external debts with the dollars. The other three countries also used the wartime balances to pay off portions of their external debts, but they waited until the postwar inflation had reduced the real value of that debt.

As in the case of the depression years, when imports were available but foreign exchange was scarce, the war-induced shortages of imports and consequent inflations most adversely affected urban residents, who were dependent on markets for virtually all of their consumer goods. And although Central America had not begun to experience the large-scale urban growth that occurred after World War II, city dwellers were beginning to be a more important component of national populations in the 1930s and 1940s. Tables 4.1 and 4.2 show the general increase in Central American population during this time and its ethnic and racial composition. Table 4.3 shows that in spite of unevenness in pace and extent, the urban populations of all five nations were sizable by the end of World War II.

Much of the economic and political activity of the depression and war years reoriented national life toward the cities, especially the capital cities. Greater urbanization was promoted by the weakness of the agricultural export sector, general population growth, rise of commerce in locally produced foodstuffs and other goods, deliberate efforts by strong Central American presidents to make the capital cities modern showcases, and especially the increases in employment and the scope of policy by the central government.

White-collar workers were an increasingly important component of the rising urban population. The political presence of this group has already been noted: Costa Rican middle classes were angered by the U.S. role in the 1919 overthrow of Tinoco in Costa Rica; Guatemalan middle classes participated in the overthrow of Estrada Cabrera in 1920; and Salvadoran middle classes supported Araujo but acquiesced in Martínez's brutal crushing of the 1932 revolt. The size and political importance of urban white-collar workers, which grew substantially during the 1930s and 1940s, warrant looking more closely at the character of this group.

TABLE 4.1 Population of Central American Nations, 1920-1960 (in thousands)

	1920	1930	1940	1950	1960
Guatemala	1,270	1,760	2,200	2,810	3,830
Honduras	720	950	1,150	1,430	1,950
El Salvador	1,170	1,440	1,630	1,860	2,450
Nicaragua	640	680	830	1,060	1,410
Costa Rica	420	500	620	800	1,250

Source: Victor Bulmer-Thomas, *The Political Economy of Central America Since 1920* (New York: Cambridge University Press, 1987), p. 310.

TABLE 4.2 Composition of Central American Populations by Geographical Origins, 1940s and 1950 (percentages)

		American Indian	European	African	Mixed	Asian	Unspecified
Guatemala	1950	53.6	--	--	--	--	46.4
Honduras	1945	6.7	2.1	1.2	89.9	0.0	--
El Salvador	1940	20.0	--	5.0	75.0	--	--
Nicaragua	1940	9.5	13.3	11.1	65.3	--	0.7
Costa Rica	1950	0.3	1.9	--	97.6	0.1	--

Source: Statistical Abstract of Latin America, 1964, Vol. 4 (Los Angeles: UCLA Latin American Center, 1964), p. 30.

In referring to urban white-collar workers, I am talking about the "modern middle class"—socially and occupationally heterogeneous white-collar workers—which includes schoolteachers, bookkeepers, administrators, managers, journalists, clerks in shops and offices, and the whole panoply of salaried employees in the public and private sectors. Although self-employed professionals (for example, physicians and lawyers) are members of this new middle class, the overwhelming character of the stratum is conditioned by the fact that the great majority of them are employees. Like wage workers, they are not possessors of property and their income is thus derived from the sale of the only commodity they do possess—their labor services.[9]

But they are not members of the working class, nor should they be considered to have an identity of interest with them. For the most part,

TABLE 4.3 Central American Urbanization, 1910-1950

	Percentage of National Populations in Cities of > 20,000			1950			
					Percentage in Cities of		
	1910	1930	1940	2,500 to 20,000	>20,000	>100,000	Capital City
Guatemala	8.9	10.3	9.8	13.8	11.2	10.2	10.2
Honduras	6.3	4.7	6.1	11.2	6.8	--	5.2
El Salvador	8.8	10.4	12.4	14.8	13.0	8.8	8.8
Nicaragua	10.9[a]	17.9[b]	21.8	19.7	15.2	10.4	10.4
Costa Rica	7.9	13.2	15.4	15.8	17.7	17.7	17.7

[a] 1920
[b] 1933

Sources: Statistical Abstract of Latin America, 1980, Vol. 20 (Los Angeles: UCLA Latin American Center, 1980), pp. 77, 78; and Richard W. Wilkie, *Latin American Population and Urbanization Analysis: Maps and Statistics, 1950-1982* (Los Angeles, UCLA Latin American Center Publications, 1984), pp. 214, 267, 280, 318, 362.

they are literate and formally educated, and the conditions of their work generally give them opportunities for advancement, an upward mobility that sharply distinguishes them from wage workers. Indeed, much of their time and energy is spent in setting themselves apart from the working classes socially and culturally, even when their earnings are but slightly, if at all, above those of better-paid wage workers. One of the chief devices they use in this effort is to affect life-styles very distinct from those of the working classes. This includes copying elite consumption patterns as closely as possible, even though Central American middle classes generally preferred U.S. rather than European models. Consumption patterns assume an importance for the middle-class workers beyond subsistence and creature comfort because they involve status and class identification.

The lack of internal group cohesion as well as unclear relations to the means of production—or to production at all—make it difficult to regard middle-class salaried workers as a class, but to avoid introducing confusing terminology I will refer to them as the middle class. But at the same time, it is crucial to remember that they are not the middle class of the English Industrial Revolution. That middle class was the industrial bourgeoisie, in the middle between propertyless workers and the landed elite, possessing the means of industrial production and rapidly becoming the most powerful economic group in the nation.

Unlike the English bourgeoisie, the modern middle class's interest in politics, in Central America as well as in Latin America as a whole, stems more from weakness than from strength. But in their political efforts, their heterogeneity causes problems in formulating a class-based political program. By the 1940s and 1950s, the middle classes in the more urbanized and industrialized South American nations, following the lead of Uruguayan and Chilean middle classes, achieved increased distance from wage workers by such statutory provisions as social security systems strongly biased toward urban salaried employees, minimum salaries (as opposed to wages), and access to consumer credit on favorable terms. These are components of a class agenda of a well-developed middle class, but in Central America during the 1930s and 1940s, national middle classes were only beginning to exercise political influence as a distinct social entity. At this stage, their disparate work situations often meant that their political goals had to be more modest. As a consequence, the goals tended to be very general, essentially oriented toward enabling individuals of the middle class to get ahead. That is, members of the middle classes organized and fought collectively to institutionalize the means for individual social mobility. Examples of these general goals are expanding government employment, establishing meritocratic standards and procedures for filling those jobs, and expanding educational opportunities for the middle class.

The first two goals are clear, but the third calls for some additional discussion. It is one thing to advocate the conditions for social mobility and another to create the conditions so that the chances for such mobility are strongly slanted toward members of the middle classes. This is the reason for the central importance of education in middle-class calculations. For this nonpropertied stratum, degrees from educational institutions are the major means by which they distinguish themselves from the working classes. As important as consumption patterns are, formal education is the ultimate certification of middle-class membership, serving as a passport to a white-collar job.

Although graduation from secondary school was sufficient for many lower-level white-collar jobs, a university degree was a much more valuable certificate. A well-developed, publicly subsidized system of higher education, disproportionately financed by the poor through regressive taxes, is particularly desirable for members of the middle class, who are not financially able to attend foreign universities. The final step, then, is for universities, which certify people for the liberal professions and good managerial and administrative posts, to maintain admission requirements that screen out all but the most fortunate and able young people of working-class backgrounds. These admissions requirements, which are not all strictly academic, are defended on the grounds of academic standards, no matter how low standards are for graduation once admitted.

It is important to distinguish the type of political program put forth by the middle classes from those of the growing working-class movements. Working-class goals at this time were necessarily collective: legitimization of unions and collective bargaining; regulation of wages, hours, and working conditions; establishment of accident and disability insurance; and other aspects of group betterment. These proposals were a definite challenge to the power of employers, and their espousal quickly became cast in overt class conflict terms. Especially (but not only) where nations had formal labor codes, the conflict became generally politicized as the state assumed responsibility for suppressing unions, breaking strikes, and disciplining recalcitrant workers.

Middle-class aspirations, in contrast, do not necessarily conflict with propertied interests, and therefore they can be cast in universal terms: meritocracy, fairness, education, honest government, competence, efficiency, democracy, and so on. Representing special interests as universal principles is not the exclusive property of the middle classes, but it is worth mentioning here because of the extent to which middle-class scholars and policymakers in the United States have believed the rhetoric and identified this politically equivocal group as the safe, democratic alternative to both right-wing and left-wing extremism—that much-desired, albeit elusive, political center.

Middle-class goals required political action because state participation, in the form of legislated procedural changes and expenditures, is necessary for their success. But even if the problem of program and disunity could be overcome, the middle class exerts little direct political influence. Its members are a minority of the population, and they do not occupy a strategic position of independent economic power from which to apply concerted political pressure. Therefore, the greatest advantage and opportunity to influence political decisions are in open campaigns and free elections. Although the middle classes are numerically a small portion of the nations' populations, their literacy, urban location, organization and communication skills, and limited goals make them a much larger and more weighty proportion of the politically active population. Moreover, access to occupations such as legislator and party worker is desirable in itself.

But the numerical and situational weakness of the middle class usually requires them to ally with other constituencies in order to achieve political prominence. With the working classes this can be risky. The Mexican revolution was a cautionary tale for all Latin American middle classes. It graphically demonstrated how the middle class, in the course of building coalitions to advance its quest for political power, could inadvertently unleash political forces that could not be contained within the orderly framework upon which the middle classes depended. Middle-class reformers in Mexico were able to topple Porfirio Diaz rather easily in 1910, but when they subsequently came up against strong conservative resistance, the reformers helped to mobilize campesinos to help them. These new allies overwhelmed the conservative resistance and the middle-class reformers, and much of postrevolution Mexican history revolves around the strenuous and not entirely successful efforts to depoliticize the campesinos.

The need to ally with more powerful social classes, then, requires that middle-class politicians constantly monitor and adjust their alliances. This accounts for the opportunism that has characterized the political style of the middle classes throughout Latin America. The most frequently observed expression of this is when urban and rural workers' movements, initially allied with middle-class parties, threaten to disrupt orderly procedures and to institute significant alterations in the structure of social power and privilege; middle-class participants then shift their allegiances to those eager to restore "order."

The pattern of middle-class political activity, which alternatively leads the way to more open political possibilities and then to retreat, complemented the development of enlarged, centralized state systems. These are important themes in the political struggles in Central America during the 1940s and 1950s.

Reform and Reaction

The year 1944 was an extremely active year for democratic struggles in all five Central American republics. Hernández Martínez and Ubico were overthrown, Carías and Somoza faced severe challenges to their rule, and elections in Costa Rica set the stage for a civil war four years later.

El Salvador

Hernández Martínez was under increasing fire from Salvadoran middle-class civilians for the corruption, inefficiency, and the closed character of his regime and from the military, which was uneasy about the existence of presidentially supported paramilitary units. Hernández Martínez put down a military revolt in early 1944, and true to form, he retaliated by executing a number of possible participants. Unlike in 1932, however, the brutality of the retaliation was directed at few people, but because many of the victims were members of the officer corps, it provoked strong middle-class reaction from both civilian and military factions. Although there was no rural participation in the subsequent strikes and demonstrations, the U.S. government, fearing political instability, joined the chorus calling for Hernández Martínez to resign.

After picking his successor, Hernández Martínez did resign in 1944. The desire of the middle class for elections was in accord with the "spirit of the times" (that is, with U.S. foreign policy), and Roosevelt's Four Freedoms and the United Nations charter were frequently heard at political rallies. The pressure was so well orchestrated among urban groups that elections were scheduled for 1945. As the campaign heated up, however, it seemed to confirm the worst fears of the propertied class and military about the strength of radical reformism. As a result, the military drastically narrowed the range of permissible programs and participants, and there were no civilian candidates in the election. The elected regime conducted affairs in a style reminiscent of Hernández Martínez, and the regime was overthrown by a younger and more progressive group of army officers in 1948.

In the late 1940s, these young majors (soon to be colonels) established the terms that would dominate Salvadoran politics for thirty years. The politics was modern in that it allowed political competition among middle-class and oligarchical groups with programs that fell within narrowly constrained definitions of legitimacy. In addition, the government condoned closely supervised urban trade unions but prohibited rural working-class organization. The vigilance against left-wing activity was again in accord with the spirit of the times (U.S. foreign policy), which by the late 1940s and early 1950s was almost exclusively defined by zealous anticommunism. The anticommunism of the United States was compatible with interests of the Salvadoran upper classes, military, and middle classes, all of whom found it convenient to limit both programs and participants in the political arena.

Because El Salvador exemplifies some salient features of then-current U.S. thinking about economic development, this is a good point to speak of more generally. U.S. anticommunism was the beginning of large-scale foreign aid by the United States to friendly regimes. Table 4.4 shows that El Salvador received comparatively little during this period, but still, U.S. foreign aid was a potential source of economic and political resources even for governments with little domestic support. This was especially valuable for the military, for which foreign aid could reduce dependence on the local tax base, budgeting processes, and indeed domestic politics.

On the positive side, but still closely linked to postwar anticommunism, was U.S. encouragement of "economic development," the importance of which was also proclaimed by international agencies such as the United Nations Economic Commission for Latin America (ECLA, or its Spanish acronym, CEPAL) and the International Bank for Reconstruction and Development (or World Bank). The enthusiasm for economic development was propelled in good part by the firm conviction among North American academics and officials of U.S. and international agencies that economic development would transform Third World "traditional" soci-

TABLE 4.4 U.S. Foreign Aid to Central America, 1945-1960 (in $1,000)

	Total Grants and Credits	Military & Security	Economic Dev't & Tech. Assist.	Other[a]
Guatemala	111,045	59,218 (53.2)[b]	8,134	43,693
Honduras	36,609	14,526 (39.7)	14,446	7,637
El Salvador	12,334	7,326 (59.3)	1,242	3,766
Nicaragua	49,814	8,402 (16.9)	3,495	37,917
Costa Rica	72,179	11,011 (15.3)	2,490	58,678
Total	$281,981	$100,483 (35.6)	$29,807	$151,691

[a] Includes Export-Import Bank and agricultural trade credits, along with "Other" and Miscellaneous" categories.

[b] Numbers in parentheses indicate percentage of total.

Source: Statistical Abstract of Latin America, 1961, Vol. 1 (Los Angeles, UCLA Latin American Center, 1961), p. 48.

eties into "modern" societies that were stable, capitalist, democratic (but programmatically limited), and equitable. The motor of economic development, at a time of the rise of Keynesian economics among U.S. economists, was an activist state that encouraged economic growth, especially of the industrial sector.

As we have seen, the general impulse for economic growth was not new to Central America. Substitute "progress" for "modernization" and it sounds very much like the Liberal programs of the nineteenth century, including the conviction that progress is fundamentally a technical, "scientific" process rather than a social one. Nevertheless, there are some important differences between economic development in the second half of the twentieth century and economic progress in the late nineteenth century. One of them was the former's emphasis on the economic growth of urban and industrial sectors, and another is the political context in which it took place, including the role of active state policy.

Regarding El Salvador, it was noted at the end of the last chapter that comprehensive economic development is not necessarily in the interests of the export elite, as an export elite. But after all, it was to be capitalist growth, and consistent with the then-fashionable prescriptions of development economics, the major incentives for expanding production and establishing new branches of economic activity were primarily aimed to those who held most of the economic resources. The distribution of resources and benefits was not seen to be an important issue, because faith in material benefits trickling down to the majority of the population followed comfortably from underlying beliefs in social harmony. The commercial and financial branches of the Salvadoran propertied class, therefore, were in an excellent position to profit, and the landed segments were not to be threatened.

Even this conception of economic development, emphasizing the stability of existing property relations, might have been construed as risky by the already wealthy and powerful, and it is doubtful that they would have chosen such policies had they still been a true oligarchy. The important point here is that even though the Salvadoran state continued to safeguard a social structure that benefited the propertied classes, it did not do so at their behest. Nevertheless, the elite continued to exercise formidable veto power in economic affairs, and the Salvadoran state, among the five Central American nations, was the least interventionist in economic matters. Moreover, in contrast with Guatemala and even Honduras in the early 1970s, the national military in El Salvador did not possess a monopoly over the instruments of official violence. As mentioned in the last chapter, a strong National Guard existed, which was responsible for peace in the countryside and was controlled by local landowners, and the Salvadoran military did not have sure control over the urban police force.

With the end of World War II, rapid economic growth in the United States (contrary to U.S. economists' predictions) and newly opened European markets markedly increased markets for Central American exports. Coffee prices practically tripled in the years immediately after the war. Figure 4.3 records the rapid rise in the value of Salvadoran exports at this time, and Figure 4.2 shows the general expansion of national output. This economic boom was part of the more general process of putting the export economy back on track, and it gave the elite more confidence and leverage. The concentration of coffee production, as in Guatemala, Costa Rica, and Nicaragua, had increased substantially in El Salvador during the 1930s and 1940s. In El Salvador during the early 1950s, almost 42 percent of agricultural land was in holdings over 850 acres. (The corresponding figures for Guatemala and Costa Rica were 27.5 percent and 47.4 percent.)

The growth of export values in the decade after the war strengthened not only the export elites but also the fiscal position of the state. Existing taxes, based primarily on export and import volumes or values, yielded greater revenue, and the Salvadoran state instituted new taxes. These new taxes included an augmentation of Hernández Martínez's earlier income tax, which explicitly excluded coffee and cotton producers, who

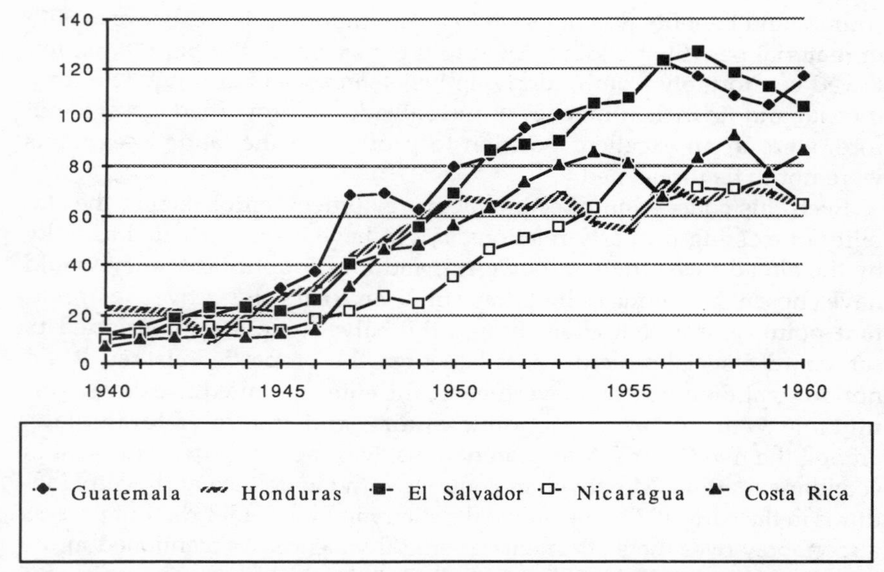

FIGURE 4.3 Value of Central American exports, 1940–1960 (U.S.$ millions). *Source:* Adapted from Victor Bulmer-Thomas, *The Political Economy of Central America Since 1920* (New York: Cambridge University Press, 1987), p. 326.

paid a special export tax. Nevertheless, the state's ability to mobilize resources was significantly strengthened in the decade after the war, and the state's promotion of economic development, primarily through roads, airports, hydraulic projects, and other infrastructural investments, was financially feasible. Industrial growth in El Salvador during the decade after the war was greater than in the rest of the region, although even by 1954 industrial production still constituted less than 15 percent of total output.

The conventional developmentalism of the Salvadoran regime and the limited political competition of the 1950s and 1960s fitted in very nicely with middle-class aspirations. Because the promotion of economic development was seen, at root, to be a technical matter, and one that correct government policy could achieve, there was ever greater need for well-trained, certified technicians in the government bureaucracy. And the extent to which growth policies with strong urban emphases were effective, more middle-class professional employment would be available in the private sector. And political competition, albeit with limited scope, ensured a prominent political place for middle-class interests and the function of political brokering.

Guatemala

Many of these same issues and forces were apparent throughout Central America. They were apparent in Guatemala, where politics was affected by many of the same ingredients apparent in El Salvador but combined in very different and more dramatic ways. University students and the urban middle class, who were most vulnerable to the scarcities and inflation of the early years of the war as well as closed out of politics by Ubico's rule, were in the forefront of the opposition to the Ubico regime. The opposition gained momentum in the urban areas when Hernández Martínez in El Salvador was overthrown in 1944 and Ubico offered him political asylum in Guatemala. As in El Salvador, the Four Freedoms and the United Nations charter made frequent appearances at antigovernment rallies. As in the case of Hernández Martínez, Ubico's violent suppression of the demonstrations and strikes galvanized anti-Ubico sentiment. He resigned in 1944, turned power over to an ally, and retired to New Orleans.

Ubico's successor was quickly deposed by young military officers allied with urban workers, students, and members of the middle class, a struggle that included their fighting Indians trucked in from the countryside by the regime. After the coup, political leadership was consolidated in a three-man junta, which included Major Carlos Arana Osorio and Captain Jacobo Arbenz. The junta sponsored the 1945 constitution, which among other provisions granted universal adult franchise, except for illiterate women, and guaranteed funding for the national university. The junta organized an open and honest election, and the overwhelming victor was Juan José Arévalo, a Guatemalan who had been teaching in an Argentine university.

Arévalo assumed the presidency in 1946 with tremendous popular enthusiasm for a reformist platform informed by his admiration for Franklin Roosevelt's New Deal and by what he described as "spiritual socialism."[10] The timing was fortuitous in that coffee prices and export values were beginning a tremendous rise, which helped to finance his ambitious program of governmentally initiated reforms. Arévalo's administration, with a cooperative legislature, implemented Guatemala's first progressive health care, social insurance, and education policies, sponsored literacy campaigns, laid extensive plans for national power and transportation systems, and provided increased credit for small businesses.

While the urban middle class was the principal beneficiary of these policies, the Arévalo government did take some important steps to improve the lot of rural inhabitants. A major step was the repeal of Ubico's vagrancy law along with legislation that reduced rents on some land and restricted some landowners' power over tenants. In addition, Arévalo's administration distributed to campesinos some of the publicly owned fincas appropriated from German nationals. Although limited in their reach, these policies were symbolically important for all campesinos and materially beneficial for some.

The most important reforms of Arévalo's term in office were political, promoting an unprecedented range of political participation. Although Guatemalan Communists were harassed a bit and not legalized during Arévalo's six-year presidential term, his presidency supported an immense increase in popular organizations, especially in urban areas. The 1947 labor code gave workers the right to organize, strike, and bargain collectively. Rural workers did not receive the same rights until the very end of Arévalo's presidency. But the institution of democratic procedures at the local level, including the popular election of municipal officials, was the source of considerable activity and mobilization of the population outside main urban centers. In some areas, however, because political decentralization occurred without significantly changing the structures of economic power, local landowners were able to reassert a control over local affairs that they had lost with Ubico's political centralization.

Arévalo's caution in confronting the power of the landlord class in the countryside reflected the fragility of his administration, which withstood more than twenty coup attempts. The largest and bloodiest one occurred at the very end of his presidential term. Much of the opposition, combining the reactionary forces of landowners, the Church, and sections of the military with urban factions that had initially supported Arévalo, had coalesced behind the leadership of Arévalo's military chief of staff, Carlos Arana Osorio, who had been a member of the junta that had overseen the transition from Ubico to Arévalo's presidency. Arana was killed in an ambush in 1949, and the resulting revolt by the heterogeneous opposition was put down in a struggle that included distributing weapons to the populace from military armories. This monumental step was taken by Arévalo's defense minister, Jacobo Arbenz, another member of the early junta and who was accused by critics of involvement in the assassination.

The revolt was decisively crushed. The euphoria of popular action was carried over to the elections of 1950, and Arbenz easily defeated the conservative candidate, General Miguel Ydígoras Fuentes, who was best known as an enforcer of Ubico's vagrancy laws. (The government took no chances, however, and harassed the opposition campaign.) Strengthened by a population whose political mobilization had been made possible by Arévalo's political reforms, the Arbenz administration turned to economic reforms and especially to the redistribution of land.

The 1952 agrarian reform law was heavily influenced by the recommendations of a study conducted by the World Bank at that time. The law was an attempt to create an agrarian capitalism in Guatemala capable of producing equitable economic growth. And it was a capitalist vision, predominantly oriented to the creation of small private landholdings. In a year and a half, almost a million acres of land were expropriated and distributed to 100,000 campesino families. The distribution of land accelerated the process of campesino political organization, and increasingly rural unions and peasant leagues became the dominant political organizations in the countryside and locus of the struggles over the distributions of land. The distribution of land was chaotic, and the lack of complementary services, such as credit, added to the organizational problems and impeded output in many of the areas affected.

The implementation of the reforms provoked sharp responses by those whose unused lands were targeted for expropriation and redistribution. The most powerful reaction came from the most powerful landowner, the United Fruit Company, whose lands constituted about one-third of the expropriations. The United Fruit Company had been unhappy with the unionization of its transportation and plantation workers, with the national transportation plan that was undermining its monopoly of commerce through the Caribbean coast, and with the first governmental audit of its books, which resulted in a large bill for back taxes.

The land reform, however, was even more serious. The Guatemalan government was prepared to compensate the United Fruit Company (albeit in government bonds) for its expropriated lands by the amount that the United Fruit Company had valued them for tax purposes. The use of self-appraisals for tax purposes as the basis for compensating landowners for expropriated land has a certain appeal, and it was also used in Colombia in the 1940s. The United Fruit Company considered it grossly unfair. The company argued that the land was actually worth more than twenty times the declared amount and demanded what in its eyes was full compensation.

This behavior was not unusual, and many other landowners protested and appealed decisions by the land reform agency. The United Fruit Company was distinctive, however, in that in addition to protesting to the Guatemalan government it appealed successfully to the U.S. government. The appeal and protest were couched in the most effective terms possible: anticommunism.

Although the buoyancy of the international economy in the postwar years made this period a good time to effect ambitious reforms that required fiscal resources, the character of international politics made the period less than optimal for serious change. The strongly democratic tide of World War II had waned, the rhetoric of preemptive reform of the Alliance for Progress had not yet arrived, and the Cold War reigned everywhere that U.S. and Soviet influence reached. Fear of communism in the United States was at a peak, complete with Senator Joseph McCarthy's witch-hunt. One of the ironies is that because Ubico and post-Ubico conservatives had so vigorously labeled any progressive initiative as Communist, Communists were probably more popular in Guatemala than their actual contributions deserved. For the same reasons, Guatemalan communism was certainly more feared outside Guatemala than its influence warranted. There is no doubt that Arbenz, along with his active and committed wife, was less concerned about the role of Communists in Guatemala than Arévalo had been, but the Communists' direct influence does not deserve the space that so much scholarship on this period of Guatemalan history, from whatever political angle, has devoted to counting Communists in and out of the administration.

During the height of the Cold War, therefore, the Eisenhower administration was very receptive to stories about the Communist menace blossoming in Guatemala, reinforced as they were by the United Fruit Company's well-financed and well-orchestrated U.S. media campaign. Moreover, the U.S. Department of State and the Central Intelligence Agency may also have been especially receptive to the stories coming from the United Fruit Company and eager to act as the company's collection agency. John Foster Dulles and Allen Dulles, Eisenhower's secretary of state and director of the CIA respectively, had been lawyers who worked for the United Fruit Company in negotiating the generous (for the United Fruit Company) contracts with the Ubico government in the 1930s, and Allen Dulles had been a member of the United Fruit Company's board of directors. At the same time, however, the U.S. Department of Justice initiated what eventually was a successful antitrust suit against the United Fruit Company.

For whatever combination of reasons, the U.S. government, through the CIA and with the cooperation of Presidents Juan Manuel Gálvez of Honduras and Somoza of Nicaragua, financed and organized an invasion of Guatemala from the Honduran border. The 1954 invasion was headed by two Guatemalan ex-military officers—Carlos Castillo Armas and Miguel Ydígoras Fuentes—and the troops were a motley assortment of mercenaries. Both leaders and troops had been recruited and paid by the CIA, straight from its recent success in Iran, where they had overthrown Mohammed Mossadegh's democratic government and installed the Shah.

Despite U.S. armaments and air support, however, the ineptitude of the invading force almost led to its early military demise. The real test was never to come, however, because after Arbenz ordered the arming of the campesinos, the Guatemalan military notified Arbenz that it would not defend his government from the invasion. Rather than subject the nation to a bloody civil war, Arbenz resigned after being assured by the Guatemalan generals that they would not allow Castillo Armas to rule and that they would protect the reforms of the post-Ubico governments. The generals, pressured by the U.S. ambassador, reneged on their promises, and Guatemala's "Ten Years of Spring" were most definitely over.

Arbenz had been losing domestic political support for a while. His economic program, though mild by the standards of revolutionary governments, certainly alienated the propertied class. Although the landlord class was critical of Arbenz and the land reform and was implicated in unsuccessful coup attempts against him, it seems to have played but a negligible role in the invasion. The attitude of the Catholic Church toward Arbenz and its role in his downfall were similar.

More important in respect to domestic politics, the Arbenz administration was beginning to be estranged from its urban middle-class base. Some of this estrangement resulted from the government's favoring rural and urban working-class constituencies in an obvious attempt to gain their support, and success of the strategy made some portions of the middle class very uneasy. That is, the very fact that organized factions of the urban working classes and especially of Indian campesinos were strong and valued supporters of the regime was disturbing to middle-class groups. This was not just a matter of snobbery and racism, although their influence cannot be dismissed. The central position of middle-class political parties was being supplanted by urban and rural working-class organizations, which were increasingly acting independent of middle-class leadership.

The Guatemalan military was another key constituency, and Arbenz worked hard to maintain its loyalty and to assure it that his distribution of arms to civilians after the assassination of Arana would never be repeated. Arbenz allowed them to disarm civilians shortly after the government beat off the 1949 coup, but many in the military remained suspicious. They remained so despite the fact that Arbenz had a military background and treated the military more solicitously than did Arévalo. But the social turbulence engendered by the political and economic reforms was threatening to senior officers, and the rise of the peasant leagues was a serious challenge to the military's traditional power in the countryside. Arbenz's effort to rearm the campesinos in 1954 could not be tolerated.

Internal divisions within the military led to its unwillingness to defend Arbenz during the invasion and sharply reduced its ability to resist the manipulations by Castillo Armas, Ydígoras, and the U.S. government after the invasion. Despite the extent to which many senior officers disliked Castillo Armas, they were outmaneuvered, and Castillo Armas became president shortly after the invasion. His administration cracked down on the political organizations, especially those in the countryside, and he severely curtailed activities by unions except tame, supposedly nonpolitical urban union activities sponsored by the international arm of the American Federation of Labor and Congress of Industrial Organizations (AFL-CIO), which in effect acted as an arm of the U.S. Department of State. Castillo Armas also reversed much of the land expropriations and superseded the 1952 agrarian reform law with the weak agrarian law of 1956. The government also restored a number of privileges to the Catholic Church, including the right to own property, which had been lost in 1871. The Guatemalan military supported Castillo Armas in these actions, but they remained uneasy about him and the other members of the so-called liberation army of 1954.

One of the most surprising accomplishments of Castillo Armas's presidency was in respect to the United Fruit Company. In exchange for restoring lands lost to the reform, the Guatemalan government imposed a 30 percent tax on United Fruit Company profits in Guatemala, and even though transfer prices made such calculations easily manipulated, it was much more tax than the company had ever had to pay in Guatemala. (Similar agreements had already been reached in Honduras and Costa Rica.) In an additional gesture of gratitude, the United Fruit Company gave back to the government 100,000 acres—almost a third of what had been expropriated.

Castillo Armas was killed in 1957 by one of his bodyguards. Confident that domestic politics were properly under control by then, the military allowed an election with essentially an urban electorate. Ydígoras, campaigning vigorously as a nationalist candidate critical of U.S. influence in Castillo Armas's administration, was elected. The ineptitude and corruption of the Ydígoras administration were legion. The Guatemalan military finally cohered enough to enable it to act in a unified manner because of the shambles of the national government, the rise of rural guerrilla activity in the east, and the likelihood of Arévalo's returning to run for president in the 1963 elections. It overthrew Ydígoras in 1963 and formally instituted military rule without the pretense of democratic elections.

Costa Rica

Although Costa Rica can be considered to have gone through a cycle of reform and reaction during the 1940s, the peak was not nearly as high nor the trough so low as in Guatemala. In fact, the crosscurrents in both reform and reaction were so strong and confusing that the parallel with Guatemala may be more misleading than clarifying.[11]

In 1940, Rafael Calderón Guardia became president through the oligarchical selection process that characterized Costa Rican politics. Despite the fiscal problems of the state brought on by the early days of World War II, Calderón moved quickly to consolidate his authority, establishing political independence from the conservative politicians who had sponsored him. His enthusiastic support for the democratic allies against the Axis in World War II was one of the early sources of tension between him and the economic and political elite, many of whom maintained strong fascist sympathies.

He was able to develop new constituencies to replace those who rapidly were becoming his opponents. One new constituency was the working class, especially those in the banana plantations organized by Communists. The Costa Rican Communist Party was not beholden to the Third International, and thereby it was not subject to rapid changes of direction reflecting the exigencies of Soviet foreign policy. After disagreements with Augusto Sandino of Nicaragua and the debacle of Farabundo Martí's revolt in El Salvador, the Third International had given up on Central America. Unlike the rest of Latin America, then, the Communist parties in the region developed more autonomously. Although some continued to adhere to the rapidly changing lines of Stalin's directives, the Costa Rican party was a more flexible and locally oriented organization.

Another source of political support was the Church hierarchy, led by an energetic and reformist archbishop. The Church's active participation in a coalition that included Communists did not stop it from initiating its own Catholic labor union movement, which competed with some success against the Communists. A third constituency was employees in the state bureaucracy and other urban middle-class groups, who were becoming sufficiently numerous and organized to have a political identity and influence.

With this support and using the powers of the state that had been expanded through the 1930s, Calderón's administration began to implement an ambitious set of reforms, which were the most extensive ever seen in Central America. In addition to such provisions as social security and workers' right to organize, they included equal wages for men and women and a general extension of civil rights. These reforms were strongly oriented toward redistributing income rather than redistributing ownership of the means of production or stimulating increased production, but they quickly earned the enmity of the propertied classes.

In the 1944 elections, which were of questionable fairness, Teodoro Picado, Calderón's choice of a successor, easily defeated León Cortés, the conservative president before Calderón and his former mentor. Calderón's heavy-handed exercise of state power had already led to accusations of authoritarianism and corruption, and these accusations became louder in the next four years.

Although Calderón had reopened the national university, which had been closed since the nineteenth century, and established a social security system favoring salaried employees, middle-class support for the reformist presidencies declined. Members of the middle class, along with those who represented them, were concerned about what they saw as their loss of political influence in the Calderón and Picado administrations. One source of this loss was the growing importance of working-class constituencies, which threatened customary political channels through which the middle classes and their parties depended for access to the political system. Another source was what was seen to be the increasingly authoritarian nature of politics, including the changes in the channels of influence as well as vote fraud and often coercive practices of the dominant coalition. Their opposition was heightened by Picado's imposition of a progressive income tax, which was most easily collected from the carefully recorded salaries of white-collar workers.

A coalition of propertied and middle-class opponents to the regime, under the banner of restoring democracy to Costa Rica, founded a party called the Social Democratic Party, even though parties with that name usually contain strong working-class participation. José Figueres, a vigorous and charismatic member of the propertied class, emerged as the spokesperson and leader of the Social Democrats' opposition to Calderonismo, as the policies of both the Calderón and Picado administrations were labeled.

Figueres was passed over as the Social Democrat Party candidate for the 1948 presidential elections, however, and the party selected a traditionally conservative candidate named Otilio Ulate to run against Calderón. The 1948 elections were hotly contested, and the results themselves were unclear. The election tribunal declared Ulate the winner, but the Calderonist legislature annulled the election. Figueres was certain that the election would be stolen, and drawing upon the arms and organization carefully prepared in advance, his opposition to the Costa Rican government became armed opposition.

The civil war was short but bloody, causing perhaps 2,000 deaths. Figueres's forces received material aid from Arévalo of Guatemala as part of a regional effort to enhance democracy. The suspicion that Arévalo's support was the beginning of a wider effort to rid the region of dictators and to establish Guatemalan suzerainty throughout the isthmus was enough for Somoza to invade in support of the Calderonists. The United States discouraged Somoza by preparing to commit troops from the Panama zone, but its intervention was limited to diplomatic mediation.

Figueres and his allies won the civil war, and Figueres led the revolutionary junta from the middle of 1948 until he turned the presidency over to Ulate at the end of 1949. This was a period of substantial reform. The junta abolished the small, weak Costa Rican army, enfranchised women, and imposed a temporary tax on the rich, including a 15 percent profit tax on the United Fruit Company. In one of its boldest moves, it also nationalized the banks. Although this action no longer threatened the export agriculture elite's control over small coffee growers, as it might have fifty years before, it did mean that entrepreneurs in the small but growing modern urban sector would no longer be handicapped by the export elite's control over credit.

It was also a period of substantial political repression. Labor unions were crushed, workers' parties disbanded, and the Communist Party outlawed. In spite of the 1942 Labor Code, employers were encouraged to fire union activists, an opportunity that the United Fruit Company welcomed, and thousands of people identified with Calderonismo were executed, jailed, exiled, denied employment, and in other ways vigorously persecuted by the government. As in Guatemala six years later, the state condoned union activities only by the nonmilitant unions sponsored by the Church and the AFL-CIO. The crackdown on working-class politics was maintained through the Ulate administration, and the union movement virtually collapsed. Figueres established a new political party, called the National Liberation Party, overcame the suspicion that the reformist side of junta policies had earned him from the conservatives, and was elected president in 1953 with solid middle-class support.

As in El Salvador in the 1950s, once Costa Rican political forces were contained within acceptable bounds, serious efforts could be made to promote capitalist economic growth. One major difference with El Salvador, however, was that "extremist" politics did not have to continue to be so closely monitored and controlled after the first few years. Upper- and middle-class access to state positions and their influence over state policymaking could be maintained while adhering to open, democratic procedures. Those procedures allowed the political interests of poor people, with few resources and extremely fragmented organizations, to compete freely with well-financed and highly organized political interests of the upper and middle classes.

This does not mean, however, that the Costa Rican state ignored the interests of the less fortunate. The presidency of Figueres was noted for attending to the welfare of the urban middle classes and (distinctively Costa Rican) rural middle classes and for sticking to a moderate, pro—United States line. Nevertheless, he did continue the long-term project of constructing a semiwelfare state that formed a net for minimum material welfare. And to help finance these programs, he doubled the tax rate on the United Fruit Company profits—from 15 to 30 percent.

The U.S. government has partially underwritten the "Costa Rican model," and Table 4.3 (in conjunction with Table 4.1) shows that during the 1950s the grants and credits that Costa Rica received from the United States were, on a per capita basis, twice those of Nicaragua (the second ranked) and over six times those of El Salvador (the fifth). In good part this was because of Figueres's staunchly anti-Communist stance and willingness to crack down on radicals. Nonetheless, in many important matters, such as giving asylum to political refugees from regimes favored by the United States (such as post-1954 Guatemala) or in dealings with the United Fruit Company, Figueres maintained a surprising independence from the U.S. State Department.

Honduras

In the 1950s, Honduras also represented an interesting model, but one that has attracted less attention. Again, 1944 was an important beginning. Honduran women organized a multicity protest against political jailings by the Tiburcio Carías regime, and the one in Pedro de Sula was met by police gunfire that killed 100 protestors.

Unlike the situations in El Salvador and Guatemala in 1944, the killings did not spur public protest against the government but probably contributed to Carías's decision not to stand for reelection yet again. Carías chose Juan Manuel Gálvez, a longtime United Fruit Company employee, to be his successor, and he was duly elected in 1948. Even though the Liberal Party had been made legal again to give the appearance of a competitive election with the National Party, the Liberals boycotted the elections after assessing their chances. But as so often is the case in Central American history, the carefully chosen successor did not turn out to be all that malleable after all. Assisted by the postwar recovery of exports, a 15 percent tax on fruit company profits, and advice from the International Monetary Fund, Gálvez began to reorganize the national government, including its financial institutions, strengthen the internal tax system, and enhance the capacity of the bureaucracy to implement and monitor state policy. Furthermore, Gálvez opened up the political process to include more genuine interparty competition between the Liberals and National parties and a much freer press.

One of Gálvez's major economic efforts was to increase coffee production and exports in order to take advantage of the spectacular rise of coffee prices in the decade after World War II, supplementing the earnings from sagging banana exports. Coffee had begun to be grown on a significant scale in Honduras only during the 1940s, but by the middle of the 1950s more acreage was devoted to coffee cultivation in Honduras than in El Salvador. But the organization of coffee cultivation in Honduras was very different from that of El Salvador (and with much lower yields per acre). In Honduras, coffee was grown primarily on medium-sized fincas, which more closely resembled nineteenth-century Costa Rica than the more highly concentrated land tenure patterns of midtwentieth-century Costa Rica, or those of Guatemala and El Salvador, where small holdings had never been a major force. Export diversification reduced the financial dependence of the Honduran state on the fruit companies and helped increase its political independence.

Nevertheless, Gálvez did work closely with Castillo Armas, Somoza, and the CIA to overthrow Arbenz in Guatemala. His involvement in that project apparently was so consuming that he interpreted the 1954 large-scale strike on the United Fruit Company railroads and plantations (and eventually the whole northern banana zone) as revenge by the Communists for his support of the Guatemalan invasion. His first reaction to the strike, therefore, was to have all the Communists on the strike committees jailed. After this had been done, and the strike continued without a pause, he began to take it more seriously as something important in its own right. With the support of the Honduran archbishop and eventually of Gálvez, the strikers won several important concessions, including the right to organize and engage in collective bargaining. These principles were contained in the 1955 labor code. The strikers also won a modest wage increase, but what they did not win was job security. Over the next four years, through mechanization and reorganization, the plantation work force was reduced by half, and thousands of former workers turned to small-scale farming in response.

With the Communist influence in the labor unions decimated, the international arm of the AFL-CIO worked with the banana unions. These unions, because of their narrow goals, were recognized by the government as potentially valuable supporters. Appealing to the plantation and transportation workers and the small urban middle class with a reformist platform, the Liberal Party ran Ramón Villeda Morales against Carías in the 1954 elections. Villeda won a plurality, but for two years he was prevented from assuming the presidency because of fraud perpetrated by Gálvez's vice-president, who had become president after Gálvez's resignation.

The period was one of stronger anticommunism and fewer political openings even for non-Communist parties, but women were enfranchised for the first time in these years. The interim government also raised the tax on fruit company profits to 30 percent. But after a particularly blatant attempt to steal the 1956 elections by the interim government and the National Party, the military overthrew the government. After some struggle within the military, the 1957 constitution was approved and a fair election in 1957 led to Villeda Morales becoming the new president.

The military, however, exacted a high price for its role in setting up new elections, allowing a majority party to take office, and returning to the barracks. The new constitution, which in several ways was a more democratic document than its predecessor, explicitly limited civilian politicians' authority over the military to little more than symbolic functions. With no role in mobilizing and controlling labor in export production, the Honduran military's corporate development had lagged behind that of the militaries in Guatemala, El Salvador, and Nicaragua. But by the 1950s, senior officers were beginning to recognize that the military had institutional interests that might not be consistent with decisions by civilian politicians and were thus eager to reduce civilian control.

Nicaragua

Events in Nicaragua were much less exciting than those in the other four republics in the 1940s and early 1950s. Anastacio Somoza García retained control of the state and National Guard, although he had to work hard to do so. Toward the end of World War II, it began to look as though Somoza's political support was eroding from all sides and that he might not last much longer as president. The overthrow of Hernández Martínez and Ubico stimulated antiauthoritarian sentiment in Nicaragua, as throughout the region. The major political force against Somoza was a coalition of propertied and middle classes. This alliance was uneasy, because the propertied classes would not cooperate with working-class organizations much less allow them to join the anti-Somoza coalition. But middle-class factions (notably the students) were extremely reluctant to cut themselves off from the labor movement, which seemed to have growing political potential. Nevertheless, the middle-class parties were not ready to declare themselves with the working classes and lose their alliance with the propertied classes.

This situation was an ideal opening for Somoza, who in 1944 fashioned a strongly populist rhetoric for the occasion.[12] This new posture included some significant concessions to union activity and led to the nominally progressive 1945 Labor Code, even though many strikes were directed at enterprises secretly owned by Somoza's family. This strategy was successful in that it increased the split between the middle class and propertied class components of the anti-Somoza coalition and at the same time led to a widening gap between the left wing of the working class and the majority of the working class. It is understandable that large segments of the organized working class were attracted to the very generous benefits from joining the governmentally sponsored labor confederation, and by isolating the left wing of the labor movement Somoza was able to keep it in reserve, as it were.

Somoza was still not sure enough of his control to risk precipitating the struggle that would occur by trying to be reelected again. So Somoza chose someone to front for him as president, but again, the chronic problem of Central American politics appeared—the puppet refused to be a puppet and acted independently. After Somoza replaced him with a more pliant president, he had to deal with the United States, which refused diplomatic recognition for this transparent political fraud. He placated the United States by withdrawing his support for the Calderonists in Costa Rica and by crushing the left wing of the Nicaraguan labor movement in an anti-Communist crusade.

The right wing of the propertied class admired Somoza's suppression of the radical faction of the labor movement and achievement of government control over most of organized labor, qualities that made him an attractive political ally after all. In the pacts of 1948 and 1950, Somoza promised these powerful groups (including the Chamorro family, whom we met in Chapters 2 and 3) that neither his family nor the government would interfere with their development of certain economic sectors. Moreover, he would guarantee the Conservative Party an agreed-upon level of political representation in governmental bodies. The result of the successful negotiations was that Somoza received the Conservatives' support for his continued rule and the ambivalent middle-class politicians were left with no coalition partners.

Somoza was a gifted and unscrupulous politician, and he constantly shifted his political alliances, all the while increasing his personal fortune. The loyalty of the National Guard required constant attention, and occasional eruptions of discontent from this quarter had to be be dealt with promptly, with either a carrot or a stick. Even though the formal institutionalization of Somoza's rule was weak, the political resilience of what Somoza built in Nicaragua was amply demonstrated in 1956, when Anastacio Somoza García was assassinated in León. The National Guard arrested and harassed thousands in a vain attempt to ferret out a movement behind the lone assassin, and among those detained and tortured was Pedro Joaquín Chamorro, the editor of *La Prensa*, the Conservative newspaper opposed to Somoza. Nevertheless, at a time of no serious internal or external challenges to Somoza rule, it was a smooth transition of political control to the former dictator's two legitimate sons. Luís Somoza Debayle, the oldest son and a graduate of Louisiana State University, took charge of public politics, and Anastacio Somoza Debayle, the younger son and a graduate of the U.S. Military Academy at West Point, took control of the National Guard.

The Political Economy of the State

In this chapter I have paid considerable attention to political processes because there was a major shift in the character of the Central American political economies in the twenty-five years between 1930 and the mid-1950s. This shift, crudely expressed, was from the nineteenth- and early twentieth-century pattern in which the economic structure conditioned and shaped politics to a situation in which political changes in the structure of the state became the context necessary for understanding economic events.

This qualitative shift had multiple sources. The one that has been emphasized in this chapter is the reaction of the propertied classes to the depression of the 1930s. They supported the development of a centralized, militarized state apparatus in order to save a social order that benefited them but that was undermined by the collapse of export markets.

The particular ways in which each nation responded to the crisis varied, in good part because each nation had its own history in respect to state power. The key differences in these dissimilar historical patterns revolved around the extent to which the state had an explicit role in mobilizing and disciplining labor for export agriculture. As described in Chapter 3, state systems in Guatemala, El Salvador, and Nicaragua had substantial responsibilities in the area of labor control—the greatest in Guatemala, less in El Salvador, and the least but still significant in the coffee-growing areas of Nicaragua. In contrast, the state structures of Honduras and Costa Rica had but little direct role in regulating labor for export agriculture, and as a consequence the coercive mechanisms (for example, the military and police) of these nations' state structures were comparatively small and undeveloped.

These different starting points, then, importantly affected the pace and extent of development of the state systems during the 1930s and 1940s, but, nevertheless, the similarities of function and often means along which that development occurred are striking. And as events in Guatemala and to a lesser degree Costa Rica illustrate, the increased authority vested in the state systems could, if captured by others, be turned against the very social order that it was established to protect.

Better road and transportation networks opened more areas of each country to direct contact with state agencies, including the military, and encouraged increased interregional commerce within nations. Modern communication devices, such as the radio—used extensively by Ubico—also brought people closer together, for better or worse. Heightened political and economic integration on the national level, then, contributed to the development of centralized state power while it was also a consequence of it.

Another factor in central state formation was the way in which changes in production and demography underlay the emergence of new political constituencies. Some of these new constituencies were actually new or recently expanded social groups, as in the case of the urban middle and working classes. Others had been around for a long time, as in the case of campesinos or the military, but were for the first time finding a political consciousness and the means for advancing their interests through national politics. Whatever the source of the new political voices, the new contenders challenged established political monopolies and the traditional exercise of power and in doing so strove to increase the capacity of central states to act as the principal arenas and arbiters of conflict.

In this chapter I have also emphasized the peculiar form of external influence. The anti-Communist fetishism of the United States after World War II made successive U.S. administrations susceptible to manipulation by Central American elites eager to have help in shutting down political activity that went beyond narrow definitions of legitimacy. Restricting the range of political activity means the capacity to exercise direct control over political activity, thus constraining the scope of political participation and strengthening the powers of the central state. The instruments used by the United States to aid its Central American allies in the fight against communism were diplomatic pressure, the beginnings of large-scale military aid, and in the case of Guatemala, invasion. The struggle against communism became synonymous with the struggle against democracy everywhere in Central America except Costa Rica.

The conception of economic development, promoted by U.S. and international agency officials, was strongly statist and also contributed to greater political centralization. Whether the source was Keynesian stabilization theory or the example of Soviet industrialization, economic development was viewed as something that required initiation and nurturing by a strong central state. This view was very different from the nineteenth-century Liberal convictions in which the state was to guarantee the social order (the "rules of the game") but to intervene only seldom and indirectly in economic affairs.

The state became increasingly independent of the economically powerful throughout the isthmus, but this independence should not be mistaken for "the autonomy of the state," as some scholars have argued.[13] Social institutions have meaning only through their relationships with other institutions in a social formation. Within a setting of interdependence and conflict, a conceptual framework that regards any social institution or actor as autonomous is a dubious guide. Moreover, as the next two decades of Central American history demonstrate, changes in the composition and social relations of production still had powerful consequences for the structure of state power.

Notes

1. For a range of interpretations about El Salvador during the three decades, see James Dunkerley, "El Salvador Since 1930," in L. Bethell (ed.), *Central America Since Independence* (Cambridge: Cambridge University Press, 1991), pp. 159–190; Victor Bulmer-Thomas, *The Political Economy of Central America Since 1920* (New York: Cambridge University Press, 1987); James Dunkerley, *Power in the Isthmus: A Political History of Modern Central America* (London and New York: Verso, 1988); Rafael Guidos Véjar (1980), *El ascenso del militarismo in El Salvador* (San Salvador: UCA Editores, 1980); and Thomas P. Anderson, *Matanza: El Salvador's Communist Revolt of 1932* (Lincoln: University of Nebraska Press, 1971).

2. In addition to the Bulmer-Thomas and Dunkerley volumes cited in note 1, see James Dunkerley, "Guatemala Since 1930," in Bethell, *Central America Since Independence*, pp. 119–159; Bulmer-Thomas, *The Political Economy of Central America Since 1920;* Dunkerley, *Power in the Isthmus;* Jim Handy, *Gift of the Devil: A History of Guatemala* (Boston: South End Press, 1984); Carol Smith (ed.), *Guatemalan Indians and the State* (Austin: University of Texas Press, 1990); and Kenneth Grieb, *Guatemalan Caudillo: The Regime of Jorge Ubico, Guatemala, 1931–1944* (Athens: Ohio University Press, 1979).

3. Quoted in Ralph Lee Woodward, *Central America: A Nation Divided,* 2d ed. (New York: Oxford University Press, 1985), p. 216.

4. For Honduras in this period, see Victor Bulmer-Thomas, "Honduras Since 1930," in Bethell, *Central America Since Independence,* pp. 191–226; Mario Posas and Rafael Del Cid, *La construcción del sector público y del estado nacional en Honduras 1870–1979* (Ciudad Universitaria Rodrigo Facio, CR: Editorial Universitaria Centroamerica, 1981); Mario Posas, *Luchas del movimiento obrero Hondureño* (San José, CR: EDUCA, 1981). The Bulmer-Thomas and Dunkerley books listed in note 1 are, as always, excellent.

5. For Nicaragua, see the Bulmer-Thomas and Dunkerley books cited in note 1; James Dunkerley, "Nicaragua Since 1930," in Bethell, *Central America Since Independence,* pp. 227–276; Richard Millett, *Guardians of the Dynasty* (New York: Orbis Books, 1977); and Jaime Wheelock, *Imperialismo y dictadura: crisis de una formación social* [on Nicaragua] (México: Siglo Veintiuno, 1975).

6. In addition to the Bulmer-Thomas and Dunkerley volumes, see Rodolfo Cerdas Cruz, "Costa Rica Since 1930," in Bethell, *Central America Since Independence,* pp. 277–326; and Mitchell Seligson, *Peasants of Costa Rica and the Development of Agrarian Capitalism* (Madison: University of Wisconsin Press, 1980).

7. Walter LaFeber, *Inevitable Revolutions: The United States in Central America,* 2d ed. (New York: W. W. Norton, 1993), pp. 60–85.

8. The economic and political patterns of this period in South America are described in F. S. Weaver, *Class, State, and Industrial Structure: The Historical Process of South American Industrial Growth* (Westport, CT: Greenwood Press, 1980), pp. 97–120.

9. C. Wright Mills, *White Collar* (New York: Oxford University Press, 1951), still stands as an interesting treatment of those whom I have called the modern middle class. A good, more recent, discussion is Anthony Giddens, *The Class Structure of the Advanced Societies* (New York: Harper, 1973), pp. 177–197.

10. Augmenting those works noted in note 2, the following focus on the "ten years of spring" and its sudden termination: Richard M. Adams (ed.), *Crucifixion by Power: Essays on Guatemalan Social Structure, 1944–1966* (Austin: University of Texas Press, 1970); Piero Gleijeses, *Shattered Hope: The Guatemalan Revolution and the United States, 1944–1954* (Princeton: Princeton University Press, 1991); Richard H. Immerman, *The CIA in Guatemala: The Foreign Policy of Intervention* (Austin: University of Texas Press, 1982); and Stephen Schlesinger and Stephen Kinzer, *Bitter Fruit: The Untold Story of the American Coup in Guatemala* (Garden City, NY: Anchor Books, 1983).

11. Some works that cover this era of Costa Rica are listed in note 6, and works that address it more specifically are John Patrick Bell, *Crisis in Costa Rica: The 1948 Revolution* (Austin: University of Texas Press, 1971); Charles D. Ameringer, *Don Pepe: A Political Biography of José Figueres of Costa Rica* (Albuquerque: University of New Mexico Press, 1978); and Burt H. English, *Liberación Nacional in Costa Rica: The Development of a Political Party in a Transitional Society* (Gainesville: University Presses of Florida, 1971).

12. For the speed and effectiveness with which Somoza could switch political gears, see Jefferey Gould, "For an Organized Nicaragua: Somoza and the Labour Movement, 1944–1948," *Journal of Latin American Studies* 19, no. 2 (1987).

13. For example, see Theda Skocpol, "Bringing the State Back In: Strategies of Analysis in Current Research," in P. Evans, D. Rueschemeyer, and T. Skocpol (eds.), *Bringing the State Back In* (New York: Cambridge University Press, 1985). For a critical treatment of the argument about state autonomy, see Paul Cammack, "Review Article: Bringing the State Back In?" *British Journal of Political Science* 19, part 2 (April 1989), pp. 262–290.

5

Economic Dynamism and Structural Transformation, the 1950s to the Early 1980s

During these years, overall economic growth and changes in the composition of production built on and altered the significance of the political changes of the previous decades. In this chapter I focus on the changes in the patterns of production in these decades and the formation of new structures, showing how the particular type of economic growth created a social and economic structure that put extreme pressure on the political order. I will draw together and build on the previous exposition to show how a set of contradictions of explosive potential was formed by the expansion and transformation of export agriculture, the development of an industrial core of a modern urban sector, the marginalization of increasing numbers of citizens, both rural and urban, and the continuing development of the state. These four elements constitute the major components of an analytical framework that I present in this chapter. The central argument is that the particular pattern of economic *growth,* not stagnation and decline, was the genesis of subsequent crises. In Chapter 6 I will explore the social and political consequences and accommodations in each nation during these decades.

General economic growth in Central America was substantial; it averaged around 6 percent a year through the early 1970s for the region as a whole. Figures 5.1 and 5.2 show the magnitude of that growth and how it began to slow in the mid-1970s, in part because of immense increases in the price of oil. Figure 5.3 illustrates the unevenness of the growth, even during the 1960s and early 1970s. Although the rates of growth fluctuated, they remained positive for extended periods of time.

Even beyond the impressive record of production increases, the specifics of Central American economic expansion conformed to the prescriptions and hopes of North American theorizing about economic development. Supported by state policies that deliberately fostered economic

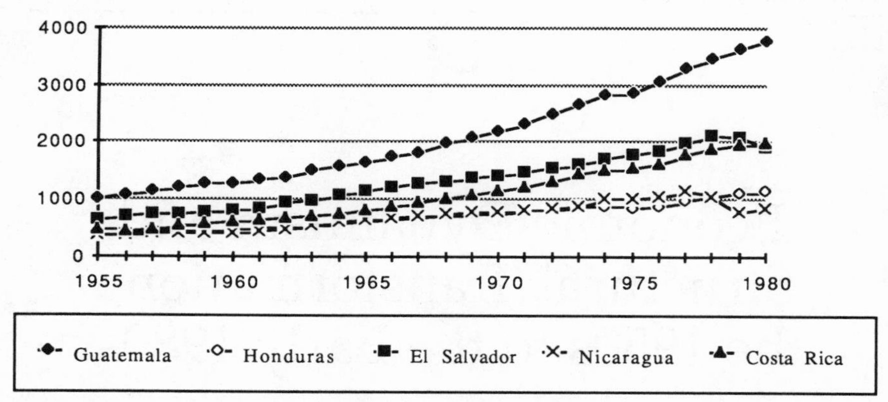

FIGURE 5.1 Gross domestic product, 1955–1980 (1970 U.S.$ millions). *Source:* Adapted from Victor Bulmer-Thomas, *The Political Economy of Central America Since 1920* (New York: Cambridge University Press, 1987), pp. 308–309.

growth, in almost textbook fashion Central America experienced considerable export diversification, agricultural modernization, and industrialization—key tenets of conventional developmental wisdom.[1] Figure 5.4 indicates the major components of Central American economic progress.

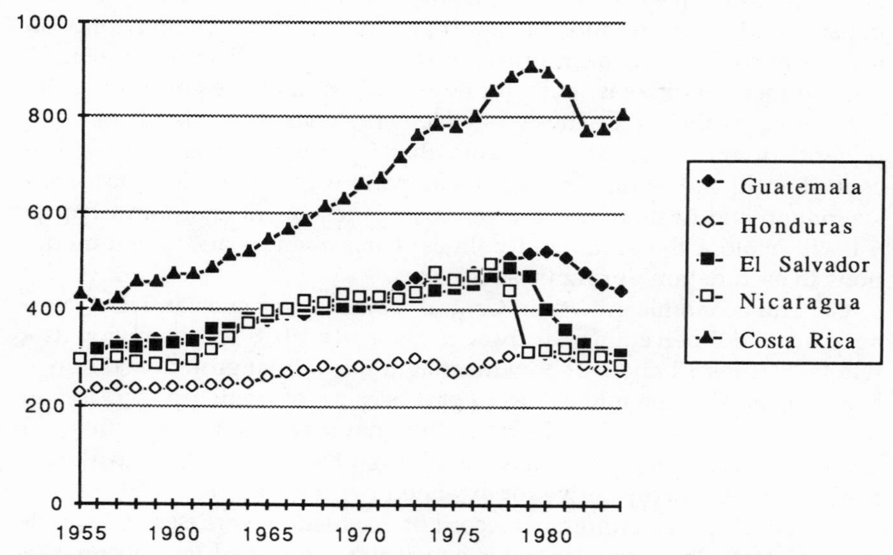

FIGURE 5.2 Per capita gross domestic product, 1955–1984 (1970 U.S.$). *Source:* Adapted from Victor Bulmer-Thomas, *The Political Economy of Central America Since 1920* (New York: Cambridge University Press, 1987), pp. 312–313.

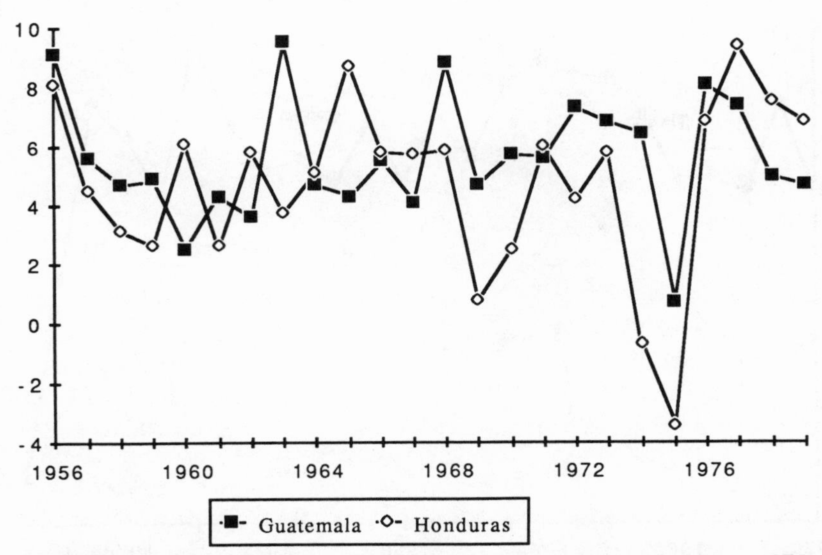

FIGURE 5.3a Rates of GDP growth: Guatemala and Honduras, 1956–1979.
Source: Adapted from Victor Bulmer-Thomas, *The Political Economy of Central America Since 1920* (New York: Cambridge University Press, 1987), pp. 308–309.

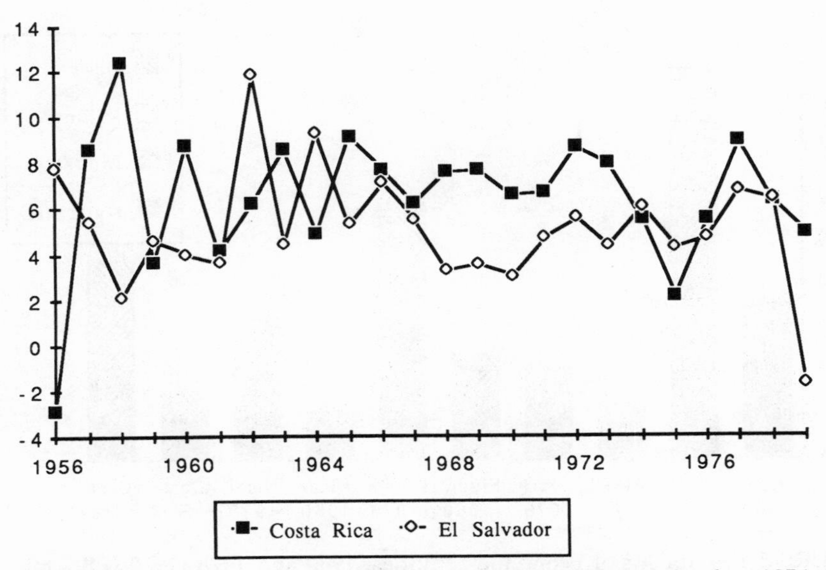

FIGURE 5.3b Rates of GDP growth: Costa Rica and El Salvador, 1956–1979.
Source: Adapted from Victor Bulmer-Thomas, *The Political Economy of Central America Since 1920* (New York: Cambridge University Press, 1987), pp. 308–309.

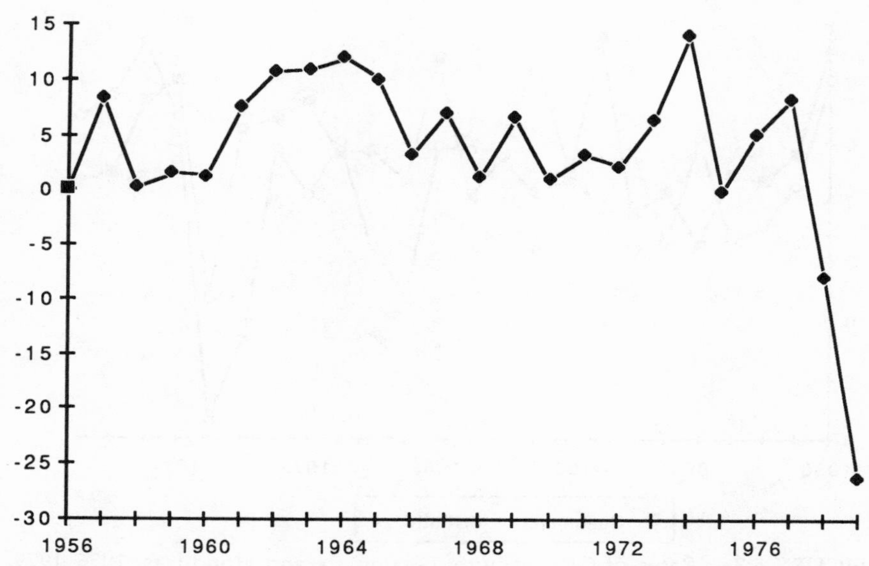

FIGURE 5.3c Rates of GDP growth: Nicaragua, 1956–1979. *Source:* Adapted from Victor Bulmer-Thomas, *The Political Economy of Central America Since 1920* (New York: Cambridge University Press, 1987), pp. 308–309.

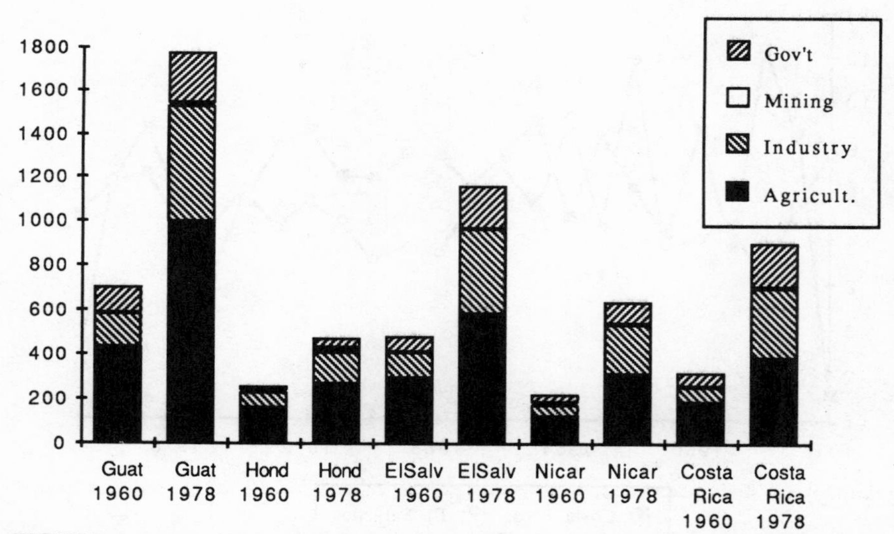

FIGURE 5.4 Four major economic activities, 1960 and 1978 (1970 U.S.$ millions). *Source:* Adapted from Victor Bulmer-Thomas, *The Political Economy of Central America Since 1920* (New York: Cambridge University Press, 1987), pp. 314–325.

A central question for this chapter, then, is why such economic success led to such severe social and political failure.

Export Diversification and Agricultural Growth

By the 1960s, the traditional exports of coffee and bananas had been joined, but not eclipsed, by manufactured exports in some of the nations and by cotton, sugar, and beef exports in all five nations.[2] Figures 5.5 and 5.6 indicate total export magnitudes and the composition of exports sent outside Central America. In this section I will focus on agricultural exports, which continued their predominance among exports sent outside the region and were central to domestic prosperity.

Cotton was cultivated in Central America before the arrival of the Spaniards in the sixteenth century, and sugar and cattle, brought to the New World by the Spaniards, were important throughout the colonial period and into the nineteenth and early twentieth centuries. The large-scale expansion of cotton, sugar, and beef production for export, however, did not begin until the late 1940s and rose to major importance in the 1960s.

Cotton for export was grown primarily along the Pacific coast plains of El Salvador, Nicaragua, and Costa Rica, an area in which the soil, tem-

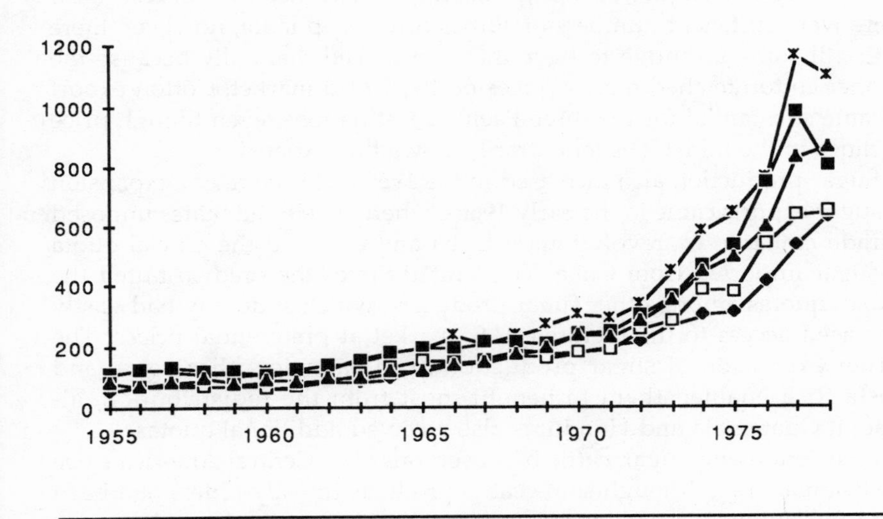

FIGURE 5.5 Value of export earnings, 1955–1978 (U.S.$ millions). *Source:* Adapted from Victor Bulmer-Thomas, *The Political Economy of Central America Since 1920* (New York: Cambridge University Press, 1987), pp. 326–327.

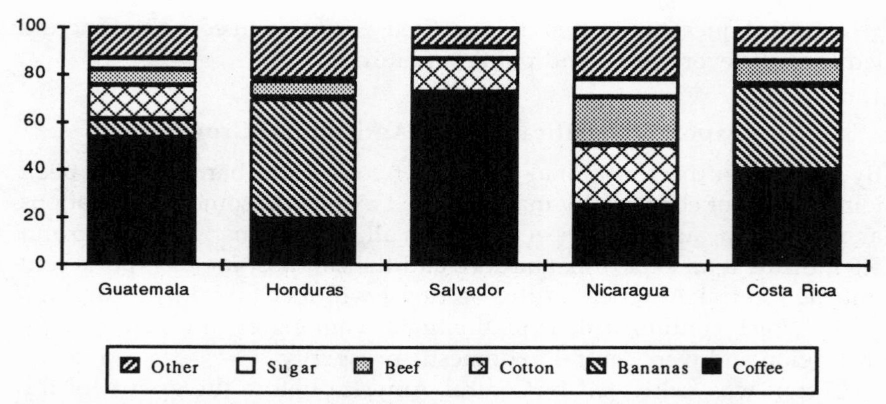

FIGURE 5.6 Percentages of value of exports sent outside Central America, 1970. *Sources:* Victor Bulmer-Thomas, *The Political Economy of Central America Since 1920* (New York: Cambridge University Press, 1987), p. 188; *Statistical Abstract of Latin America, 1978* (Los Angeles: UCLA Latin American Center, 1978).

perature, and regularity of rains proved to be ideal. The cotton could be planted just before the rainy season, and the seeds and young plants benefited from the moisture. By the time the cotton matured, however, the dry season had begun, enabling the use of machines for harvesting. If there were sufficient numbers of sufficiently cheap labor, however, there was still some incentive to have the crop picked manually because the cleaner cotton fetched higher prices on the world market. Cotton export became substantial for the three Pacific coast nations, even though price declines in the mid-1960s temporarily slowed its expansion.

Sugar production also increased in the 1950s, but the major expansion of sugar exports came in the early 1960s, when the United States imposed a trade embargo on revolutionary Cuba and canceled the official quota of sugar imported from Cuba. The United States then redistributed the Cuban quotas among other sugar producers, which suddenly had vastly increased access to the lucrative U.S. market at preferential prices. The earlier expansion of sugar production in El Salvador, Nicaragua, and Costa Rica enabled them to benefit most from the redistribution, although Guatemala and Honduras also received additional quotas.

Like cotton and sugar, cattle had been raised in Central America since the colonial era. Although some cattle products (mostly hides) had been exported within the region, the opportunity to export substantial quantities of beef to the United States did not occur until the 1950s and 1960s. U.S. consumption of low-grade beef rose dramatically in these years with the development of the fast food and convenience food industries. U.S. ranchers, oriented to raising high-grade, grain-fed beef for steaks and standing rib roasts, were not prepared to meet the rapidly rising demand for range-fed, "industrial-grade" meats appropriate for the mass production of hamburgers, burritos, frozen dinners, and so on. Although the cheapest sources of beef were from the plains of Argentina and Brazil, they had long been excluded from U.S. markets because of the fear of hoof-and-mouth disease.

With a nervous eye on the Cuban revolution, the U.S. government granted permission to Central American producers to export their beef to the U.S. market. To do so, however, Central American ranchers were required to improve the quality of their herds and adhere to U.S. Department of Agriculture standards for animal health and sanitary conditions, including slaughtering and meat packing.

Compared to traditional methods of Central American agricultural production for both export and domestic markets, the three new export crops were capital-intensive enterprises that were organizationally and technologically sophisticated. Chemical fertilizers, herbicides, insecticides, and mechanization were important in the cultivation of cotton and sugar, with all the attendant long-run environmental damages and immediate dangers to the health of agricultural workers. Sugar and cotton were grown on large estates, and although cattle were often raised on medium-sized ranches, clearing new pasturelands entailed the deforestation of large stretches of terrain. It is estimated that between 1960 and 1980, about half (40,000 square miles) of the Central American rain forest was cut, courting ecological disaster. Even when new pasturelands did not have to be cleared of trees, they usually had to be cleared of campesino cultivators, especially the land for cattle, which, unlike cotton and sugar, did well on the poor lands to which campesinos had been driven by the earlier pressures of other export agriculture crops. This clearing also could be costly, even though the same tactic used during the colonial period was often employed: Ranchers simply drove a herd into a campesino plot, and the cattle themselves would evict the family by eating their crops. High capital-labor ratios of production resulted from these initial investments, the need to increase, upgrade, and ensure the hygiene of the herds, and the low levels of employment necessary in cattle raising.

Moreover, all three of the new agricultural exports—cotton, sugar, and beef—required considerably more elaborate forward-linked processing activities than coffee and bananas, and these forward-linked processes were also quite capital intensive. High levels of investment were required for cotton ginning and packing, sugar milling and granulating, and modern facilities for the slaughter, packing, and temperature-controlled storage and transport of meat. Like coffee production, these new export activities were primarily in the hands of Central Americans, but to a large extent these Central Americans were not drawn from the ranks of the traditional agricultural export elite. Urban-based entrepreneurial groups and individuals led in the formation of these new agricultural export activities, many of them functioning as growers on rented land rather than becoming landowners in their own right.

The development of new types of export production put pressure on existing financial institutions to supply the needed credit for the new, capital-intensive agricultural exports, and as a result, banks and bankers became more prominent in the entire framework of national capitalist production. Large proportions of the necessary new infrastructure, however, such as roads, communications, and port facilities, were underwritten by domestic governments and by the material support and expert advice from the United States and the World Bank.

New entrepreneurial energy in this period was also apparent in the production of the traditional agricultural exports—coffee and bananas—although the presence of new entrepreneurs was less evident. Coffee yields (output per land area) rose substantially as a result of new investments in drainage, irrigation, and replanting and the greater use of fertilizers, herbicides, and insecticides.

The same phenomenon was seen in bananas as well. Central American banana production did not grow vigorously during this period primarily because of continuing problems with disease and the consequent shift of much of United Fruit Company banana production to uninfected locations, such as Ecuador. In the 1970s, the United Fruit Company sold off their Guatemalan banana operations to Del Monte (a subsidiary of R. J. Reynolds) and shifted their fruit plantations on the Pacific coast of Costa Rica to palm oil. United Fruit increasingly diversified its operations in Honduras and Costa Rica away from agriculture into transportation, manufacturing, and broadcasting, and reflecting this diversification in the United States as well as Latin America, the United Fruit Company became United Brands in 1970.

Along with these changes, however, bananas were still raised in large quantities on the Caribbean coasts of Honduras, Guatemala, and Costa Rica and were reintroduced on the Nicaragua coast. The three major fruit companies—United Brands, Del Monte, and Castle and Cook (Dole), which bought out Standard in the 1960s—utilized new production and shipping techniques to replace and discipline unionized workers. The changes, along with the introduction of new varieties of bananas, resulted in increased yields in banana production and fewer workers. (This reduction in employment occurred even though the new type of banana—the Cavendish—required considerably more careful, labor-intensive packing.)

Finally, although less dramatic, there were some significant initiatives in agriculture oriented to domestic markets for food, especially grains.

Whereas domestic food products continued to be grown principally on small campesino holdings, the "Green Revolution" agricultural technology of the 1970s, supported by U.S. and international aid agencies, made its appearance in Central America. This technology involved the application of an integrated package of hybrid seeds, chemical fertilizers and pest retardants, and water control, significantly increasing the intensity of cultivation and yields of food crops. As in most places where this technology was used, the innovations of the Green Revolution were more appropriate for large and middle-sized farms than small ones. This type of agricultural modernization added to the pressure on small farmers, who were already on the defensive from the expansion of export agriculture.

Such changes in the cultivation of domestic food crops were not universal, however, and these crops lagged behind export agriculture in the attention by governments and in output and productivity growth. As a consequence, food imports rose throughout the region. This rise in imports represented a problem for the welfare of the majority of the population, but the problem was not simply that of specialization in export crops at the expense of domestic food production.

As described in Chapter 3, the logic of comparative advantage suggests that each "nation" could have received more food by producing nonfood exports and using the proceeds to buy foreign-produced foods. The increase in hunger and decline in nutrition in Central America during these years occurred because export production was organized in such a fashion that many were not able to purchase adequate amounts of food, whether imported or domestically produced. That is, hunger was caused not by the process of international specialization and exchange but rather by the domestic relations of export production and the resulting concentration of income. The vastly unequal power of different groups was the reason for inadequate levels of domestic food consumption for the increasing numbers living in dire poverty. Although international forces contributed to those unequal power relations, the market patterns of commodity production and exchange were expressions of those relations and not directly the source of the increasingly serious material deprivation of the poor.[3]

In regard to production for international markets, the general modernization of export agriculture led to increases in labor productivity (output per worker), so rural employment opportunities did not increase as rapidly as the output of the five agricultural exports throughout Central America. This situation was especially dramatic in Honduran banana production. After the 1954 strike, the United Fruit Company labor force in Honduras was reduced from around 35,000 workers to around 16,000 over the next fifteen years. Although the volume of banana production did decline, its contraction was not nearly so precipitous as the loss of jobs.

The chronic labor shortage came to an end as a result of the slow growth of agricultural employment in Central American export agriculture, the appropriation of campesino lands (whether rented or owned) for export production, and rapid population growth. The labor shortage had been cited by employers for a century as a major problem, and scholars of Central American affairs had been concerned about it as recently as the late 1940s. In fact, this shortage turned into its opposite: labor surplus.

Table 5.1 shows population and urbanization figures for this period, but assertions about the role of population growth as the exclusive or principal cause of increasing impoverishment must be considered carefully. The existence of landlessness even in Honduras and Nicaragua, with their low people-to-land ratios, demonstrates that an interpretation that relies solely on the notion that landlessness was the result of too many people and too little land is seriously flawed. The social effects of population growth are always mediated by social structure, and land scarcity in Central America is a consequence of the social power of a minority to enforce the control of land to the disadvantage of increasingly large numbers of landless people. (Table 5.2 displays some comparative indexes of rural welfare in the five nations.)

People who were unable to find work in export agriculture and deprived of their lands by the expansion of export agriculture were forced to migrate to the cities or else to colonize inferior and outlying lands. This latter option—the occupation and colonization of heretofore unused lands—was supported explicitly or tacitly by the governments of Honduras and Costa Rica and to a lesser degree in Guatemala and Nicaragua. Those governments misleadingly called the process "land reform" and promoted it as long as it did not compete with the development of export agriculture. In densely populated El Salvador, however, there was

Table 5.1 Population and Urban Growth, 1960-1980

	Total Population (in 1,000s)		Per Sq.Mile	Urban Population as % of Total Population		Percentage of Urban Population in Largest City	
	1960	1980	1980	1960	1980	1960	1980
Guatemala	3,830	7,260	167	33	39	41	36
Honduras	1,950	3,691	82	23	36	31	33
El Salvador	2,450	4,750	565	38	41	26	22
Nicaragua	1,410	2,693	52	41	53	41	47
Costa Rica	1,250	2,220	109	37	43	67	64

Sources: Victor Bulmer-Thomas, *The Political Economy of Central America Since 1920* (New York: Cambridge University Press, 1987), pp. 310-311; and World Bank, *World Development Report 1981* (Washington, D.C.: World Bank, 1981), pp. 172-173.

TABLE 5.2 Four Indexes of Rural Organization and Welfare

	Land Availability, 1978-1979	Agricult. Labor, 1979	Polarization of Land Ownership	Rural Poverty 1980	
				Extreme	Total
Guatemala	1.8	56	11.6	51.5	83.7
Honduras	3.3	63	21.0	69.7	80.2
El Salvador	1.3	51	7.0	55.4	76.4
Nicaragua	4.5	44	37.5	50.0	80.0
Costa Rica	1.7	36	47.8	18.7	34.2

Notes: Column 1 shows the hectares of arable land in 1978 for each member of the agricultural work force in 1979

Column 2 shows the percentage of the national labor force employed in agriculture.

Column 3 shows the percentage of all farms in small and medium-sized holdings (roughly 20-25 acres to 300-500 acres in size).

Column 4 is the percentage of rural residents in poverty.

Source: Charles D. Brockett, "The Structure of Political Opportunities and Mobilization in Central America," *Comparative Politics* 23 (April 1991), p. 256.

so little unoccupied land that nonredistributive land reform was not feasible. For this reason, Salvadorans occupied unused Honduran land across the border, and the Honduran government considered such land to be unoccupied for the purposes of handing out land to landless Honduran families. The expulsion of Salvadoran cultivators from Honduran lands was not well received by the cultivators nor by the Salvadoran government, and this was the central issue of the 1969 "Soccer War" between Honduras and El Salvador.

The lack of redistributive land reform during this period was caused primarily by the political power wielded by propertied classes and their agents, backed up by U.S. foreign policy that favored "stability." In several of the larger Latin American nations, politically weighty urban and industrial interests rose during the 1930s and 1940s, and by the 1950s and 1960s these new interests were willing to entertain the possibility that existing land tenure patterns were retarding the growth of urban industrial activities. As a consequence, these urban political forces were open at least to the discussion of redistributive land reform that might increase agricultural production, expand domestic markets for urban products, and reduce the power of a competing elite. In Central America, the states had increased their power relative to that of the landed elite, but there were no politically significant urban and industrial classes that saw the organization of the rural economy as an obstacle to the development of their own productive resources. As a consequence, state personnel had little incentive to meddle with one of the key economic sectors.

In any case, by the 1950s and 1960s the dynamism of capitalist agricultural growth occurring without land reform seemed to justify the reluctance to engage in major structural changes in the countryside. This dynamism appeared to have reduced the need of land reform, which may seem bizarre when landlessness and rural poverty were increasing so rapidly. The social equity argument for land reform, however, was only one side of the case that had usually been made for redistributive land reform.

The second side of the case for land redistribution was productive efficiency. At least since World War II, it had been argued that land held in large holdings was ineffectively utilized and that small and medium-sized holdings, cultivated by their owners, would be more intensively worked, produce higher yields, and expand domestic markets. Even though agricultural modernization in Central America was by no means universal, it was sufficiently widespread that the production-oriented claims for redistributive land reform were definitely weakened. As in other parts of Latin America during these decades, large-scale agriculture demonstrated the capacity for capitalist modernization, raising yields and labor productivity (but not necessarily wages) in important regions and crops. As I have noted in regard to cotton, sugar, and especially beef, this process of agricultural change in Central America involved increases of land devoted to export agriculture—increases that both brought heretofore unutilized land into production and dispossessed campesinos from land that they had owned or rented for decades. The large, traditional estate, characterized by primitive productive techniques and large tracts of idle land, was no longer typical or even significant.

The major problem in rural Central America by the 1970s, then, was not the lack of capitalist agricultural development, the target of one strand of the argument for land reform. The principal problem in rural Central America in the 1970s was the *success* of capitalist agricultural development. This conclusion is cogently argued by Merilee Grindle for Latin America generally but captures the situation in Central America very well.

> [The rural poor] are not isolated, backward, or "traditional" members of society who have simply been left behind in the process of development; they do not have to be forced, trained, or cajoled into "modernity" by government programs. The growth in their unemployment, underemployment, landlessness, wage dependence, subsistence orientation, and migration is a direct result of developments in the modern capitalist sector and of state policies, and as such cannot be understood or remedied without reference to these changes.[4]

The need for land reform, then, was principally to mitigate the severe costs of that development for its victims. Basing the case for redistributive land reform exclusively on social equity considerations simply was not as compelling for Central American government bureaus and international donor agencies as were arguments for technical efficiency. Moreover, support for land reform by urban middle and working classes also weakened when it seemed as though significant alterations in land tenure would be likely to raise local food costs and to reduce foreign exchange availability. The transformation in export agriculture, therefore, was an important reason that relocating campesinos on isolated, unclaimed lands (colonization) was the only type of land reform seriously entertained.

Industrial Growth and the Central American Common Market

The industrialization side of the region's economic expansion is usually associated with the Central American Common Market. Beginning in 1950, pairs of Central American nations signed free trade treaties between them, and through these bilateral treaties all five of the nations had a free trade agreement with at least one other Central American nation. Pulling all five together into a coordinated common market, though, began in earnest in 1958. In 1961, Guatemala, El Salvador, and Nicaragua entered into a comprehensive, multilateral common market arrangement. Honduras entered in 1962, and Costa Rica completed the five-nation Central American Common Market in 1963.

The Common Market was, as its name suggests, a free trade area among the five nations with a common tariff barrier around them. But the purpose was more than a rearrangement of existing tariffs. The entire enterprise was informed by the developmentalist thinking of the United Nations Economic Commission for Latin America (or CEPAL, its Spanish acronym, which has been expanded to CEPALC to include the Caribbean). As briefly mentioned in Chapter 3, CEPAL economists argued that the particular way in which Latin America was inserted into the international economy was disadvantageous for the economic development, and particularly for industrial growth, of Latin American nations, which exported unprocessed agricultural and mineral products. Although the technical efficiency advantage of land reform was a part of the overall CEPAL strategy, they generally avoided exploring the implications of power relationships among domestic, nationally domiciled groups. The result was a set of policy prescriptions that came to be known as import-substituting industrialization (ISI).[5]

The idea of ISI is to restrict the importation of products, especially of manufactures, that might feasibly be produced domestically and, by this protection, stimulate local production to substitute for imports. CEPAL's rigorous presentation distinguished its position from earlier programs, but the basic idea certainly was not new. Alexander Hamilton in eighteenth-century United States and Friedrich List in early nineteenth-century Germany advocated precisely these policies. And in the case of List, it resulted in the 1844 formation of the Zollverein—a free trade zone among German principalities that contributed to their political unification as the nation of Germany in 1871. The European Economic Community, established in the early 1950s, was another important precedent for establishing trade blocs to protect domestic markets for the purposes of national and regional economic development.

Although the Latin American Free Trade Area and the Andean Pact also stemmed directly from the CEPAL analysis, CEPAL's emphasis on the common market in Central America, like that of the Caribbean Free Trade Area, resulted from their belief that the small size of individual national markets was an obstacle to the ISI strategy working effectively within the confines of individual national boundaries. Moreover, the common market proposal was not alien to Central America, where schemes for cooperation and unification had been frequently proposed and occasionally attempted since independence from Spain in the 1820s.[6]

In spite of the explicit ISI intentions, the common tariffs that the Central American Common Market actually did establish were not as high as the full-blown ISI efforts of, say, Argentina and Chile in the 1950s. Central American producers and consumers purchasing imported goods resisted the imposition of prohibitive tariffs, and the final common tariffs were little more than the average of already existing national tariffs. But these averages mask important changes in the tariff structures, changes that gave considerably more protection to domestic producers of final consumer goods. The tariffs of many manufactured consumer goods from outside the region were raised, and the tariffs on capital equipment and inputs (both raw and semiprocessed materials) were reduced or abolished altogether. And beyond the nominal protection favoring consumer goods, what economists call "effective tariffs" on final consumer goods offered substantial protection and significant incentives for domestic production of final consumer goods.

I will illustrate this point about effective tariff protection with a hypothetical example. Let us say that the tariff on the importation of portable transistor radios into Central America was 10 percent, certainly less than prohibitive. In addition, all the components for those radios as well as the equipment needed to assemble them could be imported into Central America duty free. Finally, let us say that the final stage of production—the assembly and packaging of the radios—constituted only 8 percent of the total cost of producing the radios. The effective tariff, therefore, on the final, assembling stage of producing radios was 125 percent—10 percent divided by 8 percent. That is, the tariff was 10 percent when calculated on the final market price of the radios, but with no tariffs on the importation of components the 10 percent tariff yielded protection exclusively to the assembly stage of production—which added only 8 percent to the total value of the transistor radios—125 percent. The structure of tariffs, therefore, must be compared to the amount of value added by each stage of production in order to identify the actual level of protection. And in these terms, the rather low nominal tariff rates of the Central American Common Market still represented quite impressive efforts at import-substituting industrialization.

But the idea of the Central American Common Market went beyond the passive notion of a common market. The plan included the agreement that the five nations, coordinated by a regional secretariat and a development bank, would cooperatively establish certain "integration industries" (actually factories) in the region. These factories were to be in product lines considered essential for the industrial development of the region as a whole but that had efficient scales of production too large to be limited to the markets of a single Central American nation. Their location was to be governed by both efficiency and political criteria. That is, the factories would be placed in locales that made economic sense but also were to be distributed among all five nations.

The United States was initially very cool, if not downright hostile, to the entire Common Market endeavor, but important shifts in the Cold War helped to bring the United States around to support the Common Market. By the late 1950s, the very nature of the Cold War was rapidly changing: There was no longer such a clear polarity of the United States and the Soviet Union. The rapid economic growth of Europe (and the formation of the European Economic Community) and of Japan meant that the United States was no longer so dominant in capitalist world markets nor the unchallenged leader of the "West." At the same time, the increasing tension between the Soviet Union and China presaged a coming rupture of a monolithic Communist bloc.

The blurring of the polarity of the Cold War led the Eisenhower administration in the late 1950s to begin to conceive the Cold War in rather more complex terms.[7] The signal of a new foreign policy stance toward Latin America in general, stimulated by the Cuban revolution, was seen in the administration's willingness to support the founding of the Inter-American Development Bank, sign a coffee agreement, and even allocate some nonmilitary foreign aid in 1959 and 1960. Although certainly not repudiating armed intervention against "leftist" governments, the Eisenhower administration's new approach to the anti-Communist campaign was also demonstrated by significantly moderating its resistance to the creation of the Central American Common Market.

The U.S. administrations of Presidents Kennedy and Johnson built on the idea of fighting Communist subversion by promoting capitalist growth, and the creation and financing of the Alliance for Progress was a monument to this thinking. This strategy, however, was a complement to, not a substitute for, the use of military power in Latin America. During the Alliance for Progress era, the ideas of the "internal enemy" and "national security state" became fashionable among certain groups; they were institutionalized in 1961 by the establishment of the Central American Defense Council (Consejo de Defensa Centroamericana, or CONDECA)—a military council sponsored by the United States to coordinate the fight against communism on a regional level. (Costa Rica did not join.) The continuing willingness to use violence as a foreign policy tool was illustrated by the the strong emphasis on counterinsurgency as well as the U.S.-initiated invasions of Cuba's Bay of Pigs in 1961 and the Dominican Republic in 1965.

The Alliance for Progress initially contained two complementary, but still distinct, strategies of how best to promote capitalist growth. The first was of a technical, even engineering nature, emphasizing infrastructural investment (roads, ports, irrigation and power systems), literacy and technical education, training programs for managers, credit availability, the transfer of technology, and so on. The second strategy for promoting capitalist growth emphasized the importance of structural reform and included such policies as redistributive land reform, taxing the wealthy, workers' rights to organize and bargain collectively with employers, and increased political participation within democratic institutions.

It was (and continues to be) argued that the first strategy, though not directly confronting established hierarchies of privilege and power, would undermine them through the very process of economic growth and development. The second strategy maintained that only by directly challenging established economic and social power would capitalist economic growth and development be possible.

As I have already described in the area of agriculture, the substantial economic growth in Central America during the 1960s seemed to show that economic growth did not require structural reform. This interpretation was eagerly advocated by Central American elites and by the lower echelons of U.S. State Department personnel responsible for implementing the Alliance. As a consequence, even when the positive side of fighting communism by promoting growth was not completely overwhelmed by whose who thought that military power should be the principal means to stamp out communism, the effort to stimulate economic growth became framed in technical modernization terms that regarded structural reforms as an unnecessary and even wasteful diversion from the principal goal of increasing economic productivity. This conception of progress, therefore, was very much like that of the Central American Liberals of the nineteenth century. Moreover, as the United States became increasingly bogged down and frustrated in the Vietnam War in the 1960s, even the narrowly conceived developmental effort became subordinated to the use of military force to suppress dissent.

The Central American Common Market did fit in nicely with the reformist aspirations of the Alliance for Progress, because it was essentially a technical arrangement—a means for expanding markets without challenging existing patterns of property rights, income distribution, social hierarchies, or political power in the region. And U.S. manufacturing interests had little objection to the Common Market as long as the integration industry component was not developed beyond a minimal level. Integration industries proved to be no problem as an idea or as a practice, however, because rivalry among the elites of the five nations severely impeded the systematic development of a coherent set of industrial enterprises for the region as a whole.

Central American agricultural exporters were initially very skeptical about the Central American Common Market, but their anxieties were assuaged by the exclusion of agricultural products, inputs needed for agricultural production, and many wage goods from the tariff lists. The costs of producing agricultural exports, therefore, would not be raised by increased prices for inputs, including labor. Moreover, because of political changes in the 1930s and 1940s and the development of new agricultural exports in the 1950s and 1960s, old-style agricultural export producers were no longer the principal political force in any of the nations.

Whatever combination of political expediency and technical assessments about the need for vigorous export growth resulted in the concessions to export agricultural interests, the result significantly deviated from a pure form of ISI: Major reallocations of resources from export agriculture to industry were not integral to the development strategy. Other Latin American nations used taxes, marketing boards, and multiple exchange rates that discriminated against agricultural exports to divert resources from exports to industry. The design of the Central American Common Market, however, contained none of these. In this sense, the entire project was a slightly modified version of good, old-fashioned export-led growth in which only positive incentives were relied upon to stimulate industrial growth. There is some question, therefore, about how much of the industrial growth that did occur can be attributed to the Common Market compared to the influence of the generally buoyant export markets of these years, which would have propelled general economic expansion in the absence of the Common Market.

In any case, the Central American Common Market was finally established. It lasted almost ten years at its most vigorous, but not without conflict among its members. Honduran governments during the 1960s continually protested what they saw to be the inordinate penetration of their domestic markets, especially by Salvadoran manufactured products and direct investors, and they petitioned the Central American Common Market (CACM) for special treatment because of the Honduran economy's backwardness. In several cases, Honduras (along with Nicaragua) was granted special exceptions, such as the right to give longer tax holidays to industrial firms locating in Honduras. Nevertheless, because the integration industry provisions did not become an effective means for industrial planning and allocation, the location of new manufacturing enterprises was determined primarily by the market and domestic governments. In Central America, the market criterion meant that any of the other four members of the Common Market were more attractive sites than Honduras because of higher incomes and better-developed transportation networks and general infrastructures. Moreover, even a pretense at rational industrial planning in Central America was defeated after Costa Rica, contrary to earlier agreements, established a tire plant that duplicated one in Guatemala sponsored by Common Market authorities.

Honduran dissatisfaction with its place in the Central American Common Market came to a head with the 1969 Soccer War, and it withdrew from the Common Market in 1970. By the mid-1970s, then, the Central American Common Market was weakened by Honduras's withdrawal, the very success of the Common Market in altering domestic structures of production, political tensions among the member nations, and changing international economic and political circumstances, and it declined in importance as an active institution, even though intraregional trade in manufactured goods continued at substantial levels throughout the 1970s.

The growth of Central American manufacturing during the 1960s and 1970s was impressive by historical standards. As suggested in the discussion of effective tariffs, the principal type of manufacturing growth induced by the Central American Common Market was so-called finishing-touches industries. That is, because only the final stages of production were protected by tariffs, plants assembling consumer goods with imported equipment, materials, and semifinished inputs dominated manufacturing growth. Even the chemicals category, which does not sound like consumer goods and constituted 15 or so percent of manufacturing production in the region, was mostly pharmaceuticals, cosmetics, and petroleum refining. Industrial chemicals constituted less than 5 percent of the total. Petrochemical production, however, did supply synthetic fibers and plastics used in the region for making clothes, shoes, building materials, and so on.

It is difficult to break this pattern of finishing-touches industry because producers of final consumer goods (like agricultural exporters) resist any extension of ISI policies to products that they use in their production, whether fuels, raw and semifinished inputs, or capital equipment. Such tariffs, whether or not they induce domestic production of the inputs, raise the costs of inputs for the final goods producers, and they may do so to the point that the amount of protection rendered by tariffs on final product imports is sharply reduced. The anomaly, then, is that new tariffs on inputs reduce the level of effective protection for final products.

The Central American Common Market led to considerable transnational corporation investment in manufacturing for the first time. Until the Central American Common Market, large international corporations preferred to serve Central American markets by sending exports from abroad, but with the establishment of the Common Market, it seemed possible that they might be closed out of these markets if they did not invest directly in productive enterprises. Direct investment in the region appeared attractive to transnational corporations, because a plant in any one of the five nations could send goods to the other four duty free—enabling a price advantage over firms supplying markets from outside the region. Transnational corporations, then, mostly based in the United States, accounted for close to one-third of total investment in Central American manufacturing by the end of the 1960s.

Transnational corporations set the pace in the use of sophisticated technology in manufacturing production, but modern, capital-intensive technology was also utilized by many domestically owned and operated manufacturing firms. As in the case of export agriculture, it limited the increase of employment associated with the growth of manufacturing production. One consequence of this form of production in manufacturing was that the growth of labor productivity in these firms outstripped productivity growth in other activities, even though the average for industry as a whole was dragged down by the vast majority of the enterprises, which continued to be small and technologically backward. Capital-intensive production was also one of the reasons that wages and salaries, as a proportion of total income, declined in favor of property income (rent, interest, and profits) in both manufacturing and agriculture through the 1960s.

When one uses conventional (neoclassical) economics, it is difficult to understand why manufacturing firms in Central America (and in the Third World generally) have demonstrated such a consistent preference for modern production techniques. Clearly it would be more reasonable, the argument goes, to use methods of production that conserve scarce capital and use relatively plentiful labor. General explanations for the perversity of entrepreneurs' choices of production techniques have included the putative scarcity of sufficiently skilled labor, inflexibility of transnational corporations accustomed to operating in advanced economies, misplaced prestige considerations, and distorted prices for capital and labor resulting from government policy.

It is unnecessary, however, to contrive special explanations for the phenomenon. First of all, the logic underlying neoclassical economists' analysis about factor proportions has been called into question, and empirical studies suggest that the technology behind high capital-labor ratios can increase the productivity of capital as well as that of labor.

But there is more to technique choice than short-run, relative price considerations. In the context of enduring labor strife, employing as few workers as possible at higher-than-usual wages can appeal to employers, no matter how many poverty-stricken workers live in the neighborhood. It may be quite rational for a firm's manager to pay wages above national averages to create a work force whose members are willing to use their political influence to protect the firm's interests and thus their own above-average standards of living.

In addition, modern production technology imported from industrially advanced nations contains within it a design of the work process that strengthens owners and their representatives by permitting maximum supervision of the work process and control of the product. The use of modern production technology in both export agriculture and modern urban sectors, therefore, makes solid class-control sense when one realizes the turbulence and conflict common in Central American workplaces.

Moreover, much of modern production technology deskills workers. That is, the machinery increasingly embodies the skills that workers used to possess and thus enables the employment of less skilled, and less expensive, production workers. An obvious example of this process in the United States is the use of bar code scanners, which automatically record the price of a product, and cash registers that calculate change, enabling grocery store owners to replace experienced checkers with part-time teenagers who do not need to know product prices or arithmetic.

Finally, large-scale, capital-intensive production contributed to the highly centralized nature of manufacturing in particular product lines, and in the 1970s manufacturing as a whole became highly centralized. Competitive markets were primarily for poor people and small enterprises. Even though modern plants in Central America were medium-sized in the context of an industrialized nation, their scale in Central America was such that most of them operated at very low proportions of their potential capacities while being able to supply most of the regional, much less national, demand for a product. As a consequence, they were able to exercise substantial market power in some product lines to the disadvantage of customers and suppliers.

The lack of competition and the low utilization of existing plants and equipment resulted in these factories being high-cost operations, and Central American purchasers paid prices considerably higher than the international prices for comparable goods. As a consequence, although exports of manufactured goods rose substantially, they were limited to the protected regional market.

The major exception to this limitation was the processing component of agricultural exports, such as the preparation of sugar, cotton, and livestock exports previously mentioned and instant coffee production in El Salvador as well. Although these stages of production are technically part of manufacturing, they are included in the agricultural commodity categories in Figure 5.6 rather than in manufacturing. Agricultural export processing, like more purely agricultural exports, had to be cost and price competitive with other suppliers in the international economy because they were sold mostly to rich nations on the international market.

An Analytical Framework

The modernization of export agriculture and the growth of manufacturing changed the economic and social landscapes of Central America in profound ways. The economic expansion of the 1960s had a dynamic very different from that of the coffee and banana export economies of the late nineteenth and early twentieth centuries, both because of the changes in social and international contexts and because of the different forms of production.

One example of this difference, emphasized in Chapter 3, is that the earlier development of export production had quite diverse effects on individual Central American nations. The greater similarity of manufacturing production among the five nations, however, meant that the social and political impacts of recent forms of economic growth have been more homogenizing. Added, then, to other forces working in the same direction, such as U.S. foreign policy, are tendencies toward convergence among the five nations, even though they have a long way to go even to approximate the homogeneous image of the region usually projected in the U.S. media.

To understand the character of this new Central American dynamic, it is useful to pull together some of the most important general features of the economic structure that resulted from the pattern of growth experienced in the 1960s and 1970s into a general framework that is still capable of distinguishing national particularities. As we have seen, a large export agricultural sector had emerged in all five nations by the beginning of the twentieth century, and important changes in the 1930s through the 1950s lay behind the development in each nation of an increasingly centralized state apparatus capable of at least limited independence from even the most powerful social groups in setting policy. An urban manufacturing sector and a transformed export agriculture came out in the 1960s and 1970s, thus completing an economic structure with specific properties and predictable contradictions.

The purpose of the general framework is to comprehend the key elements of economic growth, the implications for social organization and welfare, and the role of the state in the process. In this effort, it is crucial to identify the way in which the form of economic growth in Central America, apparently so successful, integrated increasing proportions of the population and production into market relations in a manner that generated greater disparities of economic welfare and heightened social and political tensions. For this framework, I use categories different from the conventional economic sectors of agriculture, industry, and services. Instead, I divide all productive activity into four sectors: a modern urban sector, export agriculture, a competitive sector, and a state sector.[8]

The Modern Urban Sector

The delineation of these sectors may not be very precise, but it is clear that by the early 1970s there had been established in each nation at least the beginning of a modern urban sector whose core activity was manufacturing and where production processes were characterized by (relative to the Central American context) sophisticated, capital-intensive technologies, high labor productivity, and well-organized work forces. In addition, modern urban manufacturing firms tended to be large (at least in the context of small national economies), exercise substantial market power, enjoy high profits, and provide relatively well-remunerated employment for a limited number of people. Many of their products were for upper-income consumers—for example, components and assembly of some consumer durables such as automobiles and electrical appliances as well as nondurable goods such as pharmaceuticals, designer jeans, and convenience foods. These manufacturing firms, together with the firms that supply them with energy, finance, communications, transportation, and commercial services, constitute the modern urban sector.

This sector, led by manufacturing firms, is one of the two major sources of economic growth for the economy as a whole. Because the sector's most dynamic firms, whether domestically or foreign owned, use technologically sophisticated and capital-intensive, labor-saving production processes similar to those of the industrialized nations, the sector grows primarily through capital accumulation (investment in plant and equipment) rather than by hiring proportionately greater numbers of workers. The availability of positions, not wage changes, regulates the supply of labor to the modern urban sector, with its relatively desirable jobs. Although modern urban-sector workers are capable of exerting substantial political pressure, they often limit themselves to bread-and-butter issues once they achieve collective bargaining rights.

Export Agriculture

This sector has some definite similarities with the modern urban sector: Ownership tends to be concentrated in a few hands and is a major source of social power, and the sector increasingly uses technologically sophisticated production technology and grows primarily through accumulation rather than by employment of additional labor. Ownership in both the modern urban and export agriculture sectors is "big capital," and there is considerable overlap among the people who control them.

These similarities with the modern urban sector are important, but at the same time, export agriculture possesses some striking differences. The major determinant of the sector's fortunes is foreign markets, over which domestic producers have little control. And although the dynamism or stagnation of the sector has direct and immediate effects on the general economy through the usual linkages, one of the principal functions that the sector plays in the general economy is to supply the foreign exchange necessary to pay for imports. Imports of machinery and intermediate goods used as inputs, such as fuels and chemical fertilizers, are vitally important for export agriculture and for urban manufacturing and attendant support services that constitute the modern urban sector. In 1970, over half of all five nations' imports from outside Central America were inputs for domestic production.

The dependence on imports brought about by ISI-induced industrial growth was a new and politically more dangerous kind of dependence. Instead of a slump in export markets causing a shortage of imported luxury consumer goods, as in the 1930s, a contraction of export earnings in the 1960s and 1970s resulted in difficulty in importing inputs for industrial and export production. This difficulty could cause a sharp reduction or even cessation of production by several local manufacturing firms and increased costs for export producers. For manufacturing, this means a loss of national production and income and the loss of jobs by the best-paid and most highly organized urban workers. In addition, the expansion of export agriculture's use of land and population growth constrains the ability to substitute domestically produced food for imported food, and the rise in the price of the food puts upward pressure on urban wages and further downward pressure on urban profits.

Dependence on exports means dependence on exporters—the propertied class of export agriculture. This new dependence tied industrial firms to the fortunes of export agriculture. Even after the significant industrial expansion of the 1960s led to politically consequential industrial lobbying groups, the basic commonality of interests between industry and export agriculture prevented fundamental divergences of policy advocacy. While export agriculture and industrial interests competed for public credit and favorable policies, industrialists recognized the basic commonality of interests between the two sectors.

Another, and perhaps the principal, difference between export agriculture and the modern urban sector, however, is in the workers' wages and benefits, work conditions, legislated protections (including the right to collective bargaining), and stability of employment. In all of these respects, the workers in export agriculture are not nearly as well off as their counterparts in the factories and offices of modern urban enterprises, and the agricultural export sector is the most polarized along class lines. Despite the modernization of production, export agriculture remains a sector in which low wages are centrally important for price competitiveness in international markets (at least at accustomed level of profitability for the propertied class).

But export agriculture usually is organized in enterprises that employ large numbers of workers whose labor is organized, coordinated, and supervised in ways similar to urban factory and office work. As a consequence, export agriculture workers have much greater potential for organization and political mobilization than those in the competitive sector. As we have seen in the cases of Honduras and Costa Rica, the unions among the banana plantation workers have demonstrated the capacity to be important political actors.

The Competitive Sector

In comparison with the modern urban sector and with export agriculture, firms in the competitive sector are small, low-profit, and low-wage enterprises that employ rudimentary, labor-intensive production technologies, operate in competitive markets, and demonstrate very little productivity growth. These competitive firms, in agriculture, industry, and services in both rural and urban settings, are especially important in the production of wage goods. They have weak internal growth impulses, however, with little capacity for increasing productivity and expanding output and markets by lowering production costs and product prices. As a consequence, they tend to expand only passively, in response to general economic expansion. When competitive sector firms do increase output, they do so principally through hiring additional workers rather than by accumulation.

The competitive sector employs the majority of the economically active population of each nation and is very heterogeneous. It includes small farms with wage labor or only family labor, laundries, artisanal enterprises, petty commerce, restaurants, small factories, and the entire panoply of urban services from shoe shiners to domestic workers in both formal and informal work situations, many of which are either illegal or on the edge of legality. There is typically a high turnover of employees and considerable mobility of workers between urban and rural competitive-sector employments. The scale, structure, and instability of work in this sector is as severe an impediment to organizing effective labor unions as is employer and governmental hostility. Class conflict is muted by low incomes of many proprietors as well as by the diffusion of workers among many small units.

It is important, however, that the use of the general category not obscure important dynamics and differences within the competitive sector. For instance, I have already noted the extent to which the growth of export agriculture forced small cultivators off their land and pushed them into less desirable lands in outlying areas or turned them into landless proletarians with slight prospects for employment outside the competitive sector. This situation resulted in a change of status within the rural competitive sector, and there was an analogous shift in the urban competitive sector. The industrial growth of the 1960s was led by large, capital-intensive enterprises in the modern urban sector, and their products were principally import substituting and not directly competitive with small manufacturing and artisanal enterprises. In the 1970s, however, prices of imported inputs used for manufacturing (for instance, fuel) rose considerably faster than domestic prices of final goods. The resulting profit squeeze forced many of the modern urban firms to seek new markets and to compete more aggressively and directly with the small, competitive firms. So the 1970s was the decade of significant centralization of industrial capital, pressure on independent proprietorships, rural and urban, and greater blurring of lines between wage and nonwage work for the poorest strata of workers.

But in all of this, the competitive sector is not merely an economically irrelevant residual. Its existence is critically important for both the modern urban and export agriculture sectors. The classical function of the competitive sector is to constitute a pool of reserve labor that keeps downward pressure on wage rates in all sectors. And in addition, a large part of the total marketed food as well as some direct inputs necessary for other sectors' production are produced in the competitive sector. And some firms in the modern urban sector directly utilize workers of the competitive sector by subcontracting work to these low-wage workers as individuals or as workers in small firms.

Although the functions performed by the competitive sector are vitally important to the economic system, the sector's expansion during the 1960s and 1970s was much greater than necessary for serving those functions. This overexpansion indicates the inability of the economic system to utilize profitably (exploit) the entire working population. In this technical sense, many of the unemployed and underemployed people are indeed irrelevant to the system, eking out bare existences outside the principal circuits of production. The economic irrelevance of large numbers of workers, however, becomes politically relevant when the destitution of the surplus population becomes a threat to the entire structure.

The State Sector

The logic of the development of the three private sectors generates divergent tendencies. In the modern urban sector, wages can rise, but there are relatively few employment opportunities. Yet even though wage rates in the low-wage export agriculture and competitive sectors can rise, the large number of underemployed workers dampens demand-pull impulses on wages during the up side of the business cycle and exacerbates them on the down side.

As a consequence, excess productive capacity in the modern urban sector coexists with poverty and underemployment among workers in export agriculture and the competitive sectors, generating wealth and growth at one pole and poverty and stagnation at the other. The unevenness of growth among nations, which has been an emphasis of considerable scholarship, is much less problematical than the unevenness of growth within nations. The internal unevenness produces a contradiction fundamental to late capitalism, a contradiction that can be ameliorated but not resolved by the state. While this contradiction is evident in both the First and Third worlds, it is especially severe in the Third World, where one of the key growth-inducing sectors—export agriculture—depends on low wages. Under such circumstances, present in the Central American nations, generally rising wages can impede export agriculture to the point that balance of payments restrictions choke off economic growth in the modern urban sector.

The state, acting as a political entity, implements policies to deal with the centrifugal forces of late capitalism, and the state also manages large volumes of resources and is a substantial economic actor in its own right. Although most of the state's activities are not directly productive in the conventional market sense, the state is a major employer. Wage and salary rates and conditions of work in the state sector are similar and closely linked to those in the modern urban sector, and public-sector employment, again like that in the modern urban sector, is regulated by the availability of positions rather than by wage rates.

The state sector and the modern urban sector are the major employers of those whom I have called the modern middle class. State workers are a numerically important interest group, and their numbers, strategic locations, education, and political skills make them a political force to be reckoned with in all Third World nations, although perhaps less so in Central America than in the southern cone of South America or in Africa. Teachers' unions have been the most politically active among Central American state-sector workers, and in general, as literate people used to working with people, state-sector workers can be effective mobilizers of workers in other sectors.

State employment and expenditure, when used as patronage, can be used to dampen dissent by co-optation, and its rule-making power is another source of social control. As described in the last chapter, worker protests and organizational interests have been increasingly directed at the state rather than at employers, and labor legislation has responded to and influenced this. But the role that the state plays in economic and social stabilization is best understood through expenditure policy, which can be divided into two major categories, expressing the fundamental purposes of state policy. The first is to encourage and make possible accumulation and economic growth in the modern urban and agricultural export sectors, and the second is to foster political "legitimacy" and social stability.

Among the many reasons that state policy pursues the goal of economic growth, the one that most directly and immediately affects state personnel is that economic growth results in increased fiscal revenues. This in turn means increased prosperity, security, status, and responsibility for those intimately connected to the state, whether politicians or bureaucrats. And the capacity of the state to act, of course, is directly related to its command of economic resources.

Because general economic growth of all Central American nations is tied closely to the fortunes of the export agriculture sectors and the modern urban sector, encouraging economic growth means encouraging expansion of these two sectors. When the means of production are owned privately and production is for profit, the logic of the system insists that the only way to stimulate increased production is by raising the profitability of the operations of firms. Strong emphasis on the carrot, with no stick in sight, was the particular ISI strategy favored in the Central American Common Market. One way to achieve this is to lower costs of production for modern urban and export agriculture firms. Some of the important ways in which Central American states reduced costs of production for export agriculture and modern urban sectors were investments in infrastructure (roads, power, communications) financed by domestic governments and international institutions, subsidized imports and credit, the provision of education, favorable tax treatment, and the curtailment of workers' demands.

The second way to increase profitability in order to encourage output growth is to expand markets for the products of the two sectors. Examples of this dimension of policy in Central America are trade and price agreements for agricultural exports, direct governmental purchases, and tariffs and quotas to protect modern urban-sector products from foreign competition (for instance, the CACM). Central American governments successfully pursued another important market development policy: sustaining the highly skewed distribution of income necessary for maintaining a sizable segment of prosperous customers for the products of the modern urban sector in nations with very low average incomes.

Political legitimacy and social stability entail reducing or suppressing disaffection and political unrest, primarily by workers in the export agriculture and competitive sectors and occasionally in the modern urban and state sectors as well. A high rate of economic growth in itself contributes to political legitimacy, especially among those portions of society benefiting from it. But the more important purpose of accumulation and economic growth is to provide the fiscal resources and thus the capacity of the state to effect expenditure policies to preserve legitimacy and stability.

Again there are two principal policy avenues that the state can take. One is to allocate state resources to alleviate the material hardship of the poorest (or at least the most restless) strata of society. The possibility of significant income and property redistribution in the 1960s and 1970s was severely limited by patterns of political power as well as by the market imperatives of the modern urban sector, but Costa Rica and to a lesser extent Honduras successfully maintained a sense of political legitimacy and social stability with ameliorative social policies. In thinking about this dimension of social policy and its effects, it is important that the workers and poor not be interpreted (patronizingly) as being "bought off" or "co-opted" by the powerful. People in both nations fought hard for these measures, and they won at least partial victories against very reluctant elites.

Some of the social services that help to increase political legitimacy, services such as health and education, also contribute to workers' productivity—a process that economists call "investment in human capital." This effect of such policies, however, is apparent only in the long run, whereas their political effects are immediate. So while the ameliorative policies may eventually enhance worker productivity and therefore accumulation, they are generally put into place in response to short-run political imperatives.

The second alternative—strengthening the effectiveness of the state's apparatus of violence and terror—was evident in all five nations but especially in Guatemala, El Salvador, and Nicaragua. This type of policy, however, is also expensive, and Figure 5.7 shows that U.S. military aid

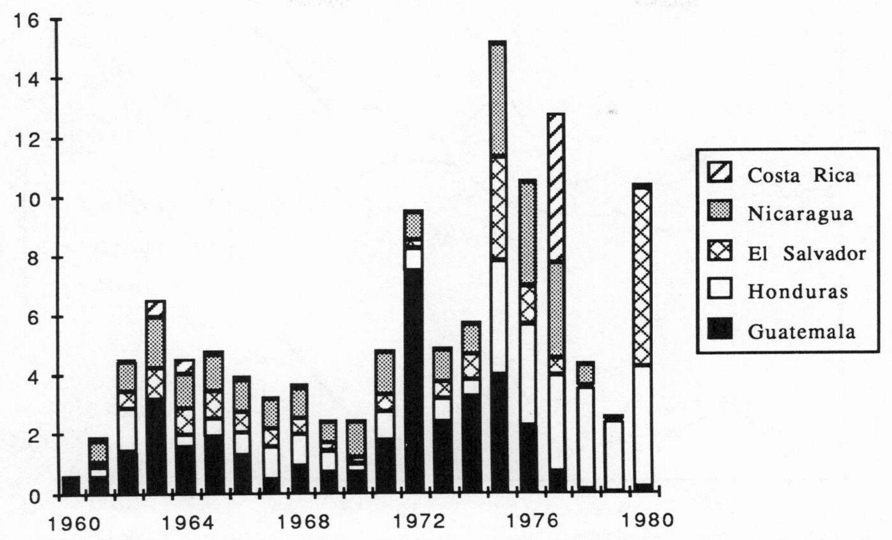

FIGURE 5.7 U.S. military assistance, 1960–1980 (U.S.$ millions). *Sources: Statistical Abstract of Latin America, Supplement 3* (Los Angeles: UCLA Latin American Center, 1974), pp. 371–376; *Statistical Abstract of Latin America,* Vol. 22 (Los Angeles: UCLA Latin American Center, 1983), p. 152.

was critically important in making repression a feasible policy option. Moreover, it has extremely slim prospects of enhancing worker productivity, and even when it is successful in ensuring social stability it probably has negative effects on workers' willingness and ability to produce.

The Fiscal Crisis

For public policy to contain the centrifugal forces embodied in modern capitalist development, the state must employ public resources effectively to promote economic growth in the modern urban and agriculture export sectors and to sustain political legitimacy or at least quiescence through social programs and a constant readiness to apply violence against the workers in the agricultural export and competitive sectors. These two dimensions of policy goals—economic growth and social stability—require large expenditures, and success in both is necessary because each requires the other. These goals become increasingly difficult to attain, as economic growth leads to greater sectoral divergence. Figure 5.8 illustrates the difficulty the states experienced in balancing state revenues and expenditures (thus the deficits) in the five nations.

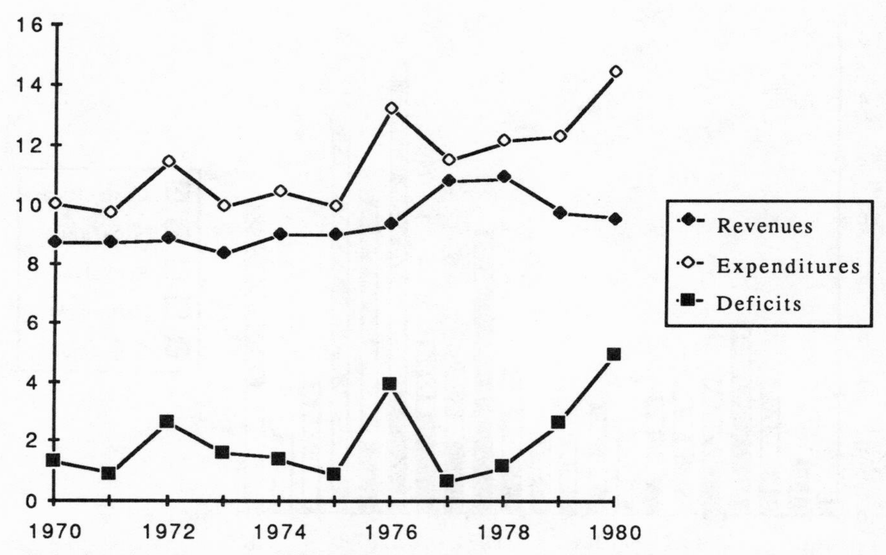

FIGURE 5.8a Revenues, expenditures, and deficits as percentage of GDP: Guatemala, 1970–1980. *Source:* Inter-American Development Bank, *Economic and Social Progress in Latin America,* annual reports for 1975 and 1980–1981.

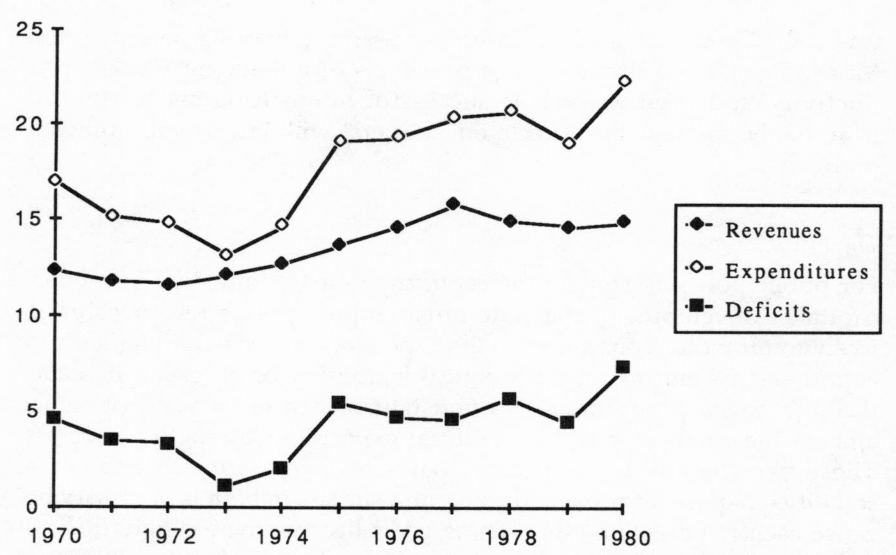

FIGURE 5.8b Revenues, expenditures, and deficits as percentage of GDP: Honduras, 1970–1980. *Source:* Inter-American Development Bank, *Economic and Social Progress in Latin America,* annual reports for 1975 and 1980–1981.

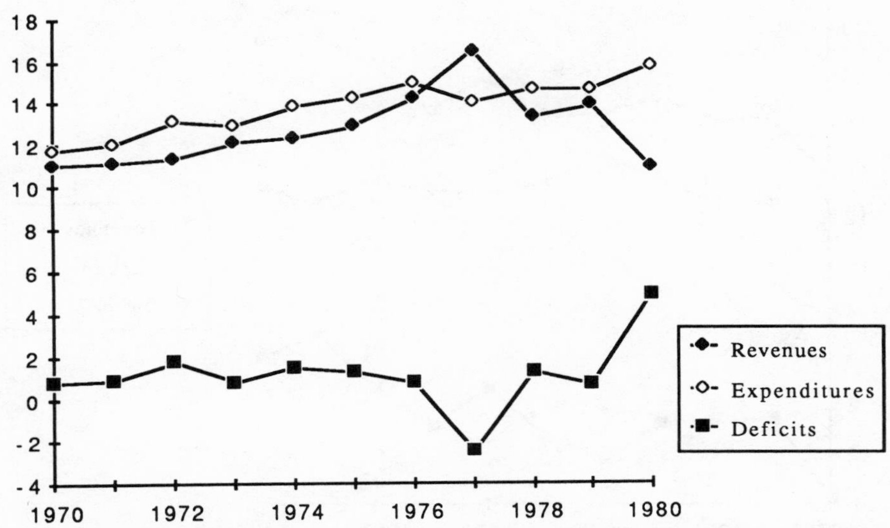

FIGURE 5.8c Revenues, expenditures, and deficits as percentage of GDP: El Salvador, 1970–1980. *Source:* Inter-American Development Bank, *Economic and Social Progress in Latin America,* annual reports for 1975 and 1980–1981.

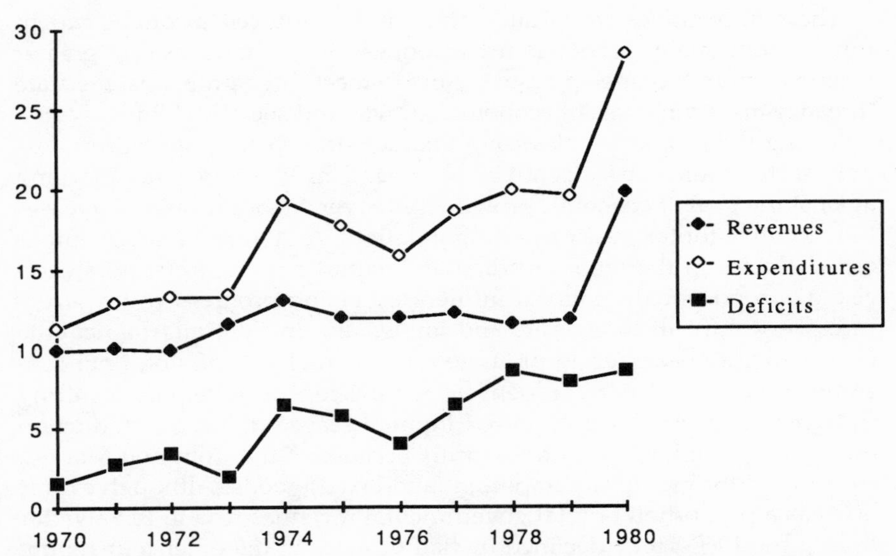

FIGURE 5.8d Revenues, expenditures, and deficits as percentage of GDP: Nicaragua, 1970–1980. *Source:* Inter-American Development Bank, *Economic and Social Progress in Latin America,* annual reports for 1975 and 1980–1981.

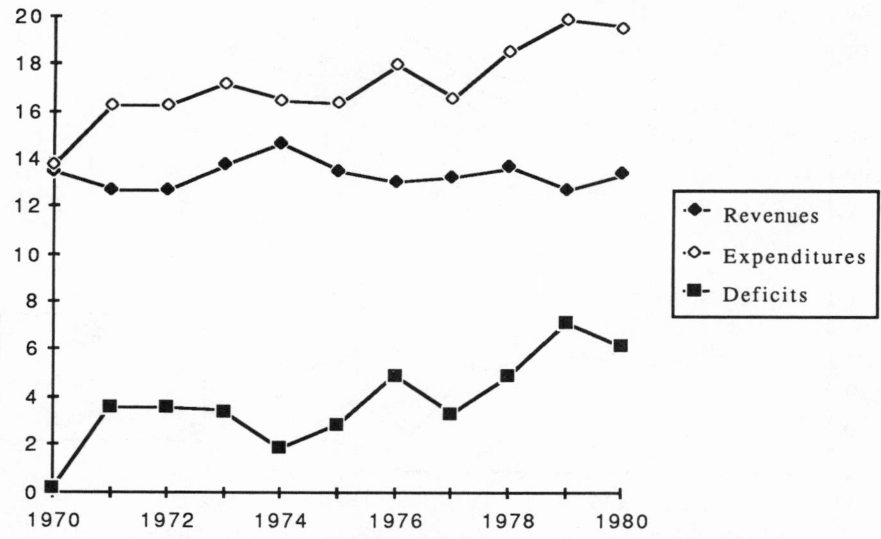

FIGURE 5.8e Revenues, expenditures, and deficits as percentage of GDP: Costa Rica, 1970–1980. *Source:* Inter-American Development Bank, *Economic and Social Progress in Latin America,* annual reports for 1975 and 1980–1981.

These imperatives chronically strain fiscal resources, as public expenditures continually press against revenues. By trying to extract greater resources from the three private sectors to meet these problems, the state threatens the twin goals of economic growth and social stability.

Taxing the propertied classes in the modern urban or agricultural export sector blunts the incentives to expand production, thus working against the goal of economic growth. Moreover, higher taxation increases the incentive for tax evasion and capital flight. And in any case, the propertied classes in the modern urban and export agriculture sectors exercise disproportionate political influence, making progressive tax structures very difficult to legislate and implement. In Central America, the tariff structure designed to promote ISI—the higher tariffs on final consumer goods—did not compensate for the loss of revenues resulting from reducing tariffs on imported inputs because domestic production (or regional production with no tariffs because of the Common Market) substituted for previously imported (and taxed) goods. Although export taxes as a proportion of total governmental revenues rose in El Salvador during the 1960s, they declined by half or more in the other four republics. In addition, the state's ability to capture sufficient resources was seriously weakened by generous tax incentives for new and existing enterprises in the city as well as in the countryside, political inability to promulgate high-yield taxes on large incomes and properties, and serious problems with administrative ineffectiveness and corruption.

Taxing the competitive sector is not easy either, because it is extremely hard and expensive to collect a little from many. This is true of employers as well as workers, especially when so many of the sector's economic activities are "informal" and only erratically recorded. In any case, reducing the incomes of the poor through taxes increases the costs of compensating policies of amelioration and repression.

Because of the difficulty of securing sufficient flows of tax revenues, state expenditure growth constantly threatens to overwhelm revenues. Public revenues in Central America continue to depend primarily on indirect (and usually regressive) taxes that yield revenues that seldom grow as rapidly as total output. Expenditure imperatives, however, often expand more quickly than total output. In response to the insufficiency of fiscal revenues, the five members of the Central American Common Market agreed in 1968 (the "San José Protocol") to increase all common tariffs by 30 percent. The across-the-board proportional increase augmented the levels of effective protection, and the entire effort was an unambiguous indication that none of the member governments was in a position to alter the level and incidence of domestic tax structures.

The consequence of chronic revenue shortfall is a strong tendency toward fiscal crisis, and the state necessarily resorts to deficit financing. If the deficit is financed domestically by borrowing from private individuals and firms, it competes with private capital formation and thereby retards economic growth in the modern urban and export sectors. But if the state borrows from the other domestic source, the central bank, it increases the amount of money in circulation and contributes to inflation and balance of payments deficits, which also impede economic growth. Inflationary impulses of this sort, unusual for Central America but common throughout the rest of Latin America, became evident in Guatemala, El Salvador, Honduras, and especially Costa Rica even before the 1973 price rise of petroleum.

If the state borrows abroad to mitigate the consequences of the basic contradictions embodied in the structure of production and power, it runs the risk of exacerbating the "two gaps"—governmental budgetary deficits and foreign exchange shortages—by mortgaging future fiscal resources in both domestic and foreign currencies. Table 5.3 shows the significant rise of foreign indebtedness among the nations of Central America during the 1970s.

The structural tendency to fiscal crisis with the continuing vulnerability to balance of payments deficits was the genesis of the international debt crisis of the 1980s. The promotion of economic growth and maintenance of social stability became more expensive as the contradictions

TABLE 5.3 External Public Debt and Debt Service Payments, 1970 and 1979

	External Public Debt				Debt Service (% of Exports)	
	U.S. $1,000,000		% of GDP			
	1970	1979	1970	1979	1970	1979
Guatemala	106	282	5.7	7.0	7.4	2.2
Honduras	90	746	12.8	36.3	2.8	12.7
El Salvador	88	397	8.6	11.5	3.6	3.2
Nicaragua	155	1,101	20.6	62.9	11.1	8.1
Costa Rica	134	1,277	13.8	33.0	9.9	23.1

Source: World Bank, *World Development Report 1981* (Washington, D.C.: World Bank, 1981), pp. 158-159, 162-163.

of economic growth proceeded through the 1960s and 1970s, and the need for fiscal resources ran up against the inability and unwillingness to implement effective tax systems. The availability of foreign sources of borrowing made foreign loans an attractive way out of the impasse.

But why was so much international credit readily available to what had to have been seen as borrowers representing considerable risk for lenders? This takes us to the supply side of the international credit market, the nature of which determined the character and pressures of the eventual debt crisis.[9]

The leaders of Middle Eastern oil-rich nations, joined by other oil-exporting nations and with the cooperation of transnational oil corporations, quadrupled the price of petroleum in 1973. This exercise of market power by oil exporters meant that the volume of foreign exchange necessary for imported oil by the five Central American nations, none of which was energy self-sufficient, rose dramatically. Meanwhile, the rise in oil prices sent the industrialized nations into a recession accompanied by inflation ("stagflation"). As shown in Figure 5.6, the newly diversified exports of Central America did quite well, compared to other Latin American nations and especially to Africa, in good part because of the sharp rise in coffee prices stemming from a massive failure of the Brazilian coffee crop in 1975. Nevertheless, the recession still slowed the growth of exports (and thus foreign exchange earnings) at the same time that the prices of imported fuel and manufactured inputs rose.

Along with domestic fiscal crises, international balance of payments difficulties propelled Central American governments into the market to borrow foreign exchange. There is a definite irony in the fact that one of the reasons leading to demands by the Central American governments for credit at the same time was the source of the supply of the needed credit. The success of the oil-exporting nations' price rises led to their depositing large amounts of U.S. dollars in European and North American private banks that were approved (i.e., had no Jewish connections). The banks, therefore, had to lend these newly swollen reserves in order to make them profitable, and the recession in the industrialized nations, induced in part by high oil prices, made this more difficult. High-pressure salesmanship by the banks to place loans in the Third World, irrespective of the prospective borrowers' creditworthiness, was one of the banks' strategies to "recycle petrodollars." This, together with Central American governments' financial straits, led to the piling up of formidable levels of debt during the 1970s and early 1980s.

The easy access to loanable funds from private banks meant that the governments did not have to borrow from the International Monetary Fund (IMF) to cover shortfalls, and thus they avoided the stringent conditions ("conditionality") that the IMF imposed on borrowers. This situation sharply reduced the IMF's ability to discipline governments whose fiscal and international financial positions were judged to be too extended. With the additional oil price boost of 1979, the more severe global recession of the 1980s, and record high interest rates, however, Third World debtors were unable to continue paying their escalating debt services. Mexico's 1982 declaration of a moratorium on debt payments, followed by others, led to a panic among the international banking community, which was seriously overextended in Third World loans that suddenly seemed vulnerable to default.

Therefore, except for negotiated "debt restructuring" agreements, new private lending to the Third World stopped completely, making it even more difficult for governments to meet their payments on previous loans. The private banks turned to the IMF, which with the support of the major industrial powers quickly assumed the role of a collection agency for the private banks in an effort to save them from the consequences of their poor judgment in placing loans. As a result, the IMF was reestablished as the most influential pillar of prudent international banking practices. For a debtor nation to qualify for even minimal debt relief, the IMF applied a set of stringent requirements, known as "structural adjustment programs," that compelled the reduction of government deficits, required privatization of spheres of economic life that had been a part of the public domain, reduced and eliminated tariffs and exchange controls, called for the withdrawal of government intervention in and regulation of markets (e.g., food subsidies), and strongly promoted the increase of exports, new or traditional, to enhance the availability of hard currencies in order to pay back the debt.

Not all of the debt contracted by the Central American governments during the 1970s went to finance economic growth, balance of payments deficits, social programs, or the protection of the social structure from assaults by the majority of the population. A large (but difficult-to-estimate) amount of funds was made available, through legal or other means, to citizens who used them for private purposes unconnected with any public goals. These funds included those for the importation of luxury goods or, perhaps more frequently, the conversion of local assets into dollars to deposit in foreign banks. This last use of dollars is called "capital flight," and insecure social and political conditions were very strong incentives for those with the means to pull their assets out of local danger. Because there were no restrictions on capital flight in any of the five Central American nations during the 1970s, a good number of the petrodollars recycled as loans to Central American governments were again recycled back as private deposits, often to the very banks that lent the dollars.

The frequency with which governmental borrowings were used by private individuals for private ends or by public agencies for suppressing the majority of the population calls into sharp question the frequent, casual statement that "Guatemala," say, borrowed money from the Chase Manhattan Bank and is contracted to repay it. An extremely unrepresentative military government borrowed the money, and specific groups and private individuals benefited from the use of it. The debt, of course, is considered to belong to Guatemala as a nation, which means that the "nation" is supposed to repay it. There is no question that the entire operation continues to involve large-scale transfers of income from the poorest to the richest within nations as well as among nations.

This situation gives an important clue to the reason that there was no large-scale defaulting on the international debt in Latin America. In spite of several historical precedents and, in some cases, solid cost-benefit reasons (at the level of the nation) for doing so, domestic governmental and economic elites were too dependent on the international system for their positions within their own nations to risk alienating those who controlled the system by defaulting on the debt. It was definitely preferable to make other citizens of their nations bear the burden of the debt.

The genesis of the debt crisis in Central America was the governmental fiscal crises, which in turn derived from the governments' efforts to respond to the structural contradictions of economic success. Foreign borrowing became a crisis only in the early 1980s, after the civil strife in Nicaragua, El Salvador, and Guatemala was well under way. But although the debt crisis was more an effect rather than a cause of political conflict in Central America, it is a critically important part of the general context in which the subsequent struggles were conducted.

Notes

1. Diana Hunt, *Economic Theories of Development: Analysis of Competing Paradigms* (Savage, MD: Barnes and Noble, 1989), is a good intellectual history of

post–World War II thought in the United States and Europe about economic development in the Third World.

2. Good on general economic growth in the period are Victor Bulmer-Thomas, *The Political Economy of Central America Since 1920* (New York: Cambridge University Press, 1987), and John Weeks, *The Economies of Central America* (New York: Holmes and Meier, 1985). For agriculture in particular, see Robert C. Williams, *Export Agriculture and the Crisis in Central America* (Chapel Hill: University of North Carolina Press, 1986); and Charles Brockett, *Land, Power, and Poverty: Agrarian Transformation and Political Change in Central America* (Boulder, CO: Westview Press, 1990).

3. Cf. Bulmer-Thomas, *The Political Economy of Central America Since 1920.*

4. Merilee S. Grindle, *State and Countryside: Development Policy and Agrarian Politics in Latin America* (Baltimore, MD: Johns Hopkins University Press, 1986), p. 7. This book is a good study of agriculture development throughout Latin America.

5. Cristóbal Kay, *Latin American Theories of Development and Underdevelopment* (New York: Routledge, 1989), surveys CEPAL thinking, and Osvaldo Sunkel (ed.), *Development from Within: Toward a Neostructuralist Approach for Latin America* (Boulder, CO: Lynne Rienner Publishers, 1993), is an interesting collection of articles by Latin American economists working in the CEPAL tradition responding to the assault on CEPAL programs by the neoclassical doctrines promoted by the IMF, World Bank, and U.S. and European governments.

6. Thomas L. Karnes, *The Failure of Union: Central America, 1824–1960* (Chapel Hill: University of North Carolina Press, 1961), is a history of the attempts at union. In addition to the works cited in note 2, W. R. Cline and A. I. Delgado (eds.), *Economic Integration in Central America* (Washington, D.C.: Brookings Institution, 1978), contains a number of useful studies of the Central American Common Market.

7. Walter LaFeber, *Inevitable Revolutions: The United States in Central America*, 2d ed. (New York: W. W. Norton, 1993), describes this shift in U.S. strategy.

8. Similar analytical frameworks are formulated and applied to the United States in Robert T. Averitt, *The Dual Economy: The Dynamics of American Industry Structure* (New York: W. W. Norton, 1968); David M. Gordon, Richard Edwards, and Michael Reich, *Segmented Work, Divided Workers: The Historical Transformation of Labor in the United States* (Cambridge: Cambridge University Press, 1982); and especially James O'Connor, *The Fiscal Crisis of the State* (New York: St. Martin's, 1973).

9. An excellent outline of the international circumstances leading to the Latin American debt crises is in William L. Canak, "Debt, Austerity, and Latin America in the New International Division of Labor," in W. L. Canak (ed.), *Lost Promises: Debt, Austerity and Development in Latin America* (Boulder, CO: Westview Press, 1984), pp. 9–27.

6

Economic Dynamism and Political Decay, the 1950s to the Early 1980s

The categories of the model presented in the preceding chapter were designed to identify the conditions necessary to promote economic growth and reproduce the social order and emphasized the role of the state and the way in which key social and economic elements interact through the process of economic growth. As noted earlier, the increasing economic integration and interdependence of the nations' populations, both in product and labor markets, do not automatically lead to increased social coherence, harmony, or stability. Even though economic growth in Central America during the 1960s and 1970s included qualities considered by economists to be very desirable—export diversification, agricultural modernization, and industrialization—the particular manner in which people and production have been integrated through the market has exacerbated sectoral divergence, conflict, and social disruption.

In considering the responses of the state to these tendencies, however, it must be understood that the categories of the model neither specify nor restrict the social base of the state. That is, the model does not require the state to be in the hands of propertied classes, popular classes, or state bureaucrats, be authoritarian or democratic in regime type, or be reactionary or progressive in its policies. But the state must deal with the contradictions embodied in the uneven growth of the sectors and with the chronic tendency to fiscal crisis. As we will see shortly, there are a number of ways in which the state can try to mitigate the contradictions of capitalist growth. The social composition of the state's principal constituencies is one of the principal determinants of which policy choices are favored.

As has already been mentioned, the pattern of modern capitalist growth accumulates wealth and power at one pole and poverty, anger, and despair at the other. Not all poverty is in the competitive sector, and certainly not everyone in the competitive sector is poor, as in the case of proprietors of some small-scale enterprises. Nevertheless, most material deprivation is located there. The expansion of export agriculture led to the dispossession of many campesino agriculturalists in all five nations without corresponding increases in export-sector jobs. Like export agriculture, manufacturing growth produced many more goods than employment opportunities and its modern form may have actually reduced manufacturing jobs in the region by driving small-scale, labor-intensive manufacturing firms out of business.

Although the organization of the competitive-sector work force (including the dispersal of the workers among a large number of small production units) makes them the most difficult to organize at work sites, the circumstances of the 1960s and 1970s galvanized thousands of the previously unorganized into major political actions, overcoming the obstacles presented by the sector's organization and official hostility. The formation of regional and national peasant leagues and urban initiatives throughout the isthmus were the major political news of the two decades.

The Politics of Religion

Before looking more closely at events in individual nations, it is worth mentioning at the general level that these efforts were supported and encouraged throughout Central America by another development that was happening at the village and neighborhood level. Catholic priests and nuns, energized by the Church's newly articulated social gospel ("liberation theology"), were important catalysts of political and self-help movements among the poorest. In the late 1950s and early 1960s, Pope John XXIII emphasized the social responsibility of the Church and approved the political actions necessary to carry out these responsibilities. The doctrines of Vatican II both reflected and influenced the work of priests, nuns, and lay readers in Latin America, and the Second Bishops' Conference in Medellín, Colombia, in 1968 was a high point. The conference formally declared the intention of implementing these new social teachings in Latin America.

The 1960s and early 1970s, then, were a time in which many Catholic clergy helped poor people to form cooperatives, explore the social teachings of the Bible themselves, organize community action projects, and press authorities for the redress of grievances. But it is important to understand that this activity was not all the creation of papal decree. Since the 1940s, Catholic Action workers in Guatemala had been involved in these kinds of activities, initiated to maintain some Church influence in the newly democratic and reformist regimes of Arévalo and Arbenz.

After 1954, foreign priests were again allowed to enter the country, an opportunity that the Church hierarchy responded to quickly to expand its influence in the Guatemala governed by Castillo Armas. To the dismay of many, the new young priests joined with progressive Catholic Action workers to form a significant group committed to grassroots organization, self-help activities, and the social gospel.

Despite the conservative intentions behind these moves by the Church hierarchy during the 1940s and 1950s, the ground had been laid for the formal acceptance of the responsibilities of the social gospel in the 1960s. But as soon as Church activists found new support and effectiveness, the successes of the Christian base communities brought them and the Church as an institution, sometimes including even bishops and archbishops, into direct opposition to the state and made them targets for brutal reprisals.

The enthusiasm for social reform among the upper reaches of the Church hierarchy did not last long. The 1979 bishops' conference in Puebla, Mexico, compared to the 1968 meeting, was a rather tepid affair. Perhaps in part because of the brutality of the response to the Church's efforts, Pope John's successors have backed away from the social gospel and Pope John Paul II has virtually repudiated social and political commitments.

Civil War, Revolution, and Reform

Clerical activism, like other influences, worked out differently in each of the five Central American nations, and we must look at the individual countries to understand the significance of the economic transformation that occurred during the 1960s and 1970s to appreciate the differences of social contexts.

Guatemala

The decade of the 1960s was marked by significant economic growth, export diversification, and armed struggle.[1] The Guatemalan state, under military control in the 1960s and 1970s, actively promoted economic growth and export diversification through the provisions of the Central American Common Market as well as active credit and infrastructural investments within a generally interventionist stance toward the economy. Although fiscal problems in the second half of the 1960s forced the state to reduce its developmental efforts, they were renewed with vigor in the early 1970s, tipping more toward industry than export agriculture.

The armed struggle part of the story began in 1960, when several young army officers tried to overthrow the corrupt and inept Ydígoras administration, reacting to the government's contribution to the U.S.

Central Intelligence Agency's training of pilots for the invasion of Cuba (the Bay of Pigs debacle of 1961). The coup failed, in part because some of those very same CIA pilots helped to defend the government.

Two of the coup's leaders, Lieutenants Marco Antonio Yon Sosa and Luís Turcios Lima, retreated to the countryside in the south and east to organize a guerrilla campaign along what were understood to be the tactical lines of the Cuban revolution. The areas selected were ladino areas where expanding cattle ranches had put the campesinos on the defensive, but the guerrilla leaders made minimal efforts to involve the Indians of the northern and northwestern highlands.

A disagreement between Yon Sosa and Turcios split the movement, and neither ever achieved large-scale grassroots support. Nevertheless, by the early 1960s there was no question among the Guatemalan military that the countryside needed serious attention. This made the army high command unwilling to tolerate Ydígoras, especially his allowing Juan José Arévalo, president from 1944 to 1948, to return to Guatemala as a presidential candidate in the forthcoming elections. In 1963, General Enrique Peralta Azurdia led a successful coup against Ydígoras, a move approved by the Kennedy administration in the United States, which was also deeply concerned about the possibility of Arévalo's presidential candidacy.

The military would probably have moved against Ydígoras and destroyed even the semblance of political democracy without U.S. support, but the U.S. government had become an important constituent of the Guatemalan military, and its opinion mattered. Table 4.4 showed that the Guatemalan military benefited from generous military grants and loans from the United States during the late 1950s, helping the military government that it had installed in 1954. This support enabled the military to act with greater independence of the propertied classes in the countryside and in the burgeoning modern urban sector than would have been feasible without it. Although the Guatemalan military was heavily indebted to U.S. military aid and training for its development, it was gaining a much stronger sense of itself as an independent institution with its own interests and mission, and senior officers increasingly resented taking orders from the U.S. Pentagon.

The growing self-consciousness of the Guatemalan military as well as its ability to govern effectively were enhanced by the end of the schism between the regular army and the participants in the CIA-sponsored "liberation" of 1954. The army's decision at that time not to defend the constitutional government of Jacobo Arbenz against a U.S.-sponsored invasion of irregulars damaged the reputation, internal coherence, and morale of the Guatemalan military. Peralta's coup came from the regular army, and it defined the beginning of the systematic institutionalization of military rule. This institutionalization included tightening command structures, reducing corruption, and reorganizing the military so that it could be more effective in governing and counterinsurgency. The last activity was actively supported by U.S. aid, which also encouraged military civic action projects such as constructing roads, schools, and health clinics.

In spite of their wariness of U.S. influence, the benefits Peralta and the military derived from the Alliance for Progress and military aid came at a price that still had to be paid. The U.S. government added to the pressure from domestic groups, notably the urban middle class, to hold elections. As a consequence, the military reluctantly agreed to national elections to be held in 1966 after drawing up a new constitution.

To the military's surprise, its limiting the range of approved parties and voters, censoring the media, and threatening all involved were not enough to ensure the election of the military candidate. Julio César Méndez Montenegro, rector of the University of San Carlos, won the election. The military did not allow him to assume office, however, until he and it had arrived at explicit understandings of the military's autonomy from civilian political control, especially in regard to fighting the guerrillas. The lesson that the guerrillas drew from this accord was that the electoral process is impotent and that armed struggle was the only possible source of reform. This lesson effectively reduced the possibility of a nonviolent political resolution.

By the mid-1960s, the guerrillas' most dramatic moves were in the cities, where the senior U.S. military attaché, the U.S. ambassador, the German ambassador, and several prominent Guatemalans, including the foreign minister, were kidnapped, assassinated, or both. A number of right-wing vigilante terrorist groups, closely connected to the police and army, emerged at the same time, and individuals suspected of reformist sentiment were victims of murder, kidnapping, and torture. The entire board of directors of the left-wing labor confederation was annihilated, and many others who were identified with the political left or center, including jurists, politicians, academics, and journalists, were vulnerable. These events were the beginning of the "disappearances" in Latin America—a tactic that was more fully reported in the United States when it occurred in Argentina ten years later.

To deal with the countryside, the army established a number of units with specialized counterinsurgency training and equipment, both supplied by the United States, which was fearful of "another Cuba." The civic action of the early 1960s was virtually abandoned, and the tactical emphasis was "pacification" of the type that the United States was practicing in Vietnam at the same time. This "pacification" included torturing and killing individuals and groups of peoples, often entire villages, who were suspected of cooperating with or of being potentially useful to the insurgents.

It was during the administration of a mildly reformist civilian president, then, that the vicious barbarism of the Guatemalan military and paramilitary units began in earnest. During the first year after the 1970 "election" of General Carlos Arana Osorio, who had earned a fearful reputation in the pacification of one province, an estimated 2,000 political murders occurred.

By 1972, when it was becoming clear that U.S. counterinsurgency efforts in Vietnam were failing, the forces of repression in Guatemala were succeeding. This success paved the way for the election of a more moderate president, General Eugenio Kjell Laugerud, whom Arana had selected in the mistaken belief that he could be controlled from behind the scenes. Kjell Laugerud reduced the pressure on urban labor unions and, while keeping firm control, allowed the development of a series of rural cooperatives, many led by parish priests.

But after the 1976 earthquake—a disaster that killed an estimated 25,000 people—Kjell Laugerud cracked down hard. Even though the national relief effort was relatively effective, especially compared to the Nicaraguan experience of a less severe quake in 1972, the earthquake destruction stimulated the formation of local reconstruction organizations that the military considered potentially dangerous. The mode of social control exercised in the second half of Kjell Laugerud's term was more like that practiced during the Arana administration: It relied almost exclusively on severe repression in both rural and urban areas. One notable urban example of the government's response to dissent was the systematic murder of workers attempting to unionize the local Coca Cola plant, murders that raised serious questions about the involvement of the U.S. managers.

These popular pressures among both rural and urban labor helped to unify the propertied classes—export agriculture and modern urban, domestic and foreign. In the context of a threat from below, the consolidated elite saw even the most modest reformist initiative as an assault on the foundations of property rights and the structure of privilege.

As a part of the hardening line toward reform during the 1970s, the military governments revived Guatemalan claims to Belize (British Honduras) in an effort to divert the opposition with a nationalist cause. The attempt was not very successful, and although Guatemalan claims to Belize were not unfounded, they were defused by Britain's granting independence to Belize in 1981.

The 1970s was also the time of the Transversal road construction project in the north of Guatemala. The road was built primarily to make the Guatemalan oil fields on the Mexican border of Chiapas more accessible, but it also opened a corridor through a large region that had been inaccessible for urbanites and made the land attractive for development. As a consequence, vast tracts of Indian lands were ruthlessly appropriated by army officers and allied civilian politicians.

This use of position for personal enrichment by military officers, however, was different from the growth of the economic power of the military as an institution. The military increasingly assumed direct control of public agencies, transportation, communications, and electrical power; operated two large diversified credit institutions and two factories producing military materiel; and controlled through regulation and supervision large proportions of economic activity. The institutional aspect of military penetration of civil society was more important than opportunism by individual officers; the Guatemalan military was beginning to aspire to be the propertied classes' partners rather than merely their instrument.

This was the situation when General Romeo Lucas García was elected in 1976. Although the election was competitive, the competition was among three generals, and factional strife within the military rather than votes by the intimidated citizenry determined the winner. But the national scene also included large numbers of increasingly angry and mobilized Indian campesinos, who had not been involved in the insurrection of the 1960s, and these forces occupied the central stage of the late 1970s and early 1980s.

During the 1960s and 1970s, then, the state was militarized to an extent heretofore unknown even in Guatemala. The state worked hard to develop the export agriculture and modern urban sectors, and in so doing it occasionally went against the interests of particular firms or segments of the propertied classes. The militarized state defended the propertied interests in both sectors, however, and it performed this task in a most uncompromising and ruthless manner, relying almost exclusively on repression rather than on ameliorating policies. An exception was the survival of the social security system (accident insurance and pensions) from the 1940s, and during the 1960s it was extended until it covered more than a quarter of the working population, much of which was in rural areas. The growth in coverage stalled in the 1970s, however, and coverage contracted in the last years of the decade.

U.S. financial and tactical assistance was crucial in the fuller development of the repressive system, but the Guatemalan military and propertied elites demonstrated their ability to sustain these efforts even when U.S. president Jimmy Carter cut off military aid to Guatemala in the late 1970s on the principled grounds of human rights violations. This decline in assistance can be seen in Figure 5.7. Although Figure 5.8 reveals some tendency toward fiscal crisis during the 1960s and early 1970s, the cutoff of military aid escalated this tendency, in spite of partially offsetting Argentine and Israeli help. Although this development is described here in terms of U.S. decisions about funding the Guatemalan military, it was the result of an explicit decision by the Guatemalan military that it did not want U.S. aid if it were to be supervised or held accountable for human rights violations. The strength of this identity and independence sharply distinguished the Guatemalan military from the Salvadoran and Nicaraguan militaries, whose human rights records were also terrible but for whom the resources were more important than any sense of corporate integrity.

Guatemalan tax effort remained very low, even compared to the region, and a good part of the fiscal deficit was financed by external borrowing, especially by decentralized governmental agencies whose debt was guaranteed by the Guatemalan government. This borrowing led to the rise of foreign debt during the 1970s, shown in Table 5.3. Reliance on violence is not inexpensive.

In addition, this approach to social unrest proved to be only temporarily effective. The relatively peaceful respite of the mid-1970s was achieved by screwing down the lid rather than reducing the pressures. That the previous problems had not gone away soon became painfully evident. Miners and sugar workers staged a massive strike in 1977 that was supported by working- and middle-class demonstrations in Guatemala City; public-sector workers went out on strike in early 1978; cotton and sugar workers struck in early 1980; and general riots broke out in Guatemala City in 1980.

Among the job actions by export- and state-sector workers and urban outbreaks, there were even more ominous rumblings among the rural Indian population, exacerbated by the army's killing more than 100 people in a small Indian village. These and other incidents marked the beginnings of a cruel civil war fought without quarter. Its most bloody period was from 1978 to 1983.

There was considerable urban political activity, to which the response was killing by death squads of hundreds of left and moderate political figures and labor leaders, but the principal war zone was in the northern and northwestern highlands, where the army lost control over large areas in the first years of the 1980s. Unlike in the previous guerrilla war, Indians were the major combatants. Once again, however, the Guatemalan army managed to clamp the lid back down by 1984. Their strategy included completely destroying a number of entire villages and indiscriminately killing anyone within certain geographical areas in scorched earth campaigns, creating new villages in which thousands of Indians were forcibly relocated, and pressing tens of thousands of men into civilian patrols that functioned as much to control the patrollers as to maintain surveillance over those not in a new village. This tactic obviously owed much to the "armored hamlets" created by the United States in Vietnam as well as to similar efforts by colonial powers in such places as Algeria, Malaya, and South Africa. The local historical precedent for Guatemala, however, was the Dominican priests' relocation of much of the Guatemalan Indian population during the sixteenth century, as described in Chapter 1. Altogether, the estimates are that 100,000 civilians were killed and around 1 million were forced to flee their homes. Many of these refugees left Guatemala altogether. Perhaps 200,000 of them entered the United States, tens of thousands of others lived in United Nations camps in Mexico, and some fewer in camps in Belize and Honduras.

U.S. military aid to Guatemala was resumed in 1983, but the Guatemalan army's human rights violations were so extensive, obvious, and continuous that the Reagan administration failed to convince the U.S. Congress to support fully the fight against the guerrillas. This was a disappointment to the Guatemalan officers, but they made no effort to change even their image until after they were satisfied that the guerrillas had been satisfactorily crushed.

Although there was middle-class participation, the war in Guatemala was much more a class struggle than was the broadly gauged Nicaraguan revolution. No doubt influenced by the success of revolutionary reforms in Nicaragua, upper-class Guatemalans continued to be substantially unified in their fears and therefore in their support for a military rather than ameliorative solution to social unrest. But the direct political influence of the upper classes should not be exaggerated. In the early 1980s, there was dissension within the ranks of the Guatemalan military officers, and dissatisfaction with the conduct of the war led to coups and countercoups in the early 1980s. In this infighting, civilian elites were increasingly marginalized in their ability to exercise a political voice in national affairs.

The demographics of the war also might have contributed to upper-class unity. It was not just poor Guatemalans challenging the social and political structure; they were Indians. This cultural ("racial") aspect of the struggle distinguished Guatemala sharply from Nicaragua, where the only strongly Indian areas are in the east and were virtually irrelevant to the revolution until after the Triumph. And of course, the Nicaraguan Indian population was very small, whereas Guatemalan Indians made up around 40 percent of the national population.

That the struggle against extant structures of privilege was being waged by "the other" probably helped upper-class unity, but it is difficult to speak precisely about the directly cultural aspects of the struggle from the side of the Indians. Certainly they were fighting to maintain a way of life, but "cultural preservation" is an elusive concept. The very definition of culture is fluid, and it is unclear about which aspects of group practices, values, and shared meanings were especially vital for the preservation of the culture. Related to these questions, some centrally important pieces of Indian culture were given up in order to mount the struggle itself. For instance, many Indian guerrillas became fluent in Spanish, conversant with the Christian Bible (often as catechists), and adept with the arms and tactics of modern guerrilla warfare, all of which are completely alien to traditional cultural practices. Yet many enlisted soldiers in the national army were of Indian background, and like Salvadoran soldiers, they seemed quite willing and able to terrorize the villages and assault the cultures of their origins.[2]

In discussing issues of culture, it is necessary to keep in mind that Guatemalan Indians were not choosing traditional ways of life over middle-class life-styles. They were resisting being cleared from their land, as in the case of the area around the Transversal highway, and as such they were fighting to preserve their very lives. The alternatives to their familiar ways of life, already altered substantially by five centuries of penetrations and by recent innovations, such as cooperatives, schools, and health clinics established with the help of radical clerics and other community organizers, were extremely bleak. The alternative was extreme degradation if not starvation, and the fight was at least as much about physical survival as it was about cultural survival.

Moreover, Guatemalan "Indians" were and are not a homogeneous group of people. There are at least five major languages and multiple important dialects among these diverse peoples, and even the politics of their revolts is unclear. Opponents of the Guatemalan regime, both domestic and foreign, claimed that the Indians were in some general sense a radical, revolutionary political force. It is ironic that they thereby agreed with the Guatemalan oppressors and their supporters, who portrayed the Indian rebels as part of some worldwide Communist conspiracy. Many of the Indian guerrillas may have been fighting more in the conservative spirit of José Rafael Carrera, whom we met in Chapter 2, than to transform society along lines envisioned by Che Guevara or Mao Tse Tung.

Costa Rica

The political processes and the resulting policies in Costa Rica during the 1960s and 1970s contrasted sharply with those of Guatemala.[3] José Figueres's first term, 1953 to 1958, was followed by the defeat of the presidential candidate of his political party, the National Liberation Party (Partido Liberal Nacional—PLN). The smooth transition to office by the conservative winner, Mario Echandi, demonstrated the stability of the political system fashioned in the years after the 1948 civil war. Supported by large-scale propertied interests in export agriculture (including processing and commerce), Echandi was elected on a platform that emphasized reducing rather than reversing the statist policies of the PLN.

The new president was not very successful in retarding state expansion, either in its interventionist operations or in the size of its budget and numbers of employees, in part because of the legislature's remaining in the hands of a PLN majority. In other ways, however, he was very effective in achieving what has been called a "democratic consolidation." He loosened restrictions on labor union activity and the Communist Party and reintegrated the Calderonistas (and Calderón himself) into national political life.

In international affairs, the president responded to the export agriculture elite's fears that the Central American Common Market would inhibit free trade and evolve into an ISI protectionist system that diverted resources from exports to domestic manufacturers. As a consequence, Echandi withdrew from the CACM negotiations. It was not until the 1962 election of Francisco Orlich, another PLN president, that Costa Rica joined the Common Market, which, as described in the last chapter, was not a full-blown ISI project.

In spite of this example, however, the differences among Echandi, Figueres before him, and Orlich after him—that is, the differences between the PLN and the principal conservative opposition—were a matter of not very great degree. The consequences of the 1962 election demonstrated the narrowness of the range of political competition and the rather remarkable degree of political consensus existing among the majority of the politically active Costa Rican population.

The narrow range of ideological difference between the major political contenders was maintained. In the next presidential election (1966), the PLN lost to another conservative candidate, José Joaquín Trejos. He again slowed down the expansion of the public sector, and only the legislature prevented him from privatizing the banking system. The PLN, however, did win the next two presidential elections, a second term for José Figueres (1970) and a term for Daniel Oduber (1974). In 1978, the presidency went back into conservative hands with the election of Rodrigo Carazo.

Although the president and his party could make a difference, the policy program of the PLN constituted the basic framework for both allies and opponents. By the early 1960s, the PLN had developed what came to be its general program, adhering to a tricky middle that embraced both an antioligarchical reformism and a strong anticommunism. The motor for modernization was the state, which promoted and regulated the process with a large number of semiautonomous agencies and organizations. The state was to be the principal guarantor of accumulation in both the modern urban and export agriculture sectors. And at the same time, it maintained the system's legitimacy in the eyes of even the poorest, primarily through extensive ameliorative policies (social security, education, health, and so on). The similarity to the ideals of the Alliance for Progress is remarkable.

The PLN's focus was urban manufacturing, especially during the two successive PLN governments in the 1970s, and its generous support of accumulation was quite successful in stimulating high rates of growth in the modern urban sector. But export agriculture was not ignored, and state subventions and support to the sector were also generous. Nevertheless, the domestic and transnational propertied interests who benefited most from these policies remained ambivalent about much of the project. They eagerly sought and enjoyed direct subsidies and the benefits of more extensive transportation, communication, and other public services, but the pervasiveness of state intervention made them uneasy. Their doubt was heightened in the late 1970s, when a series of poor decisions by the government led to the creation of several state enterprises that quickly proved to be failures.

The propertied classes saw a number of disadvantages in the PLN program. First of all, the PLN program was expensive, and Costa Rican taxes were higher than those of other Central American nations. Government regulations also contributed to Costa Rican wages being the highest in Central America. In addition, the state was plagued by bureaucratic inefficiency and corruption, and dealings with public agencies were time consuming, costly, and irritating. And finally, although the public takeover of electrical power led to highly subsidized rates for industrial users and consumers (not true in petroleum refining, however), such nationalizations seemed to call into question the security of large private property. This uncertainty was true in the countryside as well. There were some instances when official forces responded harshly to campesinos' land seizures, but the government's response was often sympathetic, and the state sponsored extensive colonization efforts.

These were real disadvantages for the economic elite, but the system clearly still worked well for the urban and rural propertied, and it did so in tangible ways. Perhaps the most important aspect of its success in the eyes of the privileged was that disruptive protests, strikes, and property seizures were only sporadic and isolated. Accumulation through most of the 1970s was vigorous, and large quantities of foreign direct investment entered urban production regardless of high taxes and wages. And the wealthy were allowed to retain much of the benefits from this growth.

Even though Costa Rica had a reputation and actually was a welfare state somewhat, income distribution in Costa Rica was not substantially different from its neighbors. These income distributions are shown in Table 6.1. It must be kept in mind that income distribution figures are difficult to compile even when a nation has a well-administered, comprehensive income tax.

Part of the explanation for the seeming paradox that the pattern of income distribution in Costa Rica was less equal than that of, say, El Salvador was, apart from the shakiness of the figures, the much higher per capita income in Costa Rica, as displayed in Figure 5.2. In 1976, for instance, per capita income in Costa Rica was more than 75 percent greater than that of El Salvador, so that even though the poorest 20 percent of the Costa Rican population received a proportion of total income two percentage points less than the poorest 20 percent in El Salvador, their absolute level of material deprivation was less. Moreover, state policies in such areas as health, social security, education, and food prices contributed to the material welfare of the poor in ways that were neither registered in income distribution statistics nor available to the poor in other Central American republics.

The Costa Rican state, therefore, worked hard to support accumulation and simultaneously to maintain social stability through political legitimacy, opting for social ameliorative measures over repression. The mix was effective through the two decades in stimulating economic growth while dampening unrest by those who benefited least from the growth.

Governmental revenues did not keep up with expenditures in spite of the comparatively high tax rates. This situation was a result of part of the government's growth strategy as well as the need to make the social policy politically palatable to big capital by minimizing tax costs. The Costa

TABLE 6.1 Estimated Patterns of Income Distribution for Honduras, El Salvador, and Costa Rica, Late 1960s and Early 1970s

		Percent of Income Received by					
		Bottom 20%	Next 20%	Next 20%	Next 20%	Top 20%	Top 10%
Honduras	1967	2.3	5.0	8.0	16.0	67.8	50.0
El Salvador	1976-77	5.5	10.0	14.8	22.4	47.3	29.5
Costa Rica	1971	3.3	8.7	13.3	19.9	54.8	39.5

Source: World Bank, *World Development Report 1981* (Washington, D.C.: World Bank, 1981), pp. 182-183; World Bank, *World Development Report 1987* (Washington, D.C.: World Bank, 1987), p. 252.

Rican state was aided in its ambitious programs by the lack of an expensive military establishment and by U.S. foreign aid, which in per capita terms was second only to Israel. U.S. support for the Costa Rican experiment continued in spite of successive Costa Rican governments' (especially Figueres's) consistent criticism of U.S.-supported dictators in Latin America and the Caribbean, less-than-complete hostility toward Castro's Cuba in the 1960s, and the establishment of diplomatic and commercial relations with Russia and Eastern Europe in the 1970s. Even though Costa Rican governments have not proven to be loyal team players, the Costa Rican example was too important for the United States to ignore.

Here was a politically stable, poor nation in which democratically elected, anti-Communist governments were directing a growing economy and implementing widespread social and welfare policies without challenging the institution of private property in production and thereby the structure of private privilege and power. The U.S. State Department's ability to use Costa Rica to make invidious comparisons with potentially obstreperous client states was too valuable to be threatened by a few uncooperative gestures.

A final Costa Rican advantage in the financial realm was that the state's stability and legitimacy enabled it to confront the U.S.-owned fruit companies and wring more taxes out of them than was the case of its neighbors.

These factors were real and important, but they were not sufficient to pay for the multipronged program of the Costa Rican state, and the threat of fiscal crisis was a continuing fact of Costa Rican public finances. The state, and especially the decentralized agencies, borrowed heavily during the 1970s. Much of the borrowing was from domestic sources, but increasingly large amounts were secured from private international banks. This borrowing became a crisis only in the late 1970s and early 1980s, when export agriculture prices declined sharply and reduced export earnings, a major pillar of the entire strategy. As a consequence, the entire Costa Rican experiment of growth with a democratic welfare state was jeopardized.

The system seemed even more fragile because of the suddenness with which Chile and Uruguay in the 1970s had been transformed from historically solid democracies with rather progressive social policies into harsh military dictatorships. These examples demonstrated that a long democratic legacy did not guarantee the resilience of a politically open and socially responsive society. Costa Rican political institutions and policies, albeit with some compromises, have nevertheless proved able to withstand severe battering.

Costa Rica in the 1960s and 1970s, then, was like Guatemala in that economic development was perceived to be the product of an active and interventionist state. The divergence between the two nations' approaches is equally obvious: Political legitimacy and social stability in Costa Rica were preserved principally through ameliorative social policies and formal democracy. This does not mean that there was no severe destitution in Costa Rica or that violence was never used by the state to put down civil unrest. Nevertheless, the contrast with Guatemala indicates the qualitatively different character of Costa Rican success in preserving and expanding a social order characterized by major inequalities.

El Salvador

In 1960 a coup was led by a group of young army officers with reformist intentions, and, as in the coup of 1944, these intentions were not realized.[4] Three months later, Colonel Julio Adalberto Rivera led a countercoup. His administration tried to institute a single-party state modeled on Mexico but allowed some space for parties of the political center and right to operate, especially at the local level.

The Christian Democratic Party (Partido Democrática Cristiana—PDC) thus managed to obtain a foothold in Salvadoran politics, and its most illustrious candidate, José Napoleon Duarte, was elected mayor of San Salvador in 1964 and served in that office until 1970. Although the position lacked any real authority, it gave Duarte and the mildly reformist Christian Democratic program national exposure.

When national elections were again held in 1967, Colonel Fidel Sánchez Hernández was elected. He was the candidate of the military party, as were the next two presidents. Already tensions were building up with Honduras over Salvadoran immigrants and Honduras's chronic trade deficit with El Salvador. Two years later, with the Honduran expulsion of 25,000 Salvadoran immigrants, together with the explosiveness of the two nations facing each other in an early round of the World Cup soccer competition, the so-called Soccer War broke out. Salvadoran troops, despite severe organizational problems, managed to move a few miles into Honduran territory. Mediators from the Organization of American States (OAS) succeeded in stopping the war after three days of fighting, with about 100 Salvadoran casualties and ten times that number of Honduran casualties. The OAS also effected the withdrawal of Salvadoran troops from Honduras, and the Salvadoran government declared victory.

The nationalist fervor created by the war was promoted and capitalized upon by Sánchez Hernández and his government, and all of the opposition parties, including the Christian Democrats and illegal Communists, enthusiastically joined the cheering section. The similarity with the domestic political use of the 1991 Persian Gulf War by the U.S. government is clear, as is the extent to which it was a Pyrrhic victory. The war did not prevent the Honduran government from expelling more Salvadorans, and in a few months 80,000 to 100,000 more Salvadorans returned to El Salvador from Honduras. With already serious problems of landlessness and unemployment, the influx posed serious problems for the Salvadoran government. Moreover, Honduras's embargo on Salvadoran imports hit the Salvadoran economy, contributing to the recession in the early 1970s (see Figures 5.1 and 5.2).

The hollowness of the victory was thus painfully evident by the time of the 1972 presidential elections. Even though it seems clear that Duarte won the election, General Arturo Armando Molina was declared the winner. Massive public protests followed the announcement, and a group of dissident army officers staged a coup. The coup attempt was defeated, in good part by the National Guard (rural police directly beholden to landowners), the national police force (closely linked to the urban elites), and Guatemalan and Nicaraguan troops under the auspices of CONDECA. Duarte was arrested, badly beaten, and exiled.

By this time, the polarization of Salvadoran society was increasingly expressed politically. Urban unions and student groups became linked with illegal but vital rural campesino organizations, and public protests and strikes mobilized tens of thousands in coordinated opposition to the military regime. In addition, an armed opposition, though still small, was becoming a threat to individuals identified with the military government and economic elites.

Allied against them was the official army, the police, and the National Guard, together with shadowy right-wing terrorist gangs. One of these, the Organización Democrática Nacionalista (ORDEN), had grown into a large, well-armed paramilitary organization by the early 1970s, and it specialized in murdering campesinos involved in peasant organizations. There were also a number of other right-wing vigilante groups, and by the mid-1970s political murders, kidnappings, disappearances, and bold atrocities were frequent. The undeclared civil war pushed Molina to propose a modest land reform in 1976, but landlord opposition effectively vetoed it.

The 1977 election had the predictable outcome of General Carlos Humberto Romero being declared the winner, and the response was another massive public protest with many deaths. Under Romero, right-wing violence escalated, and its victims now frequently included priests who had been active in organizing their parishioners in opposition to the government. Although the Church hierarchy was generally quite conservative, Archbishop Oscar Arnulfo Romero (not related to the president) suddenly began to speak out against the violence of the regime's war against the people, thus encouraging reformist commitments among priests and nuns. The military and propertied classes came to regard the

Church as an enemy, especially the large numbers of parish priests who for years had been helping the poor to organize against the economic and political forces arrayed against them and toward the Jesuit order, who ran the national university, the site of much urban opposition. The profession of religious faith by the wealthy and their hired thugs did not protect representatives of the Church from brutal reprisals if they were seen to be threats to privilege.

The increasing divisions in Salvadoran society during the 1970s and the almost exclusive reliance on violence as a political response built up to a climax in 1979. In March of that year, Archbishop Oscar Arnulfo Romero was assassinated. In the following October, El Salvador experienced yet another coup by moderate young army officers, who set up a ruling junta dominated by José Duarte and the PDC. The young officers were interested in instituting a land reform, at least in part to become eligible for aid from the Carter administration. They actually did implement some land reform, but as with the reformist officers in 1944 and 1960, they were soon overwhelmed by conservative opposition. Moreover, their reformist agenda was not supported strongly by the PDC, which was eager to establish a middle position in a polarized political setting that did not permit a stable center.

The ineffectiveness of electoral politics led to an escalation of the popular uprisings, which increasingly included large numbers of disillusioned middle-class moderates. These developments among the masses forced the highly factionalized armed opposition to come together, which they did as the Frente Farabundo Martí para la Liberación Nacional (FMLN) in late 1980.

Another important political organization was founded in the early 1980s. Roberto D'Aubuissón, closely connected with the activities of the death squads, formed the Alianza Repúblicana Nacional (ARENA). This organization was explicitly the party of property, and it opposed any social reforms and advocated a purely military solution to the conflict. Nevertheless, ARENA was an innovation and indicated that the Right was prepared to engage in electoral competition at a time when many of the most politically active of the middle class were deserting it.

In the 1970s El Salvador chose the path of Guatemala in responding with repression and military dictatorship to the contradictions of economic development. And like Guatemala, the government experienced a loss of military aid during the administration of U.S. president Jimmy Carter because of massive violations of human rights (see Figure 5.7). The result was heavy borrowing on international capital markets to compensate (see Table 5.3).

But El Salvador was unlike Guatemala in important respects. The Salvadoran military was more divided than its Guatemalan counterpart, both ideologically within the national military and organizationally between the central government's military and the National Guard. Perhaps because it was less coherent, the Salvadoran military government had less independence from the propertied classes, who did not rule but maintained an effective veto over all economic policy. Consistent with this, the Salvadoran military state was considerably less interventionist in economic matters than the Guatemalan military state, and the military had less of a corporate identity with institutional interests of its own to promote. The willingness of the wealthy to tax themselves to finance the preservation of the social order was greater than among their Guatemalan counterparts, and the pressure of fiscal crisis was therefore less severe. But by the latter half of the 1970s, it was clear that the entire strategy of repression was not working. Escalation rather than pacification was the outcome, and new approaches or much greater resources were going to be necessary to contain political conflict.

Honduras

The Liberal Party president, Ramón Villeda Morales, was elected in 1957. That election was held under the auspices of the military, which had intervened briefly to end the unconstitutional manipulations of the National Party, still heavily influenced by longtime president Tiburcio Carías Andino.[5] Villeda Morales recognized the political potential of the labor unions and campesinos, and he supported and tried to manage these groups' organizations in order to create political constituencies. He was aided in this effort by the Alliance for Progress, which in the early 1960s was tailor made for this political project. With the support of worker and campesino organizations, and against fruit company protests, he fashioned a modest program of land and fiscal reform in 1962.

The land reform program had been watered down as a result of opposition from the fruit companies and the U.S. Department of State, but its formal provisions were soon irrelevant. Ten days before the 1963 presidential elections, the military, fearful of Villeda Morales's establishment of a Civil Guard independent of the military and encouraged by the fruit companies and domestic landlords, successfully overthrew the Villeda Morales government and canceled the elections, which probably would have been won by a Liberal colleague of the president's. Although the Kennedy administration refused to grant U.S. diplomatic recognition to the new regime, the Johnson administration did so a year later. The military's intervention was significantly different from that of 1957, because the military showed every intention of staying in power and ruling this time. The leader of the military junta, Colonel Osvaldo López Arellano, was "elected" president in 1965. His candidacy was sponsored by the military and the Nationalist Party, and it was also helped by his strong-arm squads operating in rural areas.

The cessation of the land reform and any other reformist impulse happened while cotton farms and cattle ranches increasingly encroached on campesino lands. Honduran campesinos, experienced with organized protests, seized lands and led massive popular demonstrations in both rural and urban areas. These demonstrations culminated in large and coordinated strikes in 1968 and 1969 that allied the unions with industrialists and forced a response from López Arellano that went beyond repression, which clearly was not working. In the context of increased contestation of land between Salvadoran immigrants and Hondurans around the border with El Salvador, López Arellano's move was predictable. He exhumed the 1962 land reform program, which had essentially been dead since he had assumed office, and began to apply its provisions against the Salvadorans rather than the fruit companies and Honduran landlords. The 1969 war with El Salvador was a consequence.

This move was politically successful, but only in the short run. Ranchers and fruit companies were happy to have the land issue not involve their holdings, and Honduran industrial producers and retailers resented Salvadoran penetration of Honduran markets through imports as well as directly established production units and retail stores in Honduras. But the support for confronting El Salvador went far beyond those with an immediate economic stake in it. The unions and the Liberal Party enthusiastically supported this cynical ploy, and we have the depressing spectacle of both Salvadoran and Honduran workers and peasants rallying in support of oppressive military governments to fight a neighbor that had nothing to do with domestic oppression and destitution. One thousand Hondurans lost their lives and the Honduran army was disgraced in the week's hostilities, although the Honduran air force (López Arellano's branch of service) did better.

Nevertheless, the Honduran government proceeded with the expulsion of Salvadorans, blocked the importation of Salvadoran goods, and made life very difficult for Salvadoran businesses located in Honduras. In addition, the Honduran government withdrew from the Common Market and signed favorable bilateral treaties with all the members except El Salvador. The small industrial sector responded by showing more dynamism during the second half of the 1970s than it did during the 1960s, and although most foreign investment was from fruit company diversification, Honduras began receiving more direct foreign investment from other sources. By the end of the 1970s, a domestic propertied class in the modern urban sector emerged as a self-conscious political actor.

The war with El Salvador was economically disruptive, which contributed to the popular agitation that soon regained momentum. The 1971 elections were carefully choreographed by the National and Liberal parties. The parties competed for the presidency but arranged for the legislature and government posts to be evenly divided between them. López Arellano's candidate, Ramón Ernesto Cruz of the National Party, won the election. The low turnout demonstrated voters' apathy about this kind of politics. Cruz immediately began to institute the policies of López Arellano's early years. He cracked down on campesino organizations and in general responded to the wishes of the powerful cattle ranchers' organization.

The lack of success of these efforts, along with the corruption and scandal of the Cruz administration, led to the bloodless coup of 1972. Once again, López Arellano was back in the presidency, but in this incarnation he was a populist reformer. Like Villeda Morales before him, he appreciated the political potential of the organized urban and rural working classes. Land reform was back on the political agenda, and López Arellano proved adept at stimulating sugar production and in general reviving the economy. Hurricane Fifi, which devastated vast areas of the northern coast and killed perhaps as many as 5,000 people in 1974, was a major disaster, but it had an unexpected side effect. Local as well as foreign landlords abandoned thousands of acres of ruined land, and López Arellano was able to bring that land into the land reform program at relatively low financial cost and with only slight resistance from the landlords. In some areas, of course, the landholders were not willing to part with land, and their armed resistance to the land reform and campesino occupations of the land included some serious atrocities against peasant leaders and the priests who worked with them.

In early 1975, López Arellano announced a new and much more ambitious land reform program, but he was deposed before it could be put into effect. In mid-1975, a U.S. Senate investigation of the behavior of U.S. transnational corporations in the Third World, stimulated by the complicity of U.S. corporations in the 1973 coup against Salvador Allende in Chile, uncovered bribes of more than a million dollars paid by United Brands to members of the López Arellano administration to lower taxes on banana operations. The president of United Brands committed suicide, and López Arellano was removed from office by a military coup led by General Juan Alberto Melgar Castro.

The fruit companies' power had been waning over the years as bananas were becoming a much less important export, and the scandal put them on the defensive. The Melgar Castro government took the opportunity to take over some ports and railroads on the northern coast, raise taxes on the companies, and expropriate additional lands for the land reform program. But after some initial vacillations, the Melgar Castro administration drifted to the right. The internal politics of the military government were made even murkier by the attempts by Melgar Castro to project a populist image, the slowdown of land reform and harsh responses to campesino land seizures, and persistent claims that high-ranking army officers were actively involved in drug smuggling. This uncertainty was resolved but new ones created when Melgar Castro was replaced by a triumvirate of military officers in 1978.

Giving in to pressure from domestic constituencies and the Carter administration, the military triumvirate sponsored the drafting of another constitution and held elections. An indication of the fairness of the elections was that Roberto Suazo Cordova, the Liberal candidate, won and was inaugurated in 1982 even though the military had consistently been closely associated with the National Party.

The military was not giving it all away, however. Similar to the Guatemalan political system, the Honduran military retained almost complete autonomy from the political sphere. The authority of Suazo Cordova and the civilian government was narrowly circumscribed, and the military maintained direct control over its own affairs and indirect control over all important aspects of national politics through the 1980s.

As for Central Americans in general, the very end of the 1970s was a difficult time for Hondurans. Nevertheless, the decade as a whole was a time of significant industrial growth, of land reform that directly benefited 10 percent of the rural population, a social security program that included 30 percent of the economically active population, and substantial improvements in health and education indicators. These outcomes were not inconsiderable achievements for a poor nation with little or no legacy of promoting economic growth or active social policy.

Despite the use of repression, Honduran policies were closer to Costa Rican patterns than to those of Guatemala, and they were distinct from both in that the economic and political outcomes in Honduras were the result of rapid institutional innovation and shifting pressures rather than a product of previously constituted procedures and power centers. Both the extent to which the entire Honduran social and political order was in a continuing process of formation as well as the broad range of participants influencing the process were unique in Latin America, especially Central America.

Nicaragua

Economic growth in Nicaragua during the 1950s and 1960s was truly exceptional. During these two decades, the Nicaraguan economy expanded more rapidly than any economy in Latin America. Nicaragua went from having Central America's lowest per capita income from 1945 through 1950 to surpassing all but Costa Rica during certain times in the late 1960s and early 1970s (see Figure 5.2). Led by cotton, cattle, and sugar exports beginning in the 1950s and augmented by CACM-induced manufacturing production and exports in the 1960s, this exceptional growth created major social dislocations, new loci of economic power, and exceptional political tensions.[6]

Cotton was the first and immediately most profitable new agricultural export, and along the Pacific coast of Nicaragua in the 1950s land was rapidly shifted to cotton from other crops, principally food for domestic consumption. Shifting crops meant displacing the people who had been cultivating the crops, and the introduction of cotton, with its relatively capital-intensive production, sharply reduced the demand for labor. Only a small proportion of the campesinos who had been working the land became full-time wage workers in cotton cultivation and processing, and many more worked in cotton only seasonally. The seasonal workers, like full-time workers, had lost control over any means of production (land in this case), but in contrast to the full-time workers they had to migrate to other areas (frequently the cities) to sell their labor services during the off season. Many, of course, moved permanently to urban areas. The only dispossessed farm families who did not become wage workers were those who retreated to the agricultural frontier (most often the mountainous areas to the east), where they struggled to produce subsistence levels on poor and isolated lands.

In the late 1950s, cotton profits and the demand for credit needed for the expansion of cotton production (and subsequently of cattle and sugar) led to the formation of two powerful financial groups. The Somoza family and their associates were also heavily involved in cotton production, ginning, and export, and they were backed by the power of the public sector, including the National Guard. As in all other economic activities, this raised the specter of "unfair competition" by the Somoza family's entrepreneurship, which often was based on corruption, extortion, government contracts, and general misuse of state power for private gain. There was nothing new in the conflict between the economic interests of the private-sector elite and those of the Somoza family and associates, and that conflict was one of the chief reasons for the 1950 pact between Somoza and most powerful elements of the economic elites. What was new, however, was the way in which rapid economic growth consolidated the largest non-Somoza capitalist forces into two coherent and coordinated groups and at the same time raised the economic stakes in the political competition.

The two independent financial groups were prominent in urban manufacturing as well as in export agriculture, and the expansion of domestic industrial production for national and regional markets through CACM increased the scope of the groups' interests and control and enlarged the membership of the economic elite. Again, the Somoza interests had to be taken into account because the Somoza family and associates were deeply involved in industrial production from an early date.

Although the growth of urban industrial production, along with construction, transportation, commerce, and related activities, developed more capitalist and financial interests, it also significantly increased the numbers and organization of the urban working class. The expansion of the modern urban-sector working class led to a revitalization of urban labor unions, which soon outgrew the capacity of the Somoza state to control them through the government-sponsored labor confederations that had worked well for Somoza in the 1940s and 1950s. The modern urban sector, however, did not produce a combative working class, and even those influenced by Communist leadership were not particularly aggressive even in bread-and-butter economic issues until the 1970s. The majority of the urban working class, however, continued to be employed in the competitive sector and were not the highly proletarianized workers represented by the unions.

Nicaraguan politics of the 1960s and early 1970s was essentially a politics of continuity. As described in Chapter 4, Luís and Anastacio Somoza Debayle, the two legitimate sons of Anastacio Somoza García, took political control of the nation after their father was assassinated in 1956, and they retained tight control, occasionally through placing malleable allies in the presidency, until the triumph of the Sandinista revolution in July 1979. Luís was an urbane and sophisticated man who operated the quasi-legitimate political apparatus; his brother directed the National Guard and performed the duties of enforcer by applying violence when deemed necessary.

Luís Somoza, during his ten years in power, put through the only ameliorative social legislation of the post–World War II period of Somoza rule. This legislation included some social security provisions limited to workers in Managua and a minimum wage law that was not enforced. Nevertheless, through empty reforms and manipulations, Luís minimized the need for overt repression. The project of cosmetic reform fit in well with the Alliance for Progress, and the nation's vigorous economic growth made its political success possible. At the same time, however, the extent and pattern of that growth rendered woefully inadequate the minimal social reforms and welfare policy. Another factor in the political success was the continued large-scale support from the United States, in material and financial terms as well as through the consistent intervention and help of successive U.S. ambassadors.

External props to the system were especially helpful during the period of political opposition from upper- and middle-class groups in the late 1950s and early 1960s. Beginning in the early 1960s, however, the impressive rates of Nicaraguan economic growth benefited these opponents sufficiently to soothe their dissatisfactions with the regime and to postpone their efforts to gain more access to political decisions.

In the late 1960s the slowdown of the Nicaraguan economy revived opposition from these sources, and the death of Luís Somoza from a heart attack in 1967 left Anastacio Somoza Debayle in charge. This second Anastacio possessed neither the cunning of his father nor the velvet gloves of his brother, and his announced intention to become president in 1967 provoked a massive protest led by the Conservative Party. The organizers of the protest mobilized a rally of 40,000 people in Managua, and in dispersing them the National Guard killed 300.

The National Guard, led by Anastacio Somoza Debayle, was the principal instrument of official violence. The loyalty of the National Guard was key to the survival of the regime, and successive Somozas nurtured the support of both the officer corps and the Guard's rank and file. Its members were generously supplied and trained by the United States, and in a deliberate effort to isolate them from the population they and their families lived in National Guard compounds, were exempt from taxation, shopped in special stores with subsidized prices, and were allowed to prey on the population through petty corruption. The most lucrative opportunities were reserved for Guard officers and the Somoza family and associates.

Even with this solicitous care, unrest among the Guard in the late 1960s alarmed Anastacio Somoza sufficiently that he made some concessions to the Conservative Party in order to strengthen his support within civil society and to give him more leverage over the Guard. Leading members of the Conservative Party in 1971 accepted Somoza's offer of limited political participation, causing an immediate schism in the Conservative Party. Pedro Joaquín Chamorro, the editor of the opposition Conservative newspaper *La Prensa* and scion of one of the most notable families in Nicaragua, along with most of the youth groups affiliated with the Conservatives, left the party to maintain their opposition to the Somoza regime.

But by this time there were other sources of opposition brewing. The Frente Sandinista de Liberación Nacional (FSLN, or Sandinistas), dedicated to armed revolution, was formed in 1961 by three veterans of university student politics. The call for armed overthrow of the Somoza regime, however, was not the principal difference between the FSLN and the mainline opposition groups. The Sandinistas did not limit their program to political change; they advocated a major reorganization in the structure of social and economic power as well, and the revolution was to include large-scale mobilizations of popular forces both to effect the overthrow of Somoza and to implement the revolutionary program.

In a 1963 attempt at insurrection, however, the FSLN was crushed by the National Guard. After regrouping and working to build support in rural and urban areas, the Sandinistas launched another attempt, which was again smashed by the National Guard in 1967. The FSLN at this time had a very small number of cadres, and each of the defeats cost them dearly in casualties and imprisonment.

At this point, the FSLN turned away from direct armed conflict and focused on political work among campesinos in the countryside and residents in poor urban neighborhoods. They also robbed banks for funds and assassinated especially notorious members of the National Guard. The strategy of organizing the poorest was one in which none of the non-insurrectionary urban opposition groups had shown much interest, although the Church, at the grassroots level, had been forming Christian base communities among rural Pacific coast export agriculture workers. Competitive-sector urban workers, export agriculture workers, and campesinos outside the wage system, unlike the urban middle and upper classes, had not benefited from the high rates of economic growth during the 1960s and in fact had been victims of it.

The FSLN's mobilization effort was helped by the actions of the National Guard. By the late 1960s, the Guard began to see the FSLN and its organizing activities as more threatening and launched a campaign of reprisals and preemptive strikes in the countryside to destroy the FSLN and its popular support. The principal targets of this campaign were the campesinos of the cotton regions of the Pacific coast and of the coffee-growing sections of the north central part of the nation. The campesinos in the latter region had experienced considerably less displacement than their counterparts on the Pacific coast, but the mountainous terrain and the area's tradition of resistance—the site of Sandino's base fifty years earlier—made it a place of National Guard concern. The brutalization of the campesino population, which in the 1970s would account for at least 3,000 campesino deaths at the hands of the Guard, led to increased support and recruitment by the FSLN.

Another important source of opposition to the regime came from the Catholic Church when Miguel Obando y Bravo was appointed archbishop of Nicaragua in 1968. Unlike his predecessors, Obando y Bravo had serious reservations about the Somozas. In the early 1970s, he publicly declared himself in opposition to the Somoza government through a series of pastoral letters, and consistent with Vatican II and the 1968 Medellín bishops' conference, he encouraged the formation of Christian-based communities by parish priests and lay catechists and tolerated direct political action in the name of the Church. Obando y Bravo was an outspoken opponent of Somoza, and his influence was important in subsequently bringing the regime to an end. The bishop's stand, however, did not mean that he was an ally of the Sandinistas, with whom he disagreed about both program and tactics.

This range of opposition forces battered Somoza's regime in the early

1970s, but the opposition was so fragmented that Somoza might have been able to weather the storm. Again, continued strong support from the United States was crucial for the regime's durability. U.S. aid to Latin America in general declined during the administration of U.S. president Richard Nixon, whose foreign policy rhetoric included the repeated use of such phrases as "low profile" and "benign neglect." Two major exceptions to this policy were the 1973 overthrow of democratically elected president Salvador Allende in Chile and increased support for the beleaguered Somoza regime in Nicaragua. The Somoza government's employment of high-powered U.S. public relations firms along with solid friends in the U.S. Congress helped maintain a favorable attitude toward Nicaragua by U.S. policymakers.

Another, somewhat bizarre, source of support from the United States came from Howard Hughes, the recluse U.S. billionaire. In 1970, he moved to Managua, took over an entire floor of Managua's luxury hotel (owned by Somoza), and invested in a Somoza media enterprise; he moved on after the earthquake of 1972.

That earthquake, which struck two days before Christmas, significantly affected the course of the Nicaraguan struggles. The earthquake's force was concentrated in the very center of Managua, killed over 10,000 people, injured many more, and left at least 300,000 without shelter. For three days after the earthquake, the government was unable to mobilize even a full company of the National Guard, whose members either had fled the city or had stayed to loot it. After a few days, order had indeed been restored, in part because of the presence of U.S. and CONDECA troops, but the character of that order was increasingly obvious. The preoccupation by the Somozas and upper-echelon officials with profiting from real estate speculation, construction contracts, and theft of the international aid for earthquake relief was an important factor in the ineffectiveness of the government to deal with relief and reconstruction.

The earthquake was an important turning point for the opposition to Somoza by the middle and upper classes. Rural and urban propertied classes were becoming increasingly weary of the Somoza government's inefficiency and corruption, and the inability to control the National Guard after the earthquake indicated that the government could not even be counted on to preserve law and order (protect privilege). Moreover, the Somoza group's greed threatened to close the two powerful private financial groups out of lucrative economic opportunities, as indicated by its tight control of contracts for the reconstruction of Managua.

The middle class was alienated by the economic uncertainties resulting from the earthquake, the 1973 petroleum price increases on international markets and consequent domestic inflation, and the government's post-earthquake legislation mandating longer workweeks and salary freezes. The Somoza political pact with the Conservatives in 1971 offered nothing to middle-class political parties, which were increasingly shut out from political power. Larger numbers of the upper and middle classes were coming to the conclusion that Somoza had to go. In addition, the construction workers, taking advantage of their importance in the rebuilding of Managua, successfully struck against the extended workweek and low wages, and this encouraged job actions by other unions.

The general dislike, fear, and disgust with the Somoza regime finally led to the formation of a broad-based opposition coalition that included urban labor unions (including those under Communist auspices) as well as middle-class and propertied class organizations. The coalition of organizations representing poor urban neighborhoods and campesinos, many allied with the FSLN, and the FSLN itself were deliberately excluded.

The dramatic move by the FSLN in 1974 was probably a reaction to this exclusion. A small number of FSLN cadres attacked a party held for the U.S. ambassador shortly after the ambassador had left, and they captured the entire party. With a significant proportion of the elite of Somoza society held as hostages, the government was forced to capitulate to FSLN demands. The government guaranteed safe passage for the Sandinista participants and several FSLN cadres who had been imprisoned (one of whom was Daniel Ortega Saavedra), paid a ransom of $5 million, and published an FSLN statement. This bold FSLN action succeeded in catapulting the small FSLN into national and international prominence as a courageous and effective opposition force that could not be ignored.

The incident embarrassed Somoza and Guard officers. At this point the most brutal and indiscriminate governmental repression began. The Guard raged through urban and rural areas, arresting, brutalizing, and often killing young men at random because they were regarded as likely candidates for FSLN recruitment. This campaign of terror had its own logic, and Nicaragua slid into civil war over the next four years. In the case of Nicaragua at this time, it is clear that systemic tendencies to fiscal crisis were overwhelmed by immediate political crises.

The outcome of the civil war was the revolutionary Triumph of July 19, 1979, by which time the Sandinista leadership in the struggle against Somoza was so secure that it became the principal force in subsequent, postrevolutionary politics.

Even by the mid-1970s, however, the FSLN's leadership of the opposition was not an obvious outcome. At that time, the mainline opposition to Somoza, deemed legitimate by the U.S. State Department, regarded the Sandinistas as politically dangerous and in need of being neutralized, but more as an irritant than a serious threat. Moreover, after the Sandinistas' spectacularly successful kidnapping and ransom adventure in

1974, the National Guard instituted a reign of terror to destroy the FSLN. Between the mainline opposition and the Guard, then, the prospects of the Sandinistas' becoming a prominent, much less the preeminent, force in the revolt against Somoza seemed remote.

U.S. government policy toward Somoza and the insurrection contributed significantly to the ascendance of the Sandinistas. U.S. officials in the administration of President Jimmy Carter were hostile to the FSLN, but unlike the preceding administrations of Nixon and Ford, the Carter administration recognized in its first year (1977) that apart from the National Guard, Somoza had virtually no domestic support and had become a liability to U.S. interests in Latin America. Moreover, and again in contrast to all postwar U.S. administrations, the Carter administration considered the flagrant human rights violations committed by the Somoza regime to be not only embarrassing and impolitic but also morally indefensible.

U.S. aid to the Nicaraguan regime, therefore, terminated by 1978, although some previously committed U.S. aid continued to flow into Nicaragua. The Nicaraguan regime became increasingly isolated from international sources of support, and by 1979 only Spain, Portugal, and especially Israel continued to sell arms to Somoza and the Guard.

While Somoza was rapidly losing the ability to govern by any means other than the most violent, U.S. officials, right up to the end of the dictatorship, put their energy into negotiations with Somoza, trying to get him to resign and leave the country voluntarily while keeping intact the governing structure: the National Guard and the Partido Liberal Nacional (PLN), Somoza's official political party. Thus the source of the expression frequently heard in Nicaragua: "Somocismo sin Somoza" ("Somozaism" without Somoza).

Integral to this strategy, the U.S. government contributed substantially to the construction of a semicoherent coalition of domestic opposition groups willing to cooperate with the United States in this matter. The coalition was heterogeneous (for instance, it included both the Conservative and Communist political parties), very fragile, and depended heavily on U.S. support. The leadership of that coalition was heartened by the willingness of the United States to jettison Somoza and accustomed to following U.S. initiatives, but it was not able to sustain its leadership position in the anti-Somoza movement. As a result of its complicity in the negotiations, it became detached from even moderate opponents to the regime, who were increasingly unhappy with the idea of retaining the PLN and especially the Guard, the most odious of Somoza's institutions.

In any case, Somoza's intransigence condemned the entire project to failure. He was determined not to step down, even when the International Monetary Fund, at the behest of the U.S. government, made a $66 million "loan" to Somoza in early 1979, presumably as severance pay. It was not until the armed opposition militarily defeated the National Guard that Somoza finally left his bunker on the hill above Managua's luxury hotel and flew to Miami in an airplane supplied by the U.S. government. He soon moved to Asunción, the capital of General Alfredo Stroessner's Paraguay, where he was assassinated in 1980, an act with which various groups, including some close to Stroessner, have been credited.

The tactics of the U.S. government, then, compromised the mainline leadership and opened up the possibility for new sources of initiative, and this takes us back to the Sandinistas, who were never short of bold initiatives. In January 1978, Pedro Joaquín Chamorro was assassinated, most likely on the orders of Somoza's son in revenge for Chamorro's exposing how the Somozas resold abroad blood donated for earthquake relief. The assassination dramatically and powerfully mobilized domestic opposition to Somoza, and the Sandinistas built on this momentum by pulling off another daring raid. In August 1978, they captured the National Palace and took 2,000 hostages, including most of the national legislature. This successful strike once again obtained for the FSLN ransom money, the release of prisoners, and domestic and international recognition as bold and effective opponents to Somoza. This reputation set them off sharply from the timid, ineffectual, and increasingly discredited leadership of the mainline opposition.

As a consequence, the Sandinistas garnered some international support, especially in the final months of the insurrection. No doubt these foreign resources helped to strengthen the FSLN among the various anti-Somoza factions, but, as already noted, the Sandinistas were not the only anti-Somoza group to receive foreign support, and the aid to the Sandinistas was never large enough to have been decisive. Revolutionary Cuba was the best-advertised foreign supporter, although Panama under Omar Torrijos and Costa Rica under even conservative administrations contributed more and Mexico also helped.

Although inept cautiousness by the United States, timidity by the conservative domestic opponents, imaginative tactics by the Sandinistas, and a modicum of support from outside Nicaragua are important parts of the story, they are not sufficient for understanding the rise of the FSLN to dominance in the insurrection. The reason that the four factors listed here did help the FSLN to assume leadership in the struggle against Somoza was the way in which the Sandinistas combined opposition to Somoza with a social reform agenda and took both to the poor and dispossessed majority in rural and urban competitive sectors and in export agriculture. With the strength of this base and the disarray of alternatives, alliances with the FSLN became attractive to other, less revolutionary groups, such as workers in the modern urban sector, even if only for opportunistic reasons.

Not everyone in the competitive sector was an enthusiastic supporter of the FSLN, of course, and the Sandinistas were not the only people organizing the poor. In addition to spontaneous organizing among workers in export agriculture and residents in poor neighborhoods, the Catholic Church, as I have already noted, was actively bringing people together in opposition to Somoza and for instituting changes in the lives of the least fortunate. Although the Church hierarchy remained suspicious of the Sandinistas, a large number of parish priests were actively dedicated to the FSLN movement.

So the Sandinistas did not have the backing of all of the poor and were not the only ones working with the majority of the population. Nevertheless, even though the Sandinistas were rent by internal dissension during the mid-1970s, splitting temporarily into three independent "tendencies," they managed to sustain a consistent organizational effort among the poor majority of the population and eventually to ally with other, broad-based coalitions against Somoza. This was the source of their political and military strength: organizing popular constituencies around positive as well as negative change. Thus the Sandinistas, and only the Sandinistas, were in a position to assume leadership of the anti-Somoza movement when the U.S.-backed mainline leadership demonstrated their inability to remove Somoza, their unwillingness to entertain ideas of substantial social reform, and their ambivalence, even hostility, in respect to participation by the majority of the Nicaraguan people either in throwing out Somoza or in constructing a post-Somoza Nicaragua.

Eighteen years after its founding, the FSLN led the successful overthrow of Somoza. The Nicaraguan revolution was distinguished from the Cuban revolution of twenty years before by the length of time of the struggle, the large proportion of the population directly involved in the movement against the dictator, the active participation by women (a quarter to a third of combatants, several in positions of command), the defeat of the national army, and thousands of casualties and widespread physical destruction. But in another way, the Nicaraguan revolution closely resembled the Cuban revolution: Both were basically national revolts against dictators who had been strongly supported by the United States but had little domestic political support from any important constituency in civil society. Although the Nicaraguan revolt was led by the FSLN, whose key organizational base was the poorest people in Nicaragua, the character of the Nicaraguan insurrection was principally defined by its interclass alliances. The overthrow of Somoza, therefore, was essentially a nationalist project that was fully consistent with the heritage of Augusto Sandino. The class struggle phase of the Nicaraguan revolution, or perhaps the "real" revolution, began only at the moment of triumph over Somoza and the National Guard—July 19, 1979.

The phase of revolutionary social reconstruction was conditioned by indecision in Washington, D.C. After the overthrow of Somoza and the failure of U.S. efforts to undermine the FSLN, the Carter administration had great difficulty in determining a consistent policy line toward the new Nicaraguan government, led by the Sandinistas with a program of radical reform. The Carter administration had already become notorious for its inability to take decisive action on a number of fronts; it is important to recall, though, that in 1979 and 1980 there were an overwhelming number of fronts that needed decisive action. The Carter administration had to deal with the second major oil price hike by the Organization of Petroleum Exporting Countries (OPEC), the Iranian revolution (complete with U.S. hostages in Tehran), and the Soviet invasion of Afghanistan in addition to the overthrow of Somoza and the U.S. presidential election. The cumulative effect of these events was a policy overload for the Carter administration.

The year and a half between the overthrow of Somoza and the succession of President Carter by President Reagan were extremely important. Nicaragua was badly ravaged by the revolution; still had to rebuild from the 1972 earthquake; was burdened with a huge international debt contracted by Somoza; was led by young, inexperienced revolutionaries; and was surrounded by many people, domestic and foreign, who did not wish the revolution well. Nevertheless, it was in this year and half that the FSLN consolidated its rule, accomplished many of its famous reforms, and laid the bases of others. This was the time, for example, of the literacy campaign, the beginning of the land reform, the creation of local self-help and governance structures, and the first results from the creation of hundreds of health clinics and schools. Also at this time, the Sandinistas committed some of their famous errors that alienated some individuals and groups from the revolution, especially the Miskito and Suma peoples on the east coast and some peasants in the interior.

The 1980 U.S. elections made Ronald Reagan president in 1981, all ambiguity in the U.S. government's attitude toward the Sandinistas was resolved, and unremitting antagonism replaced vacillation and inconsistency. A few months after his inauguration in January 1981, President Reagan unofficially declared war on the Nicaraguan revolution.

Growth, Inequality, and Social Reform

Despite the claims and hopes of free market ideology, modern capitalist growth does not include an automatic mechanism that distributes widely the benefits of that growth. Export growth in the nineteenth century certainly did not produce such a distribution, and in the middle of the twentieth century, the expansion of manufacturing (modern urban sector) and new agricultural exports also failed to generate a tolerable level of equality.

Increased economic equality requires explicit social policy, whether such policy is regarded as co-optation of the poor or victory by the poor. The need to promote greater distributional equality to maintain the political legitimacy and stability needed for reproducing the capitalist order is recognized in all developed, industrialized societies, and that recognition is embodied in their modern welfare state apparatuses.[7] These policies are constant targets of criticism and challenge, but when they are significantly compromised, as in the United States during the 1980s, the market rapidly generates more unequal distributions of income.

This is not to say, however, that economic welfare is exclusively a matter of distribution. As the per capita income figures in Figure 5.2 indicate, simply redistributing the income available from current levels of national production would not yield high material standards of living even in Costa Rica. The trick, then, is to promote sustained economic growth with sufficiently equitable distribution so that economic growth benefits a large portion of the national population and does not tear the society apart.

In Central America, the rapid agricultural and industrial growth of the 1950s through the 1970s widened the gulfs among different groups and exacerbated strains in the social fabric. This outcome did not result from the retention of traditional forms of social relationships. The dynamic areas of the national economies were not based on coerced labor or on labor tied to haciendas through debt peonage or noneconomic bonds; they were capitalist, based primarily on wage labor. And the persistent tendency of this growth was to generate increasingly divergent levels of material welfare among different segments of the population. Rising material standards of life were experienced by the wealthiest propertied classes, large portions of the middle class serving upper-class interests in both public and private sectors, and small numbers of the working class in the modern urban sector. But for very large proportions of the national populations, vigorous capitalist growth led to displacement and degradation.

The political and social disruptions in Central America, then, stem from successful economic growth, not from economic stagnation or decline. The chronic tendency of the capitalist dynamic is to produce a social polarization that threatens the existence of the social order, and in Central America during the past three or four decades, the tendency was exacerbated by changing patterns in growth and demography. Not only did economic buoyancy fail to generate sufficient employment, but, in addition, because the economies had become labor surplus economies, land rather than labor was the most desirable productive resource in the countryside. As a consequence, the Guatemalan military and landlords began clearing the land of people, a practice more like that of nineteenth-century U.S. agrarians against indigenous peoples than like what had been feasible or desirable in Guatemala's own history of labor scarcity.

More generally, the rise of the labor surplus economy (and its intensification in El Salvador) meant that ensuring the conditions suitable for the reproduction of labor did not appear to be immediately important for the self-interest of employers or their representatives. The problem of dire poverty and early death did not threaten the supply of cheap labor. The issue was political, parallel with the changed character of land reform that I discussed in the previous chapter.

So although there may no longer be direct and immediate economic needs for ameliorative social policies (or land reform), the majority of the population can threaten the entire structure in ways that require attention. That threat can be dealt with through repressing any protests from the majority, as in Guatemala, El Salvador, and Nicaragua, or by attempting to implement ameliorative governmental policies, as in Costa Rica and to a lesser degree in Honduras. The choice, of course, is not a mutually exclusive, either/or option, nor is the choice about the mix of repression and amelioration simply dependent on the personalities of those in control of the state—that is, on whether they are nice people or nasty people. The patterns of state policy are principally the result of the structure of social power and the character of state formation, both of which are the products of historical development.

One of the major historical functions of the state and the army in Guatemala and El Salvador has been to create and then actively and directly preserve the unequal conditions underlying large-scale coffee production, where a few controlled the means of production and most worked for them. In Guatemala, coffee production entailed a system of coerced labor, mobilized through debt peonage. In El Salvador the system more approximated capitalist wage labor, but the extent of dispossession of workers from control of the land was so extreme that continued application of violence was necessary to sustain it.

In Nicaragua, the state had a function similar to that of Guatemala and El Salvador, but the intervention by the United States reoriented the state and created the National Guard, which became, with continued U.S. support, an instrument of personal rule by the Somozas, who maintained uneasy alliances with the possessing classes.

These historical formations do not mean that subsequent use of repression resulted primarily from habit, national memory, or even the selection of personnel appropriate for a particular role, although the importance of none of these can be dismissed. The principal effect of this historical function was that all social and economic patterns became structured around the presence of a repressive apparatus, and the logic of that structure itself governed future choices. In addition, of course, the repression option, led by the army, was made more feasible and attractive by being underwritten by U.S. anti-Communist policies.

A central structural implication of this form of labor mobilization was that the constant need to apply pressure on the working class, and thus the constant threat of revolt, unified the propertied classes and severely reduced the ability of the middle classes and urban working classes to forge alliances with dissident segments of the upper class that might have benefited from moderate social reforms. The beginnings of such a process, including the competition of upper-class leaders for lower-class electoral support, could be seen in El Salvador during the 1920s, but the depression of the 1930s turned it into its opposite, with disastrous effects. In Guatemala, class polarization in the countryside was exacerbated by a policy of apartheid that allowed no space for negotiating and compromising with the demands and needs of indigenous peoples. And the personalization of power in Nicaragua stunted the development of a national politics, and it eventually alienated even the propertied class. As a consequence, important fragments of that class initially led the opposition to the Somoza state, though their leadership was eventually lost to forces that their opposition helped to create.

In Honduras, in contrast, neither the army nor the state had historically served the function of coercing labor. The United Fruit Company managed its labor relations independent of the state, and for similar reasons the national economy's export base did not generate a landed class that exercized hegemony over national affairs. As a result, when the state and the army developed as significant national institutions in the 1940s and 1950s, they did so in a very different context. A working class in the banana zones began to be politically active in the 1930s, and an independent peasantry was deeply influenced by the fruit company union organizational experience and personnel. Both were feasible constituencies for the late developing Honduran state to build upon. The state and the military arm could tolerate and even support campesino efforts to protect themselves from the encroachments of expanded cattle ranching, though only sporadically and partially, and alliances between rural and urban unions and the propertied in the nascent modern urban sector were politically expedient. In more general terms, the state and the army could ally with campesinos and urban workers and with the cooperation of urban entrepreneurs create the beginning of social policies to alleviate the depredations of unrestricted economic growth. In addition, Honduran economic growth was slower than that of the other Central American states and was thus less socially and politically disruptive.

Costa Rica was similar to Honduras in that the state and the army had not been developed to control labor. Although Costa Rica was unlike Honduras in that the nineteenth-century export boom produced a national oligarchy, the wide dispersion of landownership required the state to respond to the needs and desires of small holders—education being an outstanding example. The small army was further weakened by the economic elite around the time of World War I when Tinoco showed the army's potential to damage the elite's interests. After a somewhat similar experience with the administrations of Calderón and Picado, the military was dismantled after the civil war of 1948, further weakening the state's capacity to repress. The way was clear for trenchantly anti-Communist governments to build on previous beginnings and create a welfare state focused on the middle class but much more inclusive. Only in Costa Rica were the ameliorative policies developed to the point that they might contribute to further economic growth through the education, health, and morale of the workers. Repression, of course, offers none of these possibilities.

The experience of Costa Rica is especially important because it demonstrates that the logic of modern capitalist growth does not necessarily require severe repression. This held even though the Costa Rican experience with capitalist growth included coffee exports, banana exports produced by foreign fruit companies, industrial growth with high rates of participation by transnational corporations, and substantial foreign aid and political and economic pressure from the United States.

Notes

1. For excellent comparative treatments, see Victor Bulmer-Thomas, *The Political Economy of Central America Since 1920* (New York: Cambridge University Press, 1987); and James Dunkerley, *Power in the Isthmus: A Political History of Modern Central America* (London and New York: Verso, 1988). For Guatemalan politics in recent decades, see James Dunkerley, "Guatemala Since 1930," in Leslie Bethell (ed.), *Central America Since Independence* (Cambridge: Cambridge University Press, 1991), pp. 119–158; Suzanne Jonas, *The Battle for Guatemala: Rebels, Death Squads, and U.S. Power* (Boulder, CO: Westview Press, 1991); and Michael McClintock, *The American Connection, Volume 2: State Terror and Popular Resistance in Guatemala* (London: Verso, 1985).

2. Elizabeth Burgos Debray (ed.), *I . . . Rigoberta Menchú: An Indian Woman in Guatemala* (New York: Routledge, Chapman and Hall, 1984), is a powerful testimonial by a recent winner of the Nobel Peace Prize.

3. Again, see Bulmer-Thomas and Dunkerley (note 1) for good comparative treatments. See also Rodolfo Cerdas Cruz, "Costa Rica Since 1930," in Bethell, *Central American Since Independence*, pp. 277–326; Marc Edelman and Joanne Kenen (eds.), *The Costa Rica Reader* (New York: Grove Weidenfeld, 1989); and Anthony Winson, *Coffee and Democracy in Costa Rica* (New York: St. Martin's Press, 1989).

4. For excellent comparisons of the countries, see Bulmer-Thomas, *The Political Economy of Central America Since 1920;* and Dunkerley, *Power in the Isthmus.* See also James Dunkerley, *The Long War: Dictatorship and Revolution in El Salvador* (London: Junction Books, 1982); James Dunkerley, "El Salvador Since 1930," in Bethell (ed.), *Central American Since Independence,* pp. 159–190; Enrique A. Baloyra, *El Salvador in Transition* (Chapel Hill: University of North Carolina Press, 1982); James Dunkerley, *The Long War: Dictatorship and Revolution in El Salvador,* 2d ed. (New York: Routledge, Chapman and Hall, 1985); Michael McClintock, *The American Connection, Volume 1: State Terror and Popular Resistance in El Salvador* (London: Verso, 1985); Tommie Sue Montgomery, *Revolution in El Salvador: Origins and Evolution* (Boulder, CO: Westview Press, 1982); and Joseph Tulchin and Gary Bland (eds.), *Is There a Transition to Democracy in El Salvador?* (Boulder, CO: Lynne Rienner Publishers, 1992). Good on the 1969 conflict between El Salvador and Honduras is W. A. Durham, *Scarcity and Survival in Central America: Ecological Origins of the Soccer War* (Stanford, CA: Stanford University Press, 1979).

5. Again, for excellent comparative treatments, see Bulmer-Thomas, *The Political Economy of Central America Since 1920;* and Dunkerley, *Power in the Isthmus.* See also Victor Bulmer-Thomas, "Honduras Since 1930," in Bethell (ed.), *Central America Since Independence,* pp. 191–226; Philip Shepherd, *The Depths: The United States, Honduras, and the Crisis in Central America* (Boulder, CO: Westview Press, 1993); Mark Rosenberg and Philip Shepherd (eds.), *Honduras Confronts Its Future: Contending Perspectives on Critical Issues* (Boulder, CO: Lynne Rienner Publishers, 1986); and Charles Brockett, "Public Policy, Peasants and Rural Development in Honduras" *Journal of Latin American Studies* 19, no. 1 (1987).

6. See Bulmer-Thomas and Dunkerley (note 1) for excellent comparisons of the countries. For good overviews, see Victor Bulmer-Thomas, "Nicaragua Since 1930," in Bethell (ed.), *Central American Since Independence,* pp. 119–158; and John A. Booth, *The End and the Beginning: The Nicaraguan Revolution,* 2d ed., revised and updated (Boulder, CO: Westview Press, 1986). Different aspects of the revolutionary period in particular are looked at in Carlos Vilas, *The Sandinista Revolution: National Liberation and Social Transformation in Central America* (New York: Monthly Review Press, 1986); and Anthony Lake, *Somoza Falling: A Case Study of Washington at Work* (Amherst: University of Massachusetts Press, 1990). For analyses of the decade of Sandinista rule, see Rose J. Spalding (ed.), *The Political Economy of Revolutionary Nicaragua* (Boston: Allen and Unwin, 1987); Carmen Diana Deere, Peter Marchetti, and Nola Reinhardt, "The Peasantry and the Development of Sandinista Agrarian Policy," *Latin American Research Review* 20 (1985); and Carlos Vilas, *State, Class, and Ethnicity in Nicaragua: Capitalist Modernization and Revolutionary Change on the Atlantic Coast* (Boulder, CO: Lynne Rienner, 1989).

7. An excellent study of the formation and functions of welfare systems in Western Europe and the United States is Gosta Esping-Anderson, *The Three Worlds of Welfare Capitalism* (Princeton: Princeton University Press, 1990).

7

The International Political Economy of Democracy, the 1980s to the Present

Chapter 6 completed my book's principal project—to provide a historical and comparative framework for organizing and analyzing contemporary Central American issues. I have done this by emphasizing the historical development of four major economic sectors that constitute the central elements of each nation's economic structure and have profoundly important implications for all dimensions of social life: export agriculture, state, competitive, and modern urban. This structural development has been uneven through time and among nations, and its contradictions played themselves out in different ways during the 1980s.

Reflecting the nature of those processes, the focus of this chapter is different from previous chapters. First of all, it is principally about politics. I have consistently argued that drawing a sharp line between politics and economics is difficult and analytically dubious, but it is clear that in the past fifteen years the major sources of social and political change in Central America have not stemmed chiefly from innovative changes in the social organization of production resulting from economic expansion. Instead, the 1980s and 1990s resemble the era of independence from Spain (Chapter 2) and the Great Depression and World War II (Chapter 4) in that direct political conflicts were the principal motors of change. Economic events were more background than foreground, and for that reason this chapter focuses on the state and on forms and levels of political mobilization outside the control of the state. An especially important aspect of all of this is the rapid increase in the rhetoric and hesitant practice of political democracy and popular participation in formal politics.

Another difference in emphasis is that this chapter assigns a more central role to external political pressures. As I have shown in preceding chapters, there is no question that the U.S. interventions have been important influences in Central America, but the vastly expanded scale of those interventions during the 1980s was of a qualitatively different order. Even though U.S. actions continue to be more a response to conflict in Central America than its principal determinant, the size and form of U.S. interventions in Central America during the past decade have fundamentally affected the course of the struggles and for years will indelibly color the region's future patterns and prospects.

The final difference between this chapter and the previous ones is that this last chapter is shorter. As I mentioned in the Introduction, there are a multitude of English-language books and articles on Central America in the 1980s and 1990s, and some of the works that came out of this recent explosion of literature about Central America are excellent. Nevertheless, in the authors' understandable attention to U.S. involvement in the region, they often underestimate the need to place domestic social contradictions at the center of any analysis aimed at understanding the convulsions that have occurred and will continue to occur in the region. The purpose of this chapter, then, is to make a few observations about the character and implications of recent U.S. actions in the area and to bring the political narrative up through the early 1990s. I hope that these final remarks will help readers place current arguments, claims, and debates in useful, critical perspectives informed by historical antecedents.

Electoral Politics, Democracy, and U.S. Policy

It is worthwhile to begin with a few remarks about the general global background of the events in Central America during the 1980s. Although the decade of the 1980s has been accurately labeled "the Lost Decade" for Latin America, the stagnation, uneven growth, debt crisis, and international economic restructuring that hit the larger and more industrially advanced nations of Latin America so hard were not as severe in most of Central America. The 1984 Caribbean Basin Initiative (CBI), which allowed selected exports from Central American and Caribbean nations privileged access to U.S. markets, helped a bit, especially in Costa Rica.

But Central America was not immune to the international economic forces that wreaked havoc in the rest of Latin America, and these forces, subsequent to the onset of serious instability in the region, substantially conditioned Central American political struggles. The losses of production and income as a result of depression, debt repayment, and civil war weakened the economies and made their leaders susceptible to international political pressure, especially from the United States (which ironically has the largest international debt of any nation). Political pressures from the United States exacerbated the tensions and contradictions already produced by the rapid economic growth of the 1960s and 1970s, and the result has been to prolong the conflicts and increase their severity.

Political pressure from abroad during the 1980s was a very particular type of political pressure. The governments of the United States, Western Europe, and Japan were in the hands of conservative parties that favored and encouraged the trend toward global economic integration, which had begun to be evident in the 1970s. The heightened internationalization of production had two distinct dimensions. The greater mobility of capital and products enabled corporations based in the United States and Europe to move factories from high-wage sites to, say, Hong Kong or Mexico and send the completed components and products back to U.S. and European markets. The proposal for a North American Free Trade Area is a formal extension of this process within a circumscribed region, and the effort to launch another Central America common market (La Comunidad Económica de Centroamérica, formally begun in 1990), illustrates another aspect of the same process, although such regional trading blocs do have the potential of becoming more of an impediment than a vehicle of global international integration.

The second form of economic internationalization is labor mobility. Large numbers of Latin Americans and Asians entered the United States legally and illegally, and workers from southern and eastern Europe, the Middle East, south Asia, and North Africa flowed into the Economic Community of Western Europe. Both processes—the mobility of capital and the mobility of labor—brought Asian, Latin American, and, to a lesser degree, African labor into direct competition with the higher-paid labor forces of the developed nations. This competition severely weakened the economic and political position of these nations' organized labor movements, especially in urban industry, and strengthened political conservatism in the United States and Western Europe.

With the faltering of import-substituting industrialization in the more industrialized nations of Latin America, similar shifts in the balances of power had been occurring there since the 1960s. In Argentina, Brazil, Uruguay, and Chile, however, the reactionary Right did not wait for economic changes to reduce the strength of domestic labor, and the military took power and abolished constitutional rule during the 1960s and 1970s. Acting on behalf of property, whether or not at its behest, the military fiercely smashed reformist labor and political organizations and to various degrees opened the economies to international markets. By the 1980s, the combined effects of authoritarian persecution and increased international competition had sufficiently weakened urban labor and other potentially dissident forces to enable the reestablishment of electoral politics and let elected civilian regimes deal with the debt and economic chaos created by military rule.

By increasing competition among different national pools of labor, international capital has managed to reduce labor costs and political challenges. And in Latin America, including Central America, resolute moves by the Catholic Church complemented these shifts in class balance. This can be seen most vividly in the way that the Church has systematically replaced reformist bishops and university rectors with more conservative appointments, many of whom are members of the elitist Opus Dei, which was founded in opposition to the principles of Vatican II. At the grassroots level, the Church hierarchy has reluctantly tolerated the growth of antihierarchical Charismatic Catholicism as a defense against political radicalism and also the incursions of evangelical Protestantism.

Radical clergy have been important agents of political mobilization and self-help projects in Central America, and in some areas they still are. But in other aspects, the effects of political sea changes throughout the world have been less dramatic in Central America. The political power of organized urban labor has been slight; the economies have been more open to international commerce than those of the larger Latin American nations; and the regimes were already quite conservative in the 1960s and 1970s. But because the social contradictions within these nations were so sharp, U.S. influence in Central America during the 1980s was not limited to the effects of markets and pressure from the International Monetary Fund (discussed later). The United States has been aggressively more interventionist, and given the history of such interventions, it is ironic that much recent activism was justified and aggressively implemented as the promotion of "democracy."

Although the U.S. presence was felt strongly throughout Central America during the 1980s, it focused on Nicaragua and El Salvador. The effort to remove the Nicaraguan Sandinistas from power was consistent with historic U.S. policy toward even reformist regimes such as that of Guatemala in the 1950s, much less the more revolutionary regimes of Cuba and Chile, but President Reagan made it a personal crusade. He was deeply committed to destroying the Nicaraguan revolution and never lost interest in it. Moreover, his commitment to these efforts was not merely a means to manipulate domestic U.S. politics, and he pursued them even after it became a political liability. The effort to restore conservative rule in Nicaragua included an economic embargo; aid for domestic opponents of the FSLN within Nicaragua; the prevention of aid and credit from international agencies; consistently misleading and exaggerated statements about Nicaragua released to the media; and especially the organization and financing of the Contras, mostly based over the Honduran border, whom the Reagan administration trained, coached, and supported diplomatically.

It is unclear whether President Reagan knew (or remembers that he knew) about the illegal diversion of funds to the Contras generated from the illegal sale of arms to Iran in exchange for U.S. hostages, known as the Iran-Contra scandal when the operation came to light in 1986. In any case, it was the president's single-minded devotion to the destruction of the Nicaraguan revolution that encouraged and enabled sycophantic underlings to find so many devious channels to finance the counterrevolution, especially after the U.S. Congress prohibited it. Soliciting contributions from conservative individuals, organizations, and foreign governments as well as surreptitious uses of U.S. public funds added up to a generous flow of resources to support such a project in a small nation. Once again, however, President Reagan's idiosyncratic fear of the Sandinista revolution was translated into national policy only because of the policy's more general rationales. The crusade was consistent with previous U.S. policy in the area and with general Cold War stances toward political change, but in the 1980s the decline of the United States as the world's foremost economic power meant that for the United States to lose control in its own "backyard" would have been a particularly serious blow to U.S. international prestige and authority. The president's ability to act on his convictions and fright have to be seen as a response to a generalized loss of national confidence.

Preventing FSLN aid to the guerrillas in El Salvador was an early pretext for moving against the revolutionary government of Nicaragua, but administration spokespeople seemed unable to convince even themselves that it was very significant. The absence of national elections in Nicaragua, however, was a more promising avenue for propaganda purposes. The Sandinistas were vulnerable to the charge of being antidemocratic, especially because some previous Sandinista supporters and participants had publicly criticized the FSLN for not adequately respecting earlier promises about encouraging political pluralism. Drawing from an almost 200-year-old tradition (but more recently from the Alliance for Progress and the Carter administration), the Reagan administration soon articulated a mission to promote "democracy" around the world, and it became the central rhetorical theme in destabilizing and overthrowing the Sandinistas.

The tactical use of democracy posed some credibility problems, however. First of all, the Reagan administration was staffed by individuals and represented political interests that had consistently been indifferent to, fearful of, or downright hostile to efforts to increase democratic political participation in the Third World and wary of heightened democracy in the United States. Moreover, the administration's enthusiastic choice of the Contras ("freedom fighters") in Honduras and Miami as the primary instrument for constructing democracy in Nicaragua was revealing. The original membership of the Contras was ex–National Guard who had fled over the Honduras border, and even when its ranks were expanded to 12,000 to 15,000 by men seeking paid employment and by those disaffected by Sandinista policies, the officers corps remained dominated by National Guard veterans.

Contra raids into Nicaragua from Honduras, and to a much lesser extent from Costa Rica, were known by its Washington, D.C., perpetrators as "low-intensity warfare." The warfare did not seem of low intensity to the campesino families, health workers, teachers, and so on whom the Contras harassed, wounded, or killed. Probably a better name is "proxy war," which more clearly identifies the process as a war organized and financed by the United States but that employed non-U.S. soldiers.

This choice of policy instrument clearly revealed the administration's conception of what was desirable in the way of democracy. Only by attributing cynical intentions to U.S. policymakers can one make sense of the Reagan administration's attempt to undermine and discredit the 1984 Nicaraguan national elections as well as its tepid support for some prominent defectors from the FSLN movement and government. In regard to the support of these defectors, the Sandinista revolutionary leader Edén Pastora, or even Alfredo César, Arturo Cruz, or Alfonso Robelo, could have been represented as plausible democratic opponents to FSLN rule after they left positions in the FSLN government and before some finally joined the Somocista Contras. Promoting these men as leaders in the anti-Sandinista movement, however, entailed an unacceptable risk: that they might have represented authentic democratic agendas.

The road to the failure of President Reagan's Nicaraguan policy had three principal milestones. It soon became evident even to the U.S. administration that the brutality and randomness of Contra attacks were not going to establish the Contras as a popular opposition to the FSLN, and by the mid-1980s it was clear that they were simply a terrorist operation. The Iran-Contra scandal of 1986 was a disgrace that embarrassed and politically neutralized the administration's supporters in the U.S. Congress and made channels of illegal support for the Contras more difficult to use. Finally, at the initiative of President Oscar Arias of Costa Rica and with only reluctant approval if not resistance from the Reagan administration, a regional peace plan known as Esquipulas II was signed by the governments of the five Central American nations in 1987. Although adherence to the terms of the peace plan has been very uneven, the agreement set in motion processes that have significantly reduced the levels of violence in Nicaragua and El Salvador. Moreover, it explicitly repudiated the U.S. strategy of proxy war.

The Reagan administration's combination of putative democratic aspiration and actual proxy war was not effective during Reagan's tenure in office. Nevertheless, despite setbacks, contradictions, and hypocrisy, the inability of actually existing socialisms to create authentic democratic political systems made the promotion of democracy a potent international strategy, and democracy became the principal Cold War rallying cry of U.S. and Western European conservative regimes during the 1980s. They identified democracy with "free market" capitalism, and the tactic has enabled the promotion of a sanitized, antireform type of electoral politics.

The global depression and poor countries' debt gave the elite of the industrialized nations powerful levers to use on Third World governments, and the International Monetary Fund designed and monitored "structural adjustment programs" as conditions for minimal relief in debt payments. Structural adjustment programs embody a neoliberal agenda to sell publicly owned enterprises ("privatization"), sharply reduce public regulation of the economy (including subsidies to firms and consumers and protection from international competition), and curtail public expenditures in general, although social welfare programs seem always to be the hardest hit.

As democracy was being touted, the capacity of the Central American states to play a constructive role in national life was being constrained by the antistate provisions of structural adjustment programs and by the drain of resources in the payment of the debt to creditor banks. I stress the idea of a constructive role, because although hobbling the economic and social policies of the state restricts its policy options, it does not diminish the state's imperative to achieve political stability and offset the destabilizing effects of divergent sectoral development. The net effect has been a definition of democracy as voting to elect personnel in a state with little capacity to reward supporters, co-opt opponents, or provide for general welfare. Constant surveillance, threats, and the exercise of force by the police and military—traditionally antidemocratic forces—therefore emerge (or remain) as the most feasible instruments of political stability in a nominally democratic polity. The contradictions are legion.

The advocacy of democracy by conservative regimes in the United States and Western Europe alarmed (and continues to alarm) important elements of Third World elites, but even the most reluctant are too dependent on international support to resist. But many of the elites, especially those tied to the modern urban sector and to economically progressive branches of export agriculture, have found a procedurally based, electoral definition of democracy to be an attractive alternative to redistributive reform or the loss of U.S. support.

The redistributive rhetoric of the Alliance for Progress in the 1960s did not offer a severe challenge to propertied interests in Central America, and the side of the Alliance program that promoted counterinsurgency and national security prevailed. During the 1970s, however, programs known as "development with equity" or "basic needs" became popular in World Bank and academic circles. These programs were better formulated than the Alliance's and thus potentially more threatening. The link between political democracy and tapping the energy and skills of the poor majority of a nation's population to foment economic development is that both require empowering people in complementary ways—and empowering people who have historically been excluded from active involvement in national life.

There is no question that hesitation by the privileged about democracy is based on an intelligent reading of potential challenges to authority and privilege. Both logic and evidence suggest that a genuinely participatory electoral democracy is likely to lead to social reforms and policies that will benefit the majority of the population. But the relation between democratic politics and economic growth is much murkier.[1]

The major reason that many scholars are skeptical about the ability of democracy to promote economic growth is that democratic governments with strong popular support are likely to find it difficult to resist their constituents' desire to emphasize short-run distributive policies at the expense of efforts to increase accumulation and growth. The argument is that growth-inducing policies that allocate significant resources to investment yield fewer immediate benefits for the poor majority and are thus less favorably received even though in the long run, increasing the productivity of human labor through accumulation is the only way to raise significantly the standards of material life for the population as a whole. The arithmetic of the position is clear, and in Central America, the experience of reformist regimes in Costa Rica (1940–1948) and Guatemala (1944–1954) lends some plausibility to this position.

But this familiar argument is usually based on a strict assumption about the behavior of the propertied classes, an assumption that exaggerates the extent to which the wealthy are willing and able to invest in the expansion of domestic enterprises. Moreover, at the same time it underestimates what health, education, and workers' commitment from full membership in a national society can contribute to increasing the productive powers of the work force. Moreover, the argument depends on trickle-down effects for general welfare and ignores how little the majority of the population has benefited from previous growth.

The ways in which political democracy and redistributive economic reform can contribute to accumulation and economic growth raise fascinating and important questions, but they are not the questions raised by the Reagan administration's efforts to promote democracy in Central America nor by the strategies of the Bush administration, which were similar but pursued in a less bellicose manner. The democratic content of the Reagan-Bush efforts was much narrower: an electoral political system without substantial changes in extant patterns of social power. And it is this concept of democracy, and only this concept, that was acceptable to Central American propertied classes.

But the narrow terms of procedurally defined democracy sincerely do interest the urban middle class. The numbers of the middle class grew rapidly with the increase in white-collar employment in both the state and private spheres brought about by the general advance of the economies during the 1960s and 1970s. As noted in Chapter 4, the members of this heterogeneous group do not possess real economic power (for instance, the ownership of productive assets), and their occupational prospects depend heavily on state-sector policies, expenditures, and employment. Moreover, the middle class's urban location, communication and organizational abilities, and experience dealing with people generally give them special advantages in political campaigns. In electoral politics, then, the middle class is able to exert an influence disproportionate to its numbers and economic status, both as voters and as political party activists.

Although the middle classes are often willing to form coalitions of convenience with workers and peasants, their aspirations do not necessarily conflict with the interests of property. The middle classes are very wary of massive social reforms that might destabilize the social structure in which they occupy favored but precarious positions or possibly open the political arena to an extent that the majority of the population exercises power in ways that bypass and weaken the middle classes. Some middle-class centrist parties, therefore, have cooperated with the political right in crushing the political left in exchange for instituting elections. The middle classes, then, are natural allies of efforts to establish limited, procedurally defined forms of electoral politics—their greatest hope for increased weight in the social order.

Although the desire of the Central American middle classes for electoral politics in Central America is not new, and while undemocratic elections have a long history in Central America, the electoral initiatives of the 1980s were more systematic and better choreographed than earlier sporadic episodes. In the 1980s, the principal forces for elections were not populist reform movements; instead, electoral politics has been the project of the industrialized nations' political leadership, who see electoral politics as a means to prevent social reform. And this confidence has not been misplaced. As long as democracy is defined as elections, and as long as other necessary conditions for popular political participation are successfully defeated, democracy can be highly conservative.

First of all, there are serious lapses in even the theory of democracy embodied in liberal thought. Liberal democratic theory is, of course, superior to Marxist democratic theory, because for all intents and purposes the latter hardly exists.[2] Nevertheless, by denying what Marxist theory does include—the authoritarian nature of capitalist production processes—liberal democratic theory tacitly concedes the control over a vitally important realm of social power to undemocratic mechanisms.

The family is another major dimension of social power about which liberal democratic theory is all but silent. Like the economy, the gender-based exercise of authoritarian power within the family obstructs the development of a genuinely and comprehensively democratic culture, with obvious disadvantages for democratic practice in formal political settings. The negative influence of both authoritarian institutions—the capitalist economy and the family—go beyond indirect and diffuse effects on general culture and psychology, however. In work settings, employers exercise direct power over employees, and in families, men have power over women; thus the extent to which the democratic franchise actually enables an authentic and free expression of political preferences by employees and women is often open to question.

Furthermore, there are the more obvious ways in which economic inequality affects political democracy. In societies where there are extreme differences in access to economic resources among individuals and groups, the translation of private power disparities into public power disparities has never been difficult, whether it has been done by financing explicit electoral fraud, bribing elected officials and civil servants, or variously coercing and persuading voters. Even if the upper classes are not able to determine policy outright, it has proven all too easy for them to veto substantial reforms. It is not by chance that in Latin America the only far-reaching land reforms—those in Mexico, Bolivia, Cuba, Peru, and Nicaragua—were not effected under the aegis of formally democratic governments. In the early 1970s Chile looked as though it might become an exception, but the reformist democratic government, like that of Guatemala in the 1950s, was unable to withstand the power of anti-democratic reaction.

In addition to lessening egregious inequalities in access to economic resources, another condition necessary for electoral politics to perform genuinely democratic functions is a setting in which civil liberties are protected and, therefore, elections can express voters' preferences among a range of substantive choices. There are, of course, serious questions about the validity of analogies drawn by liberal democratic theory regarding the economic market. Is it valid to view the enhancement of political democracy as parallel to that of increasing consumers' choices in the marketplace for goods and services?—that is, of enabling political consumers (voters) to choose from among a greater range of commodities (candidates)? Nonetheless, even if one accepts the terms of that conventional analogy, the electoral competition among three factions of the

Guatemalan military in the 1960s would not have qualified as democratic, even if voters had not been harassed and the votes had been tallied fairly. The protection of civil liberties must not only pertain to individuals and political parties, but it must also include the right to form other types of organizations (for instance, labor unions, neighborhood groups, religious clubs), to assemble and to disseminate information and opinion freely, and to engage in other activities that enhance the ability of individuals to participate in political life.

It is, of course, very difficult to specify how much distributional equality and civil liberty is necessary to ensure that formal electoral procedures actually express participatory politics. And at the same time, we can expand considerably the number of necessary conditions for an authentically participatory democracy without being at all confident that we have listed sufficient conditions. Nevertheless, the severe limitations of procedurally defined democracy noted previously are valid, substantial, and critically important, especially for those nations in Central America that have relied and continue to rely on repression for political stability.

The vast distances between a sanitized version of electoral politics and a truly participatory political system were especially vivid in Guatemala and El Salvador during the 1980s and 1990s. These examples demonstrate that electoral politics is compatible with immense inequalities in the distribution of economic resources and with overt repression. This compatibility suggests that limited electoral politics, in itself, is not an effective device for *creating* the conditions for a more genuinely participatory democracy. This observation, then, supports the suspicion (if not the conviction) that electoral politics without the conditions necessary for fuller democracy, even if such a politics can sustain itself, is likely to function to preserve that system—that is, to impede the establishment of a more participatory political system.

For instance, a superficial electoral system might stimulate a flow of foreign aid that strengthens a political system's capacity to repress the poor and dissident. In a more fundamental way, however, narrowly conceived systems of electoral politics can serve to legitimize an essentially undemocratic social order, at least in the eyes of such domestic participants as the urban middle classes. Moreover, it can serve to bring dissident leaders and groups into the open, and once identified, the forces of reaction can more effectively target them for co-optation and punishment. Fuller democracy requires conditions that are more likely to be promulgated by undemocratic means rather than by an electoral process, by regimes that come to power through a revolution that had politically mobilized large proportions of the population.

The dialectical possibilities of even narrow electoral systems cannot be entirely discounted, however. Even in the most restrictive settings, elections give a potential opening to dissident positions and are capable of producing surprises. And even if elections prove barren in this regard, there is very good reason to suspect that all other political systems that could conceivably operate under the social and economic conditions current in most Central American nations are much worse. Nevertheless, it is necessary to recognize the severe limitations of narrowly conceived electoral politics.

Guatemala

The Guatemalan military had no interest in even the shallowest electoral system until they had suppressed the Indian insurgents. Only after 1983 were they willing to entertain the idea of holding a carefully controlled election in order to receive more U.S. aid. Pressures from middle and upper classes uneasy about the military's increasing political insulation from the influence of even the most influential civilians also contributed to the military's decision to hold elections in 1985. The election was closely supervised and monitored by the military and emphatically did not mark the end of military power. While the actual polling may have been relatively fair, the limited spectrum of permissible candidates and platforms as well as the recent memory of raw brutality and the constant threat of new violence made the election considerably less than a fully democratic plebiscite.

The winner was Vinicio Cerezo, a Christian Democrat (Democracia Cristiana Guatemalteca—DCG) whose moderation included particular caution around the issues of land reform, investigation of the military's crimes during the civil wars, and a possible reduction of the military's place in national affairs. Although Cerezo was instrumental in achieving the Esquipulas agreement, he did not implement its provisions within Guatemala by opening negotiations with the revived guerrilla movement led by an umbrella guerrilla organization named Unidad Revolucionario Nacional Guatemalteca (URNG). Like the presidency of Julio Méndez Montenegro in the late 1960s, the civilian president was so hemmed in by the military that he was incapable of any significant social or political initiatives.

The military responded with customary savagery to the resumption of armed struggle, and the U.S. Congress again cut off military aid (against the Bush administration's wishes). This cutoff, however, was more than compensated for by an increase in other types of U.S. aid.

Another issue of national import was growing drug production and trade, which involved military officers and government officials. While drugs were not a new activity, Guatemala during the 1980s became the leading Central American producer of opium (for heroin) and marijuana and a major transshipment depot for the cocaine traffic between Colombia and the United States.

Despite these problems, the military allowed elections to be held in 1989, with constraints on issues and candidates similar to those of the previous election. One difference from 1985, however, was that the military was more openly criticized for its complicity in drug traffic and for its practice of forcibly recruiting soldiers.

Because of dissatisfaction with Cerezo's ineffectiveness and rumored links between the DCG candidate and drugs, the Christian Democrats were repudiated at the polls. After an extremely low turnout, Jorge Serrano, a center right candidate, was elected. Serrano has opened negotiations with the URNG and favored those military leaders willing to cooperate with such negotiations. His ability to play off differences of opinion within the Guatemalan military is not, of course, the same thing as establishing civilian rule. At this time of writing, the negotiations do not appear to be making substantial progress, but the agreement in El Salvador offers some hope for the process.

El Salvador

The electoral situation in El Salvador was similar to that of Guatemala. The civil war raging in El Salvador during the 1980s was also like those in Guatemala and pre-1979 Nicaragua in that it was fought against a militarized state whose chief social policy was repression. Nevertheless, without the broadly interclass national character of the Nicaraguan revolution or the crosscutting ethnic complexities of the Guatemalan struggles, the civil war in El Salvador was more clearly a class war, of the dispossessed against the privileged. Another sharp difference from the Nicaraguan and Guatemalan civil wars was, after 1981, the extent of U.S. involvement in the struggle, which for the United States was another "low-intensity conflict" or proxy war.

In spite of the fact that the nation was being torn apart by civil war, elections were held in 1982. The political left boycotted the election, because its candidates were so frequently murdered. José Duarte of the Christian Democrats (PDC), backed by the United States, won the presidency by narrowly defeating Roberto D'Aubuissón, the death squad veteran who founded the ARENA party. By this time, Duarte had dropped any mention of land reform, and he ruled out negotiations with the guerrillas unless they were first to surrender unconditionally. The Reagan administration, which had little interest in land reform or negotiations, increased U.S. aid to El Salvador until it amounted to about one-half of the national budget.

The PDC never made serious attempts to mobilize even its own electoral constituency into a popular political force, and the bankruptcy of

PDC efforts to "find a middle way" was graphically illustrated by the fierceness of the continuing war. Even with massive external assistance, the ineptitude of the Salvadoran military and the tenaciousness and popular support of the guerrillas rendered the military incapable of a Guatemalan solution. But at the same time, it became increasingly clear that the guerrillas were militarily unable to achieve a revolutionary triumph along the lines of the Nicaraguans. During the 1980s, more than 70,000 Salvadorans died in the war, and as many as 1 million Salvadorans left their native land as refugees from the continuing ravages of the war.

But even an electoral system as crippled as that of El Salvador was capable of producing surprises. During the 1980s, ARENA, founded on the hardest of hard-line principles, became less the party of politically extremist landowners and military and more the party of the modern urban sector. As such, its platform evolved into a probusiness, neoliberal stance that stressed reduced government intervention in the economy but was less intransigent about negotiation and reform. With these positions, ARENA won the congressional elections in 1988, and in 1989, the ARENA candidate—Alfredo Cristiani, president of the Legislative Assembly and member of an eminent Salvadoran family—won the presidency in an election with very low participation rates.

In addition to these changes within ARENA, the 1989 murder of six Jesuit priests and two women by Salvadoran soldiers mobilized U.S. public opinion to the extent that the U.S. Congress, against the resistance of the Bush administration, reduced military aid and put stringent conditions on continuing U.S. financial support. The new resolve by the U.S. Congress strengthened the Salvadoran moderates over the remaining hard-liners in ARENA and split the military. As a consequence, the ARENA party was willing to honor the Esquipulas conventions to the extent of entering into negotiations with the guerrillas, who since the mid-1980s had indicated a willingness to talk. Even more impressive was that after protracted talks with considerable support by the United Nations, a mutually acceptable agreement was finally hammered out by Cristiani and the guerrillas. These agreements included a reduction in the size and role of the Salvadoran army and the integration of some FMLN troops into the army. That negotiators could bargain over the army's size and composition is strikingly different from the situation in Guatemala, where the balance between military and civilian power would make such agreements, much less their implementation, extremely improbable. In fact, the Salvadoran agreement slowed progress in the Guatemalan negotiations because the Guatemalan guerrillas were asking for terms similar to those of the Salvadoran accord.

Cristiani's role in this context reminds one of Richard Nixon, a man of the political right who took the United States (and the world) off the international gold standard, established diplomatic relations with the People's Republic of China, and tacitly admitted defeat in Vietnam by withdrawing U.S. troops. The anomaly in the cases of both Cristiani and Nixon is that a president of even the political center would have had more difficulty in finding that much political latitude. We have yet to see, of course, whether these agreements between the guerrillas and the state can hold. They are vulnerable to being destroyed by either side or, more likely, by breakaway factions of either side.

Nicaragua

The February 1990 election in Nicaragua also contained surprises, but it displayed a very different dynamic. The Sandinistas lost to a conservative but heterogeneous coalition of seven parties that were united under the banner of Unión Nacional Opositora (UNO) and included the local Communist Party.[3] Violeta Chamorro, the UNO candidate and widow of Pedro Joaquín Chamorro, was elected president, and UNO won fifty-one of the ninety seats in the National Assembly. Nevertheless, the FSLN retained thirty-nine seats and is still the most powerful single party.

The 1990 election in Nicaragua was held under conditions of less economic inequality and much greater civil liberties than the elections in either Guatemala or El Salvador, and there was a much higher rate of voter participation. Although it was a more democratic election, its conservative outcome appears to conform to what we would expect from a less genuinely participatory electoral politics. To understand this seeming paradox, we must look closely at the peculiar character of the campaign and election.

The ruling Sandinistas, in a series of unprecedented moves, allowed teams of election observers from over twenty international organizations to oversee the fairness of the election, and they legalized the contributions of funds to parties and candidates from foreign sources (illegal in most other democratic nations). There is little question that the electoral procedure was honest, and there is equally little doubt that in readily visible use of official U.S. funds the level of the Bush administration's support for the UNO campaign amounted to over $10 million—around $10 a voter and $18 per UNO vote.

Reminiscent of the months before the revolutionary triumph in 1979, UNO was constructed with considerable U.S. help, including trips by its leaders to the United States for conferences and reconciliation of differences. President Bush also made campaign speeches for UNO (in the United States), promising the end of the embargo, generous aid and credit, and the end of hostilities if, and only if, UNO won the election.

The United States unquestionably contributed to the victory by UNO, but there was more to it than the U.S. purchase of the election. Although the Contras had failed militarily, continuing U.S. support for the Contra terrorists had resulted in a war of attrition against a poor nation with few reserves. As such, the war had succeeded in exhausting the economic and political resources of Sandinista Nicaragua. The diversion of financial and human resources to the war effort meant that the FSLN program of social and economic construction was severely hobbled, reducing previously planned programs in education and health. Public resources available for stimulating accumulation and economic growth were scarce and eventually nonexistent. Moreover, the military draft was increasingly unpopular, especially among those conscripted for national service and their families.

The original FSLN program called for a mixed private-public economy, and the vast majority of nationalizations were of property owned by the Somozas and their immediate cronies. As a result, most productive enterprises remained in private hands. But the fear of confiscation by the private sector as well as its hostility to the regime and its social and political program made it unwilling to support that regime and program even indirectly through the fostering of economic expansion through accumulation and innovation. In the late 1980s, the FSLN made more concerted attempts to encourage the private sector and was thus accused by some of its own members of diverting scarce resources away from the most needy and selling out the revolution. Economic stagnation and regression characterized the late 1980s, and the resources available to the public sector declined and hardship among the majority increased.

The FSLN's response to the fiscal crisis and credit blockade was to finance expenditures through an inflationary form of deficit financing, essentially printing money through a passive central bank. During the second half of the 1980s, serious inflation developed into hyperinflation; unemployment rose; scarcities of goods became common; and the purchasing power of wages and salaries, especially of those working in the public sector, a major employer, almost disappeared. A very large part of the economic problems of the FSLN regime can be attributed to the war and other forms of U.S. hostility, but there is no question that FSLN mismanagement also played an important role.

Another criticism of Sandinista rule was that early attempts to decentralize political power through a range of grassroots organizations had been abandoned and that power was highly concentrated in a few exclusive decisionmaking groups. This centralized command structure, at least in part reflecting the militarization of society and polity, was yet another cost of the Contra war, but the range and quality of public debate and political access were believed by many to be unnecessarily diminished.

The vote of February 1990 was undoubtedly influenced by the U.S.-

financed campaign, but it was also a demonstration of real dissatisfaction and desperation by the Nicaraguan population. The hope of the electorate was that the UNO, publicly backed by the U.S. administration, could bring peace and prosperity without reversing all of the revolutionary reforms.

It has not worked out too well. A major rupture within UNO soon occurred between those who believed that counterrevolutionary reforms should be done gradually and selectively and those who believed that all vestiges of the FSLN legacy should be immediately and completely stamped out. President Chamorro represents the first faction (moderates), and her vice-president is a leader of the second, hard-line faction. The split in UNO became so severe that Chamorro has had to depend politically on FSLN political support at some key junctures. In return, she supported FSLN positions, and one of the most egregious was her opposing the repeal of the infamous legislation (*la piñata*—a form of gift giving) passed in the two months between the election and the Chamorro inauguration that in effect gave significant amounts of property (houses, cars, and so on) that had been confiscated from Somocista supporters to individual FSLN and government leaders. At the same time, this cooperation has meant that the FSLN has supported Chamorro in breaking strikes by labor unions that had at least initially been FSLN unions. As a consequence of the FSLN's dual position as opposition and coalition partner, the FSLN, like UNO, is finding it increasingly difficult to sustain itself as a single political entity.

Political tensions in Nicaragua have been exacerbated by the return of many anti-Sandinista expatriates (including ex-Contra soldiers) and by the return to civilian life of thousands of demobilized FSLN military recruits. (The numbers on active military duty have been reduced from more than 216,000 in 1989 to 21,000 in early 1992.) There is strife, sometimes armed, between these two groups, neither of which has received promised benefits, and there are struggles between veterans of the Contras who had been promised land and former landowners who are trying to get back land that had been confiscated by the Sandinista land reform. And of course the land is not currently empty, and those now occupying and tilling it have an active and opposing interest to both of the other groups. In the fluid and volatile politics of postelection Nicaragua, there have been instances in which veterans of the Contras and veterans of the Sandinista army have allied against the political establishment.

In addition to internal dissension within UNO and to popular resistance to dismantling Sandinista social service and reform programs, another reason that the UNO government has been unable to move forward in a coherent counterrevolutionary direction is that after the election, U.S. interest in and support for the new Nicaraguan government have been minimal. For opposite reasons, the attitudes of both conservatives and liberals in the U.S. Congress have been ambivalent about the UNO government; some conservatives, such as U.S. Senator Jesse Helms, believe that the UNO government is too heavily influenced by the FSLN, and the liberals dislike its counterrevolutionary stance. In addition, the U.S. administration has been more interested in influencing events in the Middle East and Eastern Europe than in Nicaragua.

The irony is that even though some official U.S. aid funds have been appropriated for Nicaragua, the total amount of U.S. funds flowing into Nicaragua is probably considerably less in the early 1990s than it was in the mid-1980s. Although it is impossible to get an accurate count, pretend that we can estimate all the foreign funds—overt and covert, public and private—that at the instigation of the U.S. government were available to a wide range of individuals and organizations opposed to the FSLN. Add to this the significantly smaller amounts that were entering Nicaragua from foreign supporters of the Sandinista revolution. It is very likely that the sum would be quite a bit larger than current levels of official funds and the trickles of private moneys still coming into Nicaragua from foreign sources previously strongly committed to destroying or supporting the revolution.

UNO represents an orphaned counterrevolution, and its future is not bright.

Honduras

As noted in the last chapter, Honduran elections during the 1980s were not unlike Guatemalan elections in that they were closely supervised by the military and that the civilian presidents' authority over the military was virtually nil. But the elections were not conducted under the shadow of terror that characterized Guatemalan politics. Also unlike the situation in Guatemala, the Honduran military appeared to be truly neutral in respect to which of the two candidates won. There was no candidate from the political left, however, and substantive political differences between the National and Liberal party presidential candidates were difficult to discern.

The new Liberal Party president, Roberto Suazo Cordova, took office in 1982, the time of severe global depression, heavy U.S. buildup of the Contras on Honduran territory, and serious fighting in El Salvador that spilled over into Honduras through refugees and guerrilla training camps. The president did not have much latitude for policy initiatives, and he did not enhance Honduras's international standing by repeatedly and vigorously denying the presence of Contra bases on Honduran soil. During his tenure, progress in land reform was minimal, mostly limited to confirming land titles for campesinos.

Most of the major decisions were in the military's arena. The United States built a number of new bases in Honduras, vastly increased military aid to the Honduran military, frequently conducted joint military exercises with Honduran military personnel, and generally tried to militarize as many aspects of Honduran life as possible in order to secure Honduran support for the fight against the Sandinistas. There is no question that all of these resources and activities strengthened the Honduran military's domestic political influence, but the Honduran military appeared to have its own agenda that did not passively reflect that of the U.S. administration.

The head of the Honduran armed forces in the early 1980s was enthusiastic about entering the fray against Nicaragua, and he was interested in contriving provocations for doing so. But although the Honduras military command welcomed U.S. bases and aid, willingly hosted the Contras (under stringent conditions), and reluctantly agreed to having the United States train Salvadoran military (their recent enemies) in Honduras, they were much less interested in actually going to war against Nicaragua. As a consequence, the head of the Honduran armed forces was removed—by his officer colleagues.

Even though the Honduran military was clearly not eager to support U.S. policy to the extent desired by Washington, José Azcona Hoyo, the Liberal president who assumed office in 1986, firmly supported Reagan's Nicaraguan policy even in its dying days. He violated the Esquipulas agreement by not dismantling Contra bases on Honduran territory, and Honduras diverted some of its U.S. aid to support the Contras after the U.S. congressional prohibition. These acts apparently were his side of an explicit bargain for receiving augmented amounts of U.S. aid.

The 1989 election of President Rafael Leonardo Callejas of the National Party ended Liberal domination of the presidency. The first year of his presidency saw the largest land invasion in Honduran history, some guerrilla activity, and two major strikes. One strike was by public-sector workers and the second was against Chiquita Bananas. The banana workers' strike lasted two months and involved more than 9,000 workers until broken by the government, which imposed the company's initial offer as the final settlement.

The demise of the Reagan Nicaraguan strategy led to declines in U.S. military aid, and the Honduran military suffered budget cuts. There were more land invasions and strikes in 1991, and the Honduran record in human rights deteriorated as the military responded. This was especially so after the military command replaced the commander in chief, who was regarded as too accommodating to the budgetary reverses, and replaced him with a general who was reputedly the former head of a murder squad. In the past thirty years, the Honduran state's ability to respond to social conflicts and contradictions by means other than violence was unusual in the Central American context, reflecting the unique history of its military, weak landed class, and moderate labor and campesino organizations. In the 1990s, however, the legacy of the massive militarization of the 1980s seems to be encouraging policies of repression that were characteristic of its three troubled neighbors.

Costa Rica

The robustness of electoral institutions in Costa Rica is also a matter of continuing surprise, even wonder. The global recession hit Costa Rica hard, and its extreme dependence on external funding—both credit and U.S. aid—to maintain its expensive system of social services made Costa Rica especially vulnerable to restructuring initiatives by the IMF and the political wishes of the United States. The worst years were between 1982 and 1986, when the effects of the recession were greatest and the PLN president proved unable to resist pressure from the U.S. administration to cooperate in its effort to destroy the Nicaraguan revolution.

Oscar Arias, elected in 1986, returned the PLN to the presidency and brought more energy to the office. Although still burdened by the debt and dependence on foreign aid, Arias successfully concluded the 1987 Central American peace accord at Esquipulas, for which he was awarded the Nobel Peace Prize. On the domestic scene, he promoted new export initiatives. Significant new members of the export sector were fruit, cut flowers, labor-intensive manufactured consumer goods, and, on a different plane, tourism, all helped by the Reagan administration's Caribbean Basin Initiative. Even though some new exports included manufacturing, all of the new exports, agricultural and industrial, were characterized by low wages, well-organized work processes, and policy needs (for instance, tariff and foreign exchange policies) similar to already established commodities of the export agriculture sector, and the new entrepreneurs fitted smoothly into the agricultural export sector's politics. President Arias also implemented an IMF-sponsored structural adjustment program.

Costa Rica began to recover from the depths of the depression but at a high cost. The hardships caused by the structural adjustment program meant that Arias was not nearly as popular within Costa Rica as he was internationally, and the PLN lost the 1990 elections, in which a record number of voters abstained.

Rafael Angel Calderón, the son of Rafael Calderón Guardia (president from 1940 to 1944), won the presidency on the promise to alleviate the declines in living standards, especially among the middle classes and poor, which had resulted in good part from the cutbacks in state-sponsored social services. Once in office, however, he pursued growth and accumulation policies virtually indistinguishable from those of Arias.

Costa Rican democratic institutions have proven to be very resilient, even under conditions of substantial economic inequalities. The national consensus underlying this resilience has been strained, however, by the hardships that IMF structural adjustment policies and the dependence on international sources of credit and aid have imposed on the least fortunate members of society.

Landlessness is one area of serious struggle, and the issue has been complicated further by Costa Rica's efforts to preserve large tracts of national territory for environmental purposes. These efforts are encouraged and supported by international environmental groups and by the opportunities of a growing market in "eco-tourism." The program of environmental preservation has pitted environmentalists and their allies, both public and private, against the landless rural population.[4] Occasional occupations of national park land have brought the issues into stark relief, but the sharpness of the dichotomy, seemingly requiring either/or choices between social and environmental goals, is false. Although no doubt some trade-offs between the two sets of goals would be necessary under the most favorable conditions, an economic structure in which economic growth exacerbates the unevenness of the distribution of income and life chances and in which the state is constantly in a situation of fiscal crisis and dependent on international powers is far from being the most favorable. Necessary ecological policies will only succeed when that structure is significantly altered and the cost of such policies will not be borne disproportionately by those least able to bear them.

The End of the International Communist Conspiracy

The big international news during the late 1980s and early 1990s, of course, was the demise of the Soviet Union and the breakup of Eastern Europe. The magnitude of the triumph of capitalism is so great that it has changed important political parameters among nations and within every nation, and its effects will continue to work themselves out for years. There is no question about the positive aspects of these changes in the former Soviet Union and Eastern Europe, but there is also an ominous side to the entire process. For instance, the political potentials are sobering as workers in the former Soviet Union and Eastern Europe gain more experience with the free market—significant declines in their living standards as a result of international competition, lower wages, less job security, higher rates of unemployment, the loss of health and other social services previously provided by the state, acknowledgment of lower class status—and as the new governments have to face militant labor strike actions.

The most obvious effect on Central America is through the ways in which these changes affect U.S. foreign policy. Within the United States, red-baiting will not be as potent a means for mobilizing political support for (or discrediting dissension from) politically aggrandizing international adventures that, like those of the past two U.S. administrations, further no meaningful national or global interests. The war against drugs, the promotion of "democracy," and even environmental concerns have some potential for justifying reactionary interventionist policies, but none seem now to be feasible props for politically sustaining the undemocratic and repressive role that the United States has played in the Third World and Central America since World War II.

Naked economic interests, however, are still alive and well, and within this general category it is worth distinguishing between two types of "national economic interests." The first is where international markets or supplies of commodities are essential to a central branch or set of branches of domestic production and thus affect the situation of a broad array of U.S. constituents. The second is where the international interests of only a particular firm or fragment of U.S. capital is involved. (It is clear that the two may overlap.)

Without the threat of a Soviet nuclear deterrent, the United States is currently freer to respond aggressively to major threats to the first type of national economic interest. But the second type of national interest may be at more risk in the post–Cold War world. As previously noted, the demise of international communism as a shibboleth is likely to make it more difficult for even a powerful and clever fragment of capital to wrap their private interests in the U.S. flag and sell them to the U.S. public, convincing them that opponents are traitors.

The first kind of U.S. economic interest does not exist in Central America, and apart from the interoceanic canal it never has. The economic value of a second canal, perhaps through Nicaragua, is not compelling, and the likelihood of having to control the entire isthmus to ensure the commercial access of U.S. products to the Panama Canal and surrounding shipping routes is negligible.

The willingness of the U.S. government to respond to the second type of economic interest in Central America was graphically illustrated by the 1954 overthrow of the democratically elected government of Guatemala in support of the United Fruit Company. But the historical record of the U.S. government's protection of U.S. firms in Central America, even the United Fruit Company, is uneven, and in the past thirty years such protection has not amounted to much. This situation is unlikely to change significantly, because no powerful multinational firms currently have a significant stake in Central America and during the next decade the markets of the former Soviet Union, Eastern Europe, and China will probably become even more important relative to Latin America in general and Central America in particular.

In the twentieth century, the principal interest that the United States has had in the five nations of Central America has been strategic, revolving around the fear that communism in even a small nation could spread the contagion to others. In addition, there is the geopolitics of the interoceanic canal. The military importance of the Panama Canal is still significant but less so than it was five, much less fifty, years ago. But as in the case of commercial shipping, the military interest of the United States is that the canal not be closed to U.S. naval vessels, and with the self-destruction of the international Communist conspiracy, it will not take constant supervision and monitoring of the five Central American nations to ensure naval access.

There is no doubt that the United States will continue to desire "stability" in the isthmus, and this goal may entail meddling in internal politics, manipulating the flows of economic resources, and even, as in the recent U.S. invasion of Panama, intervening militarily. Even with these caveats, however, there is a good chance that U.S. administrations will increasingly regard the entire region as having only marginal importance. This attitude is not likely to change under the new Clinton administration, which is apparently less driven by ideological fervor. However, the Cuban exile community in the United States appears to wield considerable influence on the new administration's Latin American policy.

Neglect is not necessarily benign, of course, but given the alternatives based on the character of direct interventions in the past and the character that future interventions would be likely to have, it may not be malignant. If the United States were to desist allying with the propertied classes of these societies, the future of these nations might be less bleak than their immediate pasts.

The discussion of a future Central America without direct U.S. interventions, however, is naive on two counts. The first is that the world presence of the United States is so great that it will continue to influence the region, whether intentionally or not. Second, the history of interventions has affected the dialectics of each nation's internal development to such an extent that reducing current U.S. interference still leaves serious problems. In addition to the previous observation about Costa Rica, Nicaragua is in serious chaos, with a very uncertain future. Guatemala is peaceful only when the military's use of the instruments of violence is effective. This peacefulness is not that of a graveyard; the current struggles and potential for a rapidly escalating civil war demonstrate the inappropriateness of this common image. El Salvador is still in the beginning stages of implementing a negotiated settlement, and the balance is so fragile that it could be disrupted from a wide variety of sources. The distribution of social power is what the civil war was about, and that is yet to be addressed. In whatever forum that occurs, the new political and social institutions are going to have to be very strong to withstand the resulting tumult. While Honduras has managed to avoid the worst of the social conflicts of its neighbors, current unrest and the state's response to it are not promising.

There is, of course, the hope that without U.S. support Central American elites will have to accommodate themselves to popular pressures and needs or else be unable to defend themselves against them. The particular forms that popular initiatives will take and the U.S. response to progressive types of social and political instability remain the central questions, not whether social and political instability will occur.

Notes

1. The relation between regime type and economic growth is discussed in Georg Sørenson, *Democracy, Dictatorship, and Development: Economic Development in Selected Regimes of the Third World* (New York: St. Martin's Press, 1990). The sources of democracy in economic patterns (among others) are addressed in Dietrich Rueschemeyer, Evelyne Huber Stephens, and John D. Stephens, *Capitalist Development and Democracy* (Chicago: University of Chicago Press, 1992).

2. Two interesting studies about the tension between socialist practice and democratic politics are Samuel Bowles and Herbert Gintis, *Democracy and Capitalism: Property, Community, and the Contradictions of Modern Social Thought* (New York: Basic Books, 1986); and Carollee Bengelsdorf, *The Problem of Democracy in Cuba: Between Vision and Reality* (New York: Oxford University Press, 1993).

3. Responsible accounts of the 1990 Nicaraguan elections are Thomas W. Walker (ed.), *Revolution and Counterrevolution in Nicaragua* (Boulder, CO: Westview Press, 1991); William I. Robinson, *A Faustian Bargain: U.S. Intervention in the Nicaraguan Elections and American Foreign Policy in the Post–Cold War Era* (Boulder, CO: Westview Press, 1992); and Harry E. Vanden and Gary Prevost, *Democracy and Socialism in Sandinista Nicaragua* (Boulder, CO: Lynne Rienner Publishers, 1992).

4. Analyses of Central American environmental issues from social and political perspectives are attempted in Bill Weinberg, *War on the Land: Ecology and Politics in Central America* (London: Zed Books, 1991); and Daniel Faber, *Environment Under Fire: Imperialism and the Ecological Crisis in Central America* (New York: Monthly Review Press, 1992).

Suggested Readings

Following is a list of books and articles for further reading. This list is eclectic and includes interpretations that do not agree among themselves or with my arguments. There is, however, an essential similarity: They are all worth looking at. In addition, I have emphasized works that are likely to be available in U.S. libraries and bookstores. The bibliography begins with some background works, including general histories of Central America, and after that it is organized along the lines of the chapters of this book.

Latin America and the Third World

It is hard to know how general the general category should be, but I strongly recommend Eric Wolf, *Europe and the People Without History* (Berkeley: University of California Press, 1982), for a broadly historical and comparative work on the Third World. For compact, intelligent surveys of the major issues regarding economic development theory, see Diana Hunt, *Economic Theories of Development: Analysis of Competing Paradigms* (Savage, MD: Barnes and Noble, 1989); and Ronald H. Chilcote and Joel C. Edelstein, *Latin America: Capitalist and Socialist Perspectives of Development and Underdevelopment* (Boulder, CO: Westview Press, 1986). For an excellent analysis of Latin American thought on development that is rooted in an interpretation of Latin American political economics, see Cristóbal Kay, *Latin American Theories of Development and Underdevelopment* (New York: Routledge, 1989). A rigorous, difficult, and very intelligent and thorough survey of thinking and debates about economic development is Anthony Brewer, *Marxist Theories of Imperialism: A Critical Survey,* 2d ed. (London and New York: Routledge, Chapman and Hall, 1990).

Some of the interpretive and comparative materials in this book have been drawn from my earlier book, *Class, State, and Industrial Structure: The Historical Process of South American Industrial Growth* (Westport, CT: Greenwood Press, 1980), although substantially reworked and refined. Here I will mention only two other good sources on Latin America in general. Even though it has a tone of "official history" about it, the multivolume *Cambridge History of Latin America,* edited by Leslie Bethell (Cambridge: Cambridge University Press, 1985), is invaluable. Just pick your period, place, or topic, and it is likely that you will find a first-rate essay and bibliography in one of the volumes. The recent and magisterial work by Ruth Berins Collier and David Collier, *Shaping the Political Arena* (Princeton: Princeton University Press, 1991), is an ambitious and comprehensive treatment of political uncertainties and analytical issues in the larger Latin American nations.

In addition, there are five valuable professional journals that specialize in Latin American scholarship and are available in most U.S. research libraries. *Latin American Research Review* is especially useful, offering excellent articles surveying debates over historical and contemporary issues and extensive reviews. *Hispanic American Historical Review* and *The Americas* are the two principal historical journals, and *The Journal of Latin American Studies* and *Latin American Perspectives* are general research journals with frequently outstanding articles on historical and current topics. Finally, the regularly reported data and the special essays in *The Statistical Abstract of Latin America* (published annually by the UCLA Latin American Center) make it an extremely valuable resource for all interested in Latin America.

Central American Histories

Turning now to works on Central America with sufficient historical reach to be included in several of the chapter categories below, Edelberto Torres-Rivas, *Interpretación del desarrollo social centroamericano: Procesos y estructuras de una sociedad dependiente,* 2d ed. (San José, CR: Editorial Universitaria Centroamericana, 1971); and especially Ciro Cardoso and Hector Pérez Brignoli, *Centroamérica y la economía occidental (1520–1930)* (San José, CR: Editorial Universidad, 1977), are important works. In English, R. L. Woodward, Jr., *Central America: A Nation Divided,* 2d ed. (New York: Oxford University Press, 1985), is the standard historical narrative, and it is rich in texture and detail, especially for the earlier periods. Hector Perez-Brignoli, *A Brief History of Central America* (Berkeley: University of California Press, 1989), is gracefully written and brief, and Thomas L. Karnes, *The Failure of Union: Central America, 1824–1960* (Chapel Hill: University of North Carolina Press, 1961), is the best account of efforts to unify the nations politically.

There are, however, three extensive English-language books on Central American history that stand out. One is a compilation of the essays on Central America from the *Cambridge History of Latin America* and published separately as Leslie Bethell (ed.), *Central American Since Independence* (Cambridge: Cambridge University Press, 1991). The other two are large-scale comparative works on the twentieth century: Victor Bulmer-Thomas, *The Political Economy of Central America Since 1920* (New York: Cambridge University Press, 1987); and James Dunkerley, *Power in the Isthmus: A Political History of Modern Central America* (London and New York: Verso, 1988). Both are truly impressive, although the sheer volume of information in them at times blurs interpretation. Bulmer-Thomas's construction of economic time-series data is an important service for scholars, and his arguments are provocative and well supported. Dunkerley's meticulous sorting of the relationships among broader social forces, organizations, and personalities is outstanding. I have benefited greatly from the three books, and my debt to them should be clear to those familiar with them.

Walter LaFeber, *Inevitable Revolutions: The United States in Central America,* 2d ed. (New York: W. W. Norton, 1993), is a popular book on the history of U.S. foreign policy. It contains much useful information, but the book is marred by the author's apparent conviction that the United States has been the only source of initiation and change in Central America. Dana G. Munro, *The Five Republics of Central America: Their Political and Economic Development and Their Relations with the United States* (New York: Oxford University Press, 1918), is still very valuable.

Each edition of the annual *Handbook of Latin American Studies* contains good bibliographic essays, and the Woodward and Bethell volumes cited earlier include excellent bibliographies. Kenneth Grieb, *Central America in the Nineteenth and Twentieth Centuries: An Annotated Bibliography* (Boston: G. K. Hall, 1988), is also useful. The *Hispanic American Periodicals Index,* published by the UCLA Latin American Studies Center, covers 250 journals and is also available on-line.

National Histories

Turning now to histories of individual Central American nations, and beginning with Guatemala, Jim Handy, *Gift of the Devil: A History of Guatemala* (Boston: South End Press, 1984), is a lively account, and Carol Smith (ed.), *Guatemalan Indians and the State* (Austin: University of Texas Press, 1990), is a set of innovative essays on the social and political history of indigenous Guatemalans.

David Browning, *El Salvador, Landscape and Society* (Oxford: Oxford University Press, 1971); and Rafael Guidos Véjar (1980), *El ascenso del militarismo in El Salvador* (San Salvador: UCA Editores, 1980), have very distinct emphases that provide fruitful contrasts.

For the other nations of Central America, see O. N. Bolland, *The Formation of a Colonial Society: Belize from Conquest to Crown Colony* (Baltimore: Johns Hopkins University Press, 1977); Mario Posas and Rafael Del Cid, *La construcción del sector público y del estado nacional en Honduras 1870–1979* (Ciudad Universitaria Rodrigo Facio, CR: Editorial Universitaria Centroamerica, 1981); Mario Posas, *Luchas del movimiento obrero Hondureño* (San José, CR: EDUCA, 1981); E. Bradford Burns, *Patriarch and Folk: The Emergence of Nicaragua, 1798–1858* (Cambridge: Harvard University Press, 1991); Jaime Wheelock, *Imperialismo y dictadura: Crisis de una formación social* (México: Siglo Veintiuno, 1975); Carolyn Hall, *Costa Rica: A Geographical Interpretation in Historical Perspective* (Boulder, CO: Westview Press, 1985); Mitchell Seligson, *Peasants of Costa Rica and the Development of Agrarian Capitalism* (Madison: University of Wisconsin Press, 1980); Philippe Bourgois, *Ethnicity at Work: Divided Labor on a Latin American Plantation* [on Costa Rica and Panama] (Baltimore: Johns Hopkins University Press, 1989); and Walter LaFeber, *The Panama Canal: The Crisis in Historical Perspective,* updated edition (New York: Oxford University Press, 1989).

Chapter 1: 1500 to 1700

John H. Parry, *The Age of Reconnaissance: Discovery, Exploration, and Settlement* (Berkeley: University of California Press, 1981), is short and readable on European global expansion during the fifteenth through the seventeenth centuries, and I recommend the same author's *The Spanish Seaborne Empire* (New York: Knopf, 1971), for the political economy of the Spanish American colonies. There are two intriguing books on the impact that the New World had on European thought: Anthony Pagden, *The Fall of Natural Man: The American Indian and the Origins of Comparative Ethnology* (New York: Cambridge University Press, 1986), is an illuminating account of conceptions of what constitutes "humanness"; and Alfred W. Crosby, *The Columbian Exchange: Biological and Cultural Consequences of 1492* (Westport, CT: Greenwood Press, 1972), is fascinating on the relationships between biology and culture. Finally, George Foster, *Culture and Conquest: America's Spanish Heritage* (New York: Quadrangle Books, 1960), which I describe in Chapter 1, raises important questions.

On sixteenth- and seventeenth-century Central America, M. J. MacLeod, *Spanish Central America: A Socioeconomic History, 1520–1720* (Berkeley and Los Angeles: University of California Press, 1973), is without doubt the most important source. Also worth consulting are W. L. Sherman, *Forced Labor in Sixteenth Century Central America* (Lincoln: University of Nebraska Press, 1979); the three essays by MacLeod, Sherman, and R. J. Carmack in M. J. MacLeod and R. Wasserstrom (eds.), *Spaniards and Indians in Southeastern Mesoamérica: Essays on the History of Ethnic Relations* (Lincoln: University of Nebraska Press, 1983); and Linda Newson, *The Cost of Conquest: Indian Decline in Honduras Under Spanish Rule* (Boulder, CO: Westview Press, 1986).

Chapter 2: 1700 to 1850

John Lynch, The Spanish American Revolutions, 1808–1826, 2d ed. (New York: W. W. Norton, 1986), and the essays by John Lynch, Timothy Anna, and Tulio Halperín Donghi, in L. Bethell (ed.), *The Cambridge History of Latin America, Volume 3: From Independence to c. 1870* (New York: Cambridge University Press, 1985), are good for general background on the eighteenth-century Bourbon reforms and the early nineteenth-century independence movements and consequent turmoil throughout Latin America.

I found the following especially helpful for Central America in the late eighteenth and early nineteenth centuries: Miles L. Wortman, *Government and Society in Central America, 1680–1840* (New York: Columbia University Press, 1982); Mario Rodríguez, *The Cádiz Experiment in Central America, 1808–1826* (Berkeley: University of California Press, 1978); Robert S. Smith, "Financing the Central American Federation, 1821–1838" *Hispanic American Historical Review* 43, no. 4 (1963); Ralph L. Woodward, *Class Privilege and Economic Development: The Consulado de Comercio of Guatemala, 1793–1871* (Chapel Hill: University of North Carolina Press, 1966); Keith Miceli, "Rafael Carrera: Defender and Promoter of Peasant Interests in Guatemala, 1837–1848," *The Americas* 31, no. 1 (1974); and E. Bradford Burns, *Patriarch and Folk: The Emergence of Nicaragua, 1798–1858* (Cambridge: Harvard University Press, 1991).

Chapter 3: 1850 to 1930

There is a massive literature of various political flavors on dependency theory, and very good surveys of the key arguments can be found in the previously cited books by Diana Hunt, Ronald H. Chilcote and Joel C. Edelstein, Cristóbal Kay, and Anthony Brewer.

For rural Guatemala, see J. C. Cambranes, *Coffee and Peasants: The Origins of the Modern Plantation Economy in Guatemala, 1853–1897* (Stockholm: Institute of Latin American Studies, Monograph No. 10, 1985). And of the several good pieces by David McCreery, I especially like "Coffee and Class: The Structure of Development in Liberal Guatemala," *Hispanic American Historical Review* 56, no. 3 (1976); and "Debt Servitude in Rural Guatemala, 1876–1936," *Hispanic American Historical Review* 63, no. 4 (1983). On urban developments, see Paul J. Dosal, "The Political Economy of Guatemalan Industrialization, 1871–1948: The Career of Carlos F. Novella," *Hispanic American Historical Review* 68, no. 2 (1988).

Excellent and complementary works on the Salvadoran export economy are David Browning, *El Salvador, Landscape and Society* (Oxford: Oxford University Press, 1971); Hector Lindo-Fuentes, *Weak Foundations: The Economy of El Salvador in the Nineteenth Century* (Berkeley and Los Angeles: University of California Press, 1990); and E. Bradford Burns's two articles, "The Modernization of Underdevelopment: El Salvador, 1858–1931," *Journal of Developing Areas* 18 (1984), and "The Intellectual Infrastructure of Modernization in El Salvador," *The Americas* 41, no. 3 (1985).

Good places to begin a more extensive study of the Costa Rican coffee economy are Lowell Gudmundson, *Costa Rica Before Coffee: Society and Economy on the Eve of the Export Boom* (Baton Rouge: Louisiana State University Press, 1986); and Ciro F.S. Cardoso, "Formation of the Coffee Estate in Nineteenth-Century Costa Rica," in K. Duncan and I. Butledge (eds.), *Land and Labour in Latin America: Essays on the Development of Agrarian Capitalism in the Nineteenth and Twentieth Centuries* (New York: Cambridge University Press, 1977).

Charles Kepner, *Social Aspects of the Banana Industry* (New York: Columbia University Press, 1936), is still an important source on fruit company activities in Honduras. In addition to the entries for Honduras and Nicaragua listed in the previous national histories section, see K. V. Finney, "Rosario and the Election of 1887: The Political Economy of Mining in Honduras," *Hispanic American Historical Review* 59, no. 1 (1979); and C. L. Stansifer, "José Santos Zelaya: A New Look at Nicaragua's 'Liberal' Dictator," *Revista/Review Interamericana* 7 (1977). Finally, Thomas D. Schoonover, *The United States in Central America, 1880–1911: An Episode of Social Imperialism and Imperial Rivalry in the World System* (Durham, NC: Duke University Press, 1991), explores interesting questions about U.S. influence during this period.

Chapter 4: 1930 to the 1950s

Several of the entries in the next section, for the 1960s and beyond, have good historical backgrounds on the 1930s, 1940s, and 1950s. The works listed here, therefore, are those that focus particularly on the 1930s through the 1950s, even though several of them bring the story up to more recent times.

Kenneth Grieb, *Guatemalan Caudillo: The Regime of Jorge Ubico: Guatemala, 1931–1944* (Athens: Ohio University Press, 1979), focuses on the regime that politically defined the 1930s and early 1940s in Guatemala. Richard M. Adams (ed.), *Crucifixion by Power: Essays on Guatemalan Social Structure, 1944–1966* (Austin: University of Texas Press, 1970), looks closely at the "ten years of spring" and subsequent years in the Guatemalan countryside. The best English-language studies of the U.S. policy toward the reformist regime, including the invasion that ended the era, are the following, which have different emphases: Piero Gleijeses, *Shattered Hope: The Guatemalan Revolution and the United States, 1944–1954* (Princeton: Princeton University Press, 1991); Richard H. Immerman, *The CIA in Guatemala: The Foreign Policy of Intervention* (Austin: University of Texas Press, 1982); and Stephen Schlesinger and Stephen Kinzer, *Bitter Fruit: The Untold Story of the American Coup in Guatemala* (Garden City, NY: Anchor Books, 1983).

Thomas P. Anderson, *Matanza: El Salvador's Communist Revolt of 1932* (Lincoln: University of Nebraska Press, 1971), describes the failed uprising and resulting massacres in El Salvador.

Donald C. Hodges, *The Intellectual Foundations of the Nicaraguan Revolution* (Austin: University of Texas Press, 1986), is a lengthy attempt to demonstrate that Augusto César Sandino had a coherent and revolutionary program. The classic study of the National Guard is Richard Millett, *Guardians of the Dynasty* (New York: Orbis Books, 1977). Jefferey Gould, "For an Organized Nicaragua: Somoza and the Labour Movement, 1944–1948," *Journal of Latin American Studies* 19, no. 2 (1987), is an excellent study of Somoza at his most creative in political manipulation.

The standard studies of the watershed changes in Costa Rican political life and of Figueres and his political party are John Patrick Bell, *Crisis in Costa Rica: The 1948 Revolution* (Austin: University of Texas Press, 1971); Charles D. Ameringer, *Don Pepe: A Political Biography of José Figueres of Costa Rica* (Albuquerque: University of New Mexico Press, 1978); and Burt H. English, *Liberación Nacional in Costa Rica: The Development of a Political Party in a Transitional Society* (Gainesville: University Presses of Florida, 1971).

Chapters 5, 6, and 7: The 1950s to the Present

The explosion of writings during and about the most recent decades makes selection especially important and difficult. Beginning at the level of Latin America, Rhys Jenkins, *Transnational Corporations and Uneven Development* (Pittsburgh: University of Pittsburgh Press, 1987), is a compact and stimulating argument about the role of transnational corporations in Latin America. A good introduction to recent changes in Latin American political economies is Jeffry A. Frieden, *Debt, Development, and Democracy: Modern Political Economy and Latin America, 1965–1985* (Princeton: Princeton University Press, 1991).

Earlier versions of the four-sector model presented in Chapter 5 can be seen in various of my earlier publications, and these ideas have their roots in works focused on the United States. See especially Robert T. Averitt, *The Dual Economy: The Dynamics of American Industry Structure* (New York: W. W. Norton, 1968); David M. Gordon, Richard Edwards, and Michael Reich, *Segmented Work, Divided Workers: The Historical Transformation of Labor in the United States* (Cambridge: Cambridge University Press, 1982); and, most important, James O'Connor, *The Fiscal Crisis of the State* (New York: St. Martin's Press, 1973).

Samuel Bowles and Herbert Gintis, *Democracy and Capitalism: Property, Community, and the Contradictions of Modern Social Thought* (New York: Basic Books, 1986), poses the difficult theoretical and historical questions about the tensions between capitalist accumulation and political democracy in Europe and the United States and pursues these questions provocatively and interestingly. Central issues about the relationships between capitalist development and political democracy in the Third World are addressed in Georg Sørenson, *Democracy, Dictatorship, and Development: Economic Development in Selected Regimes of the Third World* (New York: St. Martin's Press, 1990); and Dietrich Rueschemeyer, Evelyne Huber Stephens, and John D. Stephens, *Capitalist Development and Democracy* (Chicago: University of Chicago Press, 1992). The latter makes some suggestive arguments about these issues. Both of them, however, have weak chapters on Central American politics. These books serve as a good background for Edelberto Torres-Rivas, *Repression and Resistance: The Struggle for Democracy in Central America* (Boulder, CO: Westview Press, 1989); and John A. Booth and Mitchell Seligson (eds.), *Elections and Democracy in Central America* (Chapel Hill: University of North Carolina Press, 1989).

Merilee S. Grindle, *State and Countryside: Development Policy and Agrarian Politics in Latin America* (Baltimore, MD: Johns Hopkins University Press, 1986), is a provocative and interesting study of recent changes in Latin American agriculture, although the author pays insufficient attention to how urban interests affected agrarian policy.

The Economist Intelligence Unit, *World Outlook,* in the portions devoted to individual Central American nations, is a very good source for current events, with some analysis. The Inter-Hemispheric Education Resource Center ("The Resource Center") in Albuquerque, New Mexico, publishes "Country Guides" for each of the five Central American nations. These books, authored by Tom Barry and periodically updated, are informative introductions to political and economic conditions in each nation and are good for a general overview of recent years. The North American Congress on Latin America (NACLA), *Report of the Americas,* has timely and hard-hitting articles on Latin America, with frequent essays on Central America. Finally, the reports of both Amnesty International and of Americas Watch are important sources about human rights and political conditions in Central America.

Extensive surveys of the recent literature on Central America, with a strong political economy emphasis, are Carol A. Smith and Jefferson Boyer, "Central America Since 1979: Part I," *Annual Review of Anthropology* 16 (1987), pp. 97–221; and Carol A. Smith, Jefferson Boyer, and Martin Diskin, "Central America Since 1979: Part II," *Annual Review of Anthropology* 17 (1988), pp. 331–364. Such surveys are quickly dated, but these are extremely good reviews of a large bibliography, and the way in which the authors pose the central questions makes them worth reading in their own right.

John Weeks, *The Economies of Central America* (New York: Holmes and Meier, 1985), is a useful economic survey of the 1960s and 1970s, with well-organized tables. W. R. Cline and A. I. Delgado (eds.), *Economic Integration in Central America* (Washington, D.C.: Brookings Institution, 1978), is an extensive study of the Central American Common Market. Morris J. Blachman et al., *Confronting Revo-*

lution: Security Through Diplomacy in Central America (New York: Pantheon, 1986), is a series of informative and interesting essays that could serve as effective introductions to the region. The essays in Damián J. Fernández (ed.), *Central America and the Middle East: The Internationalization of the Crises* (Miami: Florida International University Press, 1990), are good on an important international dimension of the Central American conflicts.

Robert C. Williams, *Export Agriculture and the Crisis in Central America* (Chapel Hill: University of North Carolina Press, 1986); and Charles Brockett, *Land, Power, and Poverty: Agrarian Transformation and Political Change in Central America* (Boulder, CO: Westview Press, 1990), are outstanding, complementary studies of changes in the Central American countryside, and they make good companion readings with Merilee Grindle's book cited earlier. Bill Weinberg, *War on the Land: Ecology and Politics in Central America* (London: Zed Books, 1991), is one of the very few books on environmental issues that directly confront the difficult political questions about the relation between environmental concerns and the material welfare of the poor.

An entire issue of *Journal of Latin American Studies* 15, part 2 (1983), is devoted to Central America, and although there is no effort at comprehensiveness or coherence, the individual articles are very good on politics and economics. George Irwin and Stuart Holland (eds.), *Central America: The Future of Economic Integration* (Boulder, CO: Westview Press, 1989), is a good collection of essays on the vicissitudes and potentials of regional economic cooperation.

Philip Berryman, *The Religious Roots of Rebellion: Christians in Central American Revolution* (New York: Orbis Books, 1984); and David Stoll, *Is Latin America Turning Protestant? The Politics of Evangelical Growth* (Berkeley and Los Angeles: University of California Press, 1990), are good places to begin exploring the significance of continuing changes in Central American religious life and institutions.

For studies of individual countries, I recommend the following books and articles. Suzanne Jonas, *The Battle for Guatemala: Rebels, Death Squads, and U.S. Power* (Boulder, CO: Westview Press, 1991); and Elizabeth Burgos Debray (ed.) *I . . . Rigoberta Menchú: An Indian Woman in Guatemala* (New York: Routledge, Chapman and Hall, 1984). The material of these books ranges from structural analysis to personal testimony. Also see Michael McClintock, *The American Connection, Volume 2: State Terror and Popular Resistance in Guatemala* (London: Verso, 1985).

On Honduras, good analyses of contemporary tensions and prospects can be found in Mark Rosenberg and Philip Shepherd (eds.), *Honduras Confronts Its Future: Contending Perspectives on Critical Issues* (Boulder, CO: Lynne Rienner Publishers, 1986); and Charles Brockett, "Public Policy, Peasants and Rural Development in Honduras," *Journal of Latin American Studies* 19, no. 1 (1987).

W. A. Durham, *Scarcity and Survival in Central America: Ecological Origins of the Soccer War* (Stanford, CA: Stanford University Press, 1979), is the best English-language work on the 1969 conflict between El Salvador and Honduras.

For the civil war in El Salvador and its hoped-for aftermath, there are a variety of understandings. A range of interesting interpretations of the civil war and of immediate prospects is presented in Enrique A. Baloyra, *El Salvador in Transition* (Chapel Hill: University of North Carolina Press, 1982); James Dunkerley, *The Long War: Dictatorship and Revolution in El Salvador*, 2d ed. (New York: Routledge, Chapman and Hall, 1985); Michael McClintock, *The American Connection, Volume 1: State Terror and Popular Resistance in El Salvador* (London: Verso, 1985); Tommie Sue Montgomery, *Revolution in El Salvador: Origins and Evolution* (Boulder, CO: Westview Press, 1982); and Joseph Tulchin and Gary Bland (eds.), *Is There a Transition to Democracy in El Salvador?* (Boulder, CO: Lynne Rienner Publishers, 1992).

The volume of literature on Nicaragua is overwhelming and of uneven quality. The following are good on the political and economic background of the Nicaraguan revolution and emphasize different aspects of the revolution's dynamics: John A. Booth, *The End and the Beginning: The Nicaraguan Revolution,* 2d ed., revised and updated (Boulder, CO: Westview Press, 1986); Carlos Vilas, *The Sandinista Revolution: National Liberation and Social Transformation in Central America* (New York: Monthly Review Press, 1986); and Anthony Lake, *Somoza Falling: A Case Study of Washington at Work* (Amherst: University of Massachusetts Press, 1990).

For the ten years of Sandinistas in power, see Rose J. Spalding (ed.), *The Political Economy of Revolutionary Nicaragua* (Boston: Allen and Unwin, 1987); Carmen Diana Deere, Peter Marchetti, and Nola Reinhardt, "The Peasantry and the Development of Sandinista Agrarian Policy," *Latin American Research Review* 20 (1985); and Carlos Vilas, *State, Class, and Ethnicity in Nicaragua: Capitalist Modernization and Revolutionary Change on the Atlantic Coast* (Boulder, CO: Lynne Rienner Publishers, 1989).

For explanations and the implications of the Sandinistas' loss to UNO in the 1990 election, see Thomas W. Walker (ed.), *Revolution and Counterrevolution in Nicaragua* (Boulder, CO: Westview Press, 1991); William I. Robinson, *A Faustian Bargain: U.S. Intervention in the Nicaraguan Elections and American Foreign Policy in the Post–Cold War Era* (Boulder, CO: Westview Press, 1992); and Harry E. Vanden and Gary Prevost, *Democracy and Socialism in Sandinista Nicaragua* (Boulder, CO: Lynne Rienner Publishers, 1992).

Important issues about Costa Rica are addressed in Marc Edelman and Joanne Kenen (eds.), *The Costa Rica Reader* (New York: Grove Weidenfeld, 1989); and Anthony Winson, *Coffee and Democracy in Costa Rica* (New York: St. Martin's Press, 1989). Very good, compact studies of the two Central American nations not included in my book are Andrew Zimbalist and John Weeks, *Panama at the Crossroads: Economic Development and Political Change in the Twentieth Century* (Berkeley: University of California Press, 1991); and O. Nigel Bolland, *Belize: A New Nation in Central America* (Boulder, CO: Westview Press, 1986).

As I suggested previously, students with a serious interest in any one or all of the Central American nations should, at an early stage, read Leslie Bethell (ed.), *Central America Since Independence* (Cambridge: Cambridge University Press, 1991); Victor Bulmer-Thomas, *The Political Economy of Central America Since 1920* (New York: Cambridge University Press, 1987); and James Dunkerley, *Power in the Isthmus: A Political History of Modern Central America* (London and New York: Verso, 1988). Although not easy works, they are very rewarding.

Series in Political Economy and Economic Development in Latin America

Series Editor
Andrew Zimbalist
Smith College

Through country case studies and regional analyses this series will contribute to a deeper understanding of development issues in Latin America. Shifting political environments, increasing economic interdependence, and the difficulties with regard to debt, foreign investment, and trade policy demand novel conceptualizations of development strategies and potentials for the region. Individual volumes in this series will explore the deficiencies in conventional formulations of the Latin American development experience by examining new evidence and material. Topics will include, among others, women and development in Latin America; the impact of IMF interventions; the effects of redemocratization on development; Cubanology and Cuban political economy; Nicaraguan political economy; and individual case studies on development and debt policy in various countries in the region.

About the Book and Author

Central America sprang into the consciousness of the U.S. public in the late 1970s, propelled by the Nicaraguan revolution and the brutal civil wars in Guatemala and El Salvador. The continuing debates over the nature of the conflicts and the role of U.S. policy have too seldom acknowledged the historical depths of the crises' roots, and the size of the Central American nations has often led U.S. participants in the debate to underestimate the dynamism, complexity, and heterogeneity of the social structures that underlie the political struggles.

This book presents a historical and analytical interpretation of recent Central American crises. Using a consistent comparative framework, Dr. Weaver sorts out the relations among economic growth, social organization, and political structure and offers explanations for the historically divergent developments among the five Central American nations. By setting those events in a broader Latin American context and illuminating the relationships between domestic and international influences, Weaver shows how rapid changes in the social organization of economic production in some periods affected social structures and configurations of political power while at other times, political conflicts conditioned and shaped subsequent patterns of economic expansion.

Frederick Stirton Weaver is professor of economics and history at Hampshire College.

Index